T0371594

# Beyond Bad Apples

'One bad apple spoiling the whole barrel' has become a common metaphor used with reference to risk culture in organisations. This 'inside-out' perspective begins with the individual as the unit of analysis and follows with inferences to the broader environment. Since the Global Financial Crisis (GFC) of 2008, risk culture for many has become the explanation for shortcomings, poor decisions and moral failures in organisations. This book presents an institutional perspective of the forces that shape risk culture, and culture more generally, in organisations through a multi-disciplinary examination from a variety of leading academics and subject specialists. The authors demonstrate that firms play a role as manufacturers and managers of risk, and they challenge common conceptions that attribute risk to chance circumstances or rogue behaviours. The foundational concepts needed for an institutional view of risk culture are highlighted with subsequent links to significant developments within society and firms.

MICHELLE TUVESON is Chairman and Executive Director of the Cambridge Centre for Risk Studies, Judge Business School, University of Cambridge. She is a board member, commentator and speaker, and her articles have been published in reports such as *Risk Analysis: An International Journal* and *Financial Times Special Report on Risk Management*.

DANIEL RALPH is the founding Academic Director of the Centre for Risk Studies, Judge Business School and Fellow of Churchill College, University of Cambridge. Daniel works with leading international organisations, in financial services, energy and beyond, on identifying, assessing and managing systemic risks.

KERN ALEXANDER is Professor of Banking and Financial Market Regulation at the University of Zurich. His research focuses on the regulation of financial markets. He is the author of *Principles of Banking Regulation* (Cambridge University Press, 2019) and *Economic Sanctions: Law and Public Policy* (2009), and co-author of *Brexit and Financial Services: Law and Policy* (2018).

# Beyond Bad Apples

## Risk Culture in Business

Edited by

**MICHELLE TUVESON**
*Cambridge Judge Business School*

**DANIEL RALPH**
*Cambridge Judge Business School*

**KERN ALEXANDER**
*University of Zurich*

CAMBRIDGE
UNIVERSITY PRESS

# CAMBRIDGE
## UNIVERSITY PRESS

University Printing House, Cambridge CB2 8BS, United Kingdom

One Liberty Plaza, 20th Floor, New York, NY 10006, USA

477 Williamstown Road, Port Melbourne, VIC 3207, Australia

314–321, 3rd Floor, Plot 3, Splendor Forum, Jasola District Centre,
New Delhi – 110025, India

79 Anson Road, #06–04/06, Singapore 079906

Cambridge University Press is part of the University of Cambridge.

It furthers the University's mission by disseminating knowledge in the pursuit of
education, learning, and research at the highest international levels of excellence.

www.cambridge.org
Information on this title: www.cambridge.org/9781108476102
DOI: 10.1017/9781316996959

© Cambridge University Press 2020

First published 2020

Printed in the United Kingdom by TJ International Ltd. Padstow Cornwall

*A catalogue record for this publication is available from the British Library.*

*Library of Congress Cataloging-in-Publication Data*
Names: Tuveson, Michelle, 1966– editor. | Ralph, Daniel, editor. | Alexander, Kern,
   1962– editor.
Title: Beyond bad apples : risk culture in business / edited by Michelle Tuveson,
   University of Cambridge, Judge Business School, Daniel Ralph, University of
   Cambridge, Judge Business School, Kern Alexander, University of Zurich.
Description: Cambridge, United Kingdom ; New York, NY : Cambridge University Press,
   2020. | Includes bibliographical references and index.
Identifiers: LCCN 2019049497 (print) | LCCN 2019049498 (ebook) |
   ISBN 9781108476102 (hardback) | ISBN 9781108466882 (paperback) |
   ISBN 9781316996959 (epub)
Subjects: LCSH: Risk management. | Corporate culture–Moral and ethical aspects.
Classification: LCC HD61.B49 2020 (print) | LCC HD61 (ebook) | DDC 658.15/5–dc23
LC record available at https://lccn.loc.gov/2019049497
LC ebook record available at https://lccn.loc.gov/2019049498

ISBN 978-1-108-47610-2 Hardback
ISBN 978-1-108-46688-2 Paperback

# Contents

# Figures

# Contributors

## Editors

**Michelle Tuveson** is Chairman and Executive Director at the Cambridge Centre for Risk Studies at the Cambridge Judge Business School, University of Cambridge. Tuveson chairs the centre's advisory board and the Cambridge Chief Risk Officers Council and is a former IEEE Standards Committee member on the General Ethical Principles for Artificial Intelligence and former advisory board member to the World Economic Forum's *Global Risks Report.* She is the director of the advisory board of Elevate City, an organisation aligned with the UK HM Treasury's Women in Finance Charter. She has worked in corporations within the technology and consulting sectors. During Tuveson's tenure, the Cambridge Centre for Risk Studies has become a world-leading provider of research and thought leadership in scenario-based modelling of multidisciplinary risks to society and businesses. Her research topics include risk culture and governance and emerging risk profiling through scenario-based modelling. She is a frequent commentator and speaker, and her articles have been published in reports such as *Risk Analysis: An International Journal, Banking & Financial Services Policy Report* (Wolters Kluwer) and *Financial Times Special Report on Risk Management.* She has earned degrees from the Massachusetts Institute of Technology, Johns Hopkins University and University of Cambridge.

**Daniel Ralph** is Academic Director at the Cambridge Centre for Risk Studies and Professor of Operations Research at the Cambridge Judge Business School. He is a fellow and Director of Studies for Management Studies at Churchill College. His research interests include identification and management of systemic risk, risk aversion in investment decisions, equilibrium models in energy economics, and optimisation methods. Management stress tests and assessment of business viability, via catastrophe scenarios, is one focus of his work in the Cambridge Centre for Risk Studies. Another is the role and expression of risk management within organisations. Ralph engages across scientific and social science academia, a variety of commercial and industrial sectors, and government policymaking. He is a graduate of the University of Melbourne and University of Wisconsin–Madison. He was the editor-in-chief of *Mathematical Programming (Series B)* from 2007 to 2013.

**Kern Alexander** holds the chair for Banking and Financial Law and Regulation at the University of Zurich. He is a lawyer and economist with a research focus on the regulation of systemic risk in financial markets. His academic publications include *Principles of Banking Regulation* (Cambridge University Press, 2019) and *Global Governance of Financial Systems* (co-author, Oxford University Press, 2006). He is also co-author of *Brexit and Financial Services* (Bloomsbury, 2018). He has written extensively on UK and EU banking regulation and market abuse law and is co-editor of the *Research Handbook on International Financial Regulation* (Edward Elgar, 2012) and *Law Reform and Financial Markets* (Edward Elgar, 2011). He is also the author of *Economic Sanctions: Law and Public Policy* (Macmillan, 2009), providing a comprehensive analysis of the regulatory and governance aspects of economic and financial sanctions. Alexander's articles and commentaries have been published in the *Journal of International Economic Law, Cambridge Law Journal, European Law Review, European Business Organisation Review* and *Journal of Corporate Law Studies*. He has written several commissioned reports for the European Parliament on financial regulatory reform and the Eurozone sovereign debt crisis and was a member of the Expert Panel on Financial Services for the European Parliament (2009–14). He was Specialist Adviser to the British

Parliament's Joint Select Committee on the Financial Services Act 2012 and has served as an adviser to the UK Serious Fraud Office on the Libor investigations. He was educated at Cornell, Oxford and Cambridge universities.

## Authors

**Andrew Freeman** has been a Risk Fellow at the Cambridge Centre for Risk Studies since 2012. He works as Head of Risk Management, International Distribution, Natixis Investment Managers and from 2014 to 2019 was Chief Risk Officer at Ardian, a private equity firm. He is also Director of the Finance Foundation, a think tank, and in 2014 he co-founded Fairer Finance Ltd. Over a thirty-year career, he has written numerous articles and books, first as a journalist on *The Economist* (1992–2006) and latterly in his role as a senior knowledge expert in risk at McKinsey & Company. Between 2009 and 2011, he was Executive Director of the Center for Financial Services at Deloitte LLP, overseeing its research programme on the financial services industry. In 1998 he published *Seeing Tomorrow: Rewriting the Rules of Risk* (co-author, John Wiley & Sons). In 2016 and 2017, he published two articles on risk management in private equity co-authored with D. Sykes Wilford. Freeman is a graduate of Balliol College, Oxford, and was also elected a Domus Senior Scholar at Merton College, Oxford.

**Anthony Hotson** is Deputy Director of the Centre for Financial History and a member of Darwin College, Cambridge. Hotson worked at the Bank of England during the 1980s, including a secondment as Assistant Commissioner at the newly formed Building Societies Commission. He was employed by McKinsey & Company before joining S. G. Warburg, where he worked as a corporate financier and director during the 1990s. Thereafter, he has served as a director on a number of company boards in the financial services sector while pursuing his academic interests. His book, *Respectable*

*Banking: The Search for Stability in London's Money and Credit Markets since 1695,* was published by Cambridge University Press in 2017.

**Jennifer Howard-Grenville** is the Diageo Professor of Organisation Studies at the Cambridge Judge Business School, University of Cambridge. She contributes to organisation theory through in-depth studies of how people work from within to change organisations, communities and occupations. By focusing on the processes through which people seek change, her scholarship advances theoretical understanding of organisational routines, culture, identity and identification, as well as transformations required to tackle grand challenges, like environmental sustainability. She is recognised as a leading qualitative researcher with a focus on process theorising and has served as an associate editor (2013–16) for *Academy of Management Journal,* as guest editor-in-chief for *Academy of Management Discoveries* for a special issue on the UN Sustainable Development Goals and will be joining *Academy of Management Journal* as deputy editor in 2019–22. Her work has been published extensively in top management journals, and she is the author or co-author of four books. Howard-Grenville received her PhD at MIT, her MA at Oxford and her BSc (Eng.) at Queen's University, Canada.

**Stelios Kavadias** is the Margaret Thatcher Professor in SME Studies, Growth and Innovation, Director of Research and Director of the Entrepreneurship Centre at the Cambridge Judge Business School. He serves as an associate editor for *Management Science*'s entrepreneurship and innovation department, and as the department editor for the R&D, New Product Development and Project Management department of *Production and Operations Management.* At Georgia Tech's Huang Executive Education Center, he regularly contributed to open enrolment and custom executive programmes on innovation and project management and was the academic director of their GE Energy PLMP programme. He has authored several case studies through close collaboration with major firms across multiple industries.

**Kostas Ladas** is an associate at the Entrepreneurship Centre at Cambridge Judge Business School, University of Cambridge. He served as project manager at Cambridge JBSEEL on the relationship of technology and innovation. Previously he was head of network strategy – responsible for the fixed network – at OTE, the incumbent telecom operator in Greece. He has more than twenty years' experience in a broad range of high-level management positions in telecommunications and defence industries and has served as adviser to the CEO responsible for technology selection and collective labour agreements negotiations. Ladas holds an MPhil from the Cambridge Judge Business School on Technology Policy, and a PhD in electrical engineering from Northeastern University, Boston, MA, USA. He has authored several papers in electromagnetics, mathematics and business journals.

**Anette Mikes** joined Saïd Business School in 2019, having most recently been Professor of Accounting, Control and Risk Management at HEC Lausanne, University of Lausanne, and previously Assistant Professor at Harvard Business School. She received her PhD from the London School of Economics, where her dissertation on risk management in financial institutions was the first field-based research in this area of studies. Between 2007 and 2010, Mikes directed a research programme that investigated evolving directions in risk management in the banking sector on both sides of the Atlantic. She has also studied risk management practices in various non-financial organisations, from NASA to the Royal Navy. She was the 2017 laureate of the prestigious ACA Prize of the University of St.-Gallen for her contribution to the field of risk management and financial governance. She won the David Solomons Award ('Best Paper in Management Accounting Research') twice: in 2010 (for her article 'Risk Management and Calculative Cultures') and in 2016

(for the article 'How Do Risk Managers Become Influential?').
Her research documentary on a man-made disaster ('The Kursk
Submarine Rescue Mission') won the Most Outstanding Short Film
Award at the Global Risk Forum in Davos in August 2014. The
latter project signifies her continuing interest in man-made disasters,
and her current research ('Values at Risk: Management Accounting
in the Age of Corporate Purpose') focuses on the interface between
risk management, business ethics and management control.

**Duncan Needham** is a senior risk researcher at the Centre for Risk
Studies, Affiliated Lecturer in the Faculty of History, Director of the
Centre for Financial History and Senior Tutor of Darwin College,
University of Cambridge. Before returning to academia, he worked
as a credit trader at JP Morgan and then as a portfolio manager at
Cairn Capital. Needham lectures in economic history and teaches
undergraduate courses in history, economics and politics. His PhD
thesis was published by Palgrave Macmillan in 2014 and awarded the
Economic History Society's 2015 Thirsk–Feinstein Prize for best
doctoral dissertation.

**Michael Power** is Professor of Accounting at the London School of
Economics and Political Science and a fellow of the British Academy.
Educated at St Edmund Hall, Oxford and Girton College Cambridge,
he is a fellow of the Institute of Chartered Accountants in England and
Wales, an associate member of the UK Chartered Institute of Taxation
and an honorary fellow of the Institute of Risk Management. Formerly
on the board of St James's Place plc from 2005 to 2013 and currently a
non-executive director of RIT Capital Partners plc and Chairman of St
James's Place International. He has also held a number of advisory
positions for public bodies, including the Financial Reporting Council,
and was Director of the Centre for Analysis of Risk and Regulation at
LSE until April 2014. Power holds honorary doctorates from the
universities of St Gallen, Switzerland; Uppsala, Sweden; and Turku,
Finland. His research and teaching focus on regulation, accounting,

auditing, internal control, risk management and organisation theory. His major works are *The Audit Society: Rituals of Verification* (Oxford University Press, 1999), *Organized Uncertainty: Designing a World of Risk Management* (Oxford University Press, 2007) and *Riskwork: Essays on the Organizational Life of Risk Management* (Oxford University Press, 2016).

# Acknowledgements

The editors are grateful to the chapter authors, who have contributed their intellectual perspectives and expertise to help bring a different voice to the risk culture discussion to date. Given the multifaceted nature of the topic, it has been a privilege to have the opportunity to work across the represented disciplines.

We acknowledge the Cambridge Centre for Risk Studies for its vision for growing and fostering an environment to advance the field of risk management – a culture that supports innovative thinking and intellectual curiosity to allow the continual exploration of topics related to broad themes of risk. We are particularly grateful to the other executive directors: Dr Andrew Coburn and Simon Ruffle. We thank our stakeholder community at the centre – sponsors, researchers and affiliates – who have participated in creating and growing an interactive community. We thank our long-standing advisers at the centre, who were encouraging of our efforts to shape our Risk Summit themes that supported the concepts in this book.

We thank the academic and professional practice communities for supporting our interests in culture and organisations over the years, including Professor Sandra Dawson, for contributing their views on risk culture and personal agency; Dr Ben Hardy, for his social science sensibilities and contributions to sentiment polling during our annual risk summits; Dr David Good, for his thoughtful suggestions on the overlaps between sociology and psychology of risk culture; Professor Dan Kahan, on cultural cognition and professional judgement; Professor Martin Kilduff, on how social networks might describe organisations; and Professor

Alison Liebling, on the anti–risk management and moral culture of prison societies.

We acknowledge the chief risk officers and other senior risk professionals who participated in our CRO Council round-table discussions.

We acknowledge colleagues for supporting our broader agenda into understanding systemic risk as a backdrop to risk culture in organisations. They include Professor Elroy Dimson, Professor Christoph Loch, Professor Jochen Runde, Professor Kishore Sengupta, Professor Sir David Spiegelhalter and Dr Philip Stiles, at the University of Cambridge; and Dr Alberto Feduzi and Professor Paul Walker, from further afield. We are grateful to the Cambridge Judge Business School for hosting the Centre for Risk Studies, and Cambridge Judge Business School Executive Education for facilitating our interactions with financial services companies.

We acknowledge attendees at the Aspen Risk Forums for providing critique on some of our early ideas.

We thank Valerie Appleby and the editorial staff at Cambridge University Press for their assistance and encouragement during the book project.

Michelle Tuveson: I am enormously thankful to David for his early encouragement and support to pursue challenge as an opportunity; Katie, Marina and Tim for their inspiration on keeping a future perspective; Dr John Inglis for his valuable advice throughout the book publication process; and many other family, friends and colleagues from whom I continue to learn and gain inspiration in so many different and positive ways.

Daniel Ralph: I am grateful to my family, especially Amanda, for steadfast support of my work towards the book in my sometimes crazy schedule. My warm thanks also to many contacts and collaborators who have provided inspiration, insight and challenge during the project.

Kern Alexander: I am grateful to Dr Francesco DePascalis for his insights and comments on regulating risk culture in the financial services industry in the context of EU regulation and to Leonardo Gelli and Bruce Pollock for research assistance. A special thanks to my family, including Natasha, Kern IV and Ruth for their support.

# Introduction

## Michelle Tuveson, Daniel Ralph
## and Kern Alexander

O.I SETTING THE SCENE

The one bad apple spoiling the barrel has become a common metaphor to describe risk culture in organisations. This 'inside-out' perspective begins with the individual as the unit of analysis and follows with inferences to the broader environment. Since the global financial crisis (GFC) of 2008, risk culture for many has become the explanation for shortcomings, poor decisions and moral failures in organisations. We present an institutional perspective of some of the forces that shape risk culture in organisations.

By many accounts, the role of risk management has become more prominent in addressing the disruptive challenges facing modern businesses. The tumultuous period for the financial services, the business environment and wider society kicked off by the GFC provided jet fuel for a long running re-exploration of the foundations of risk management practices. One could argue that ascendancy of risk culture is a particular outcome of the crisis, trailing the thesis that organisational norms were responsible for the shortcomings in risk management.

Risk management processes within organisations have become increasingly formalised over time, and visibly so since the GFC. The reach of risk management processes has increased due to expansive regulatory requirements outlined in regulations such as the Dodd–Frank Act. This organising of risk management has built upon embedded controls in finance, compliance, quality, safety and so on within many firms, public bodies and third-sector entities. The requirement for stricter controls by systemically important financial institutions (SIFIs) has contributed to the growth of the risk profession even within non-SIFIs, such as the appointment of chief risk officers and the creation of risk committees at the top level of organisations. This has been interpreted as a rational governance response to managing risk and uncertainty within the wider business environment. Yet to many observers, these risk management developments overly focus on mechanical monitoring and control processes within siloed organisational structures, and lack holistic implementations that avoid misalignments between employees and customers.

The failure of firms, whether from idiosyncratic or systemic causes, engenders management soul searching and calls into question the health of the firms, including their cultures (Group of Thirty, 2015). This puts a spotlight on the role of culture in a firm versus the role of individuals and subgroups who may appear to forge idiosyncratic paths. A growing response, across the private and public sectors, has been on actively managing risk culture as a complementary approach to improving individual agency along with incentives, accountability and roles of individuals in governance structures. The underlying proposition is that the maintenance of good corporate behaviour and responsible attitudes will lead individual employees to act with higher ethical standards and take risks that are better calibrated to the risk appetite of the firm.

We believe that good risk culture can help organisations recognise their blind spots more clearly; however, the supporting development or proof of this proposition seems un-scoped, if not vexed. This book is an effort, rather than proving or disproving prevailing views on risk culture or providing an exhaustive review on topics that should touch risk culture, to contribute thoughtful perspectives on risk culture that specifically take on organisational considerations.

## 0.2    WHAT IS RISK CULTURE?

Somewhat separate from risk management, organisational culture and organisational theory are well developed and active areas for academics and practitioners. It seems natural to embed risk considerations into classical descriptions of organisational culture. For instance, the International Institute of Finance (IIF) defines risk culture as 'the norms of behaviour for individuals and groups within an organisation that determine the collective ability to identify and understand, openly discuss and act on the organisations current and future risks' (2009). This definition takes a leaf from the standard work of organisational scholars. Chapter 1 will provide discussion linking the theory of organisational theory to risk culture.

Against that, the complexities in the culture of an organisation and trade-offs intrinsic to management, and risk management in particular, suggest that a snappy definition of risk culture is not a fruitful goal. Quoting from an oft-cited UK-based report, 'Our desk research of academic and practitioner literature on risk management, management control, culture and safety issues suggested strongly that risk culture is a way of framing issues of risk and culture in organisations and not a separate object' (Power, Palermo & Ashby, 2013).

## 0.3 RISK CULTURE THEMES COVERED IN THIS BOOK

This book presents a multidisciplinary examination of risk culture from a variety of leading academics and thought leaders. They bring expertise from their individual disciplines to help formulate the perspectives and themes presented throughout these chapters. Some of the topics are drawn from the concepts and themes that helped shape the Cambridge Centre for Risk Studies summit 'Risk Culture: Challenging Individual Agency' (Cambridge Judge Business School, 2016).

This book explores risk culture from the organisational versus the individual perspective. Taking the organisation as our unit of analysis is a departure from what we see hitherto as a focus on individuals, be they the proverbial 'bad apples', whose behaviours imply threats to an organisation as a whole, or board members who set the 'tone at the top' to pre-empt poor behaviours and encourage good behaviours. We draw attention to the role of firms as manufacturers and managers of risk versus risk being the passive recipients of chance circumstances or individuals' rogue behaviours, supporting the institutional view of risk management (Ashby, Palermo & Power, 2014; Banks, 2012).

The book comprises two parts. The first part, 'Risk Culture Conceptual Underpinnings', presents four topics that provide the foundational concepts needed for an institutional view of risk culture. These include notions of culture, hence risk culture; the role of information and information processes in the realisation of risk culture; how culture is diffused from the ubiquitous 'tone at the top' through the organisation; and the essential role of risk in innovation and thus in innovation management. The intention is to convey that risk culture is more wide-reaching than what might appear in linear risk appetite statements. We hope the more nuanced and subtle view will provide challenge to the way risk culture is currently viewed.

The second part, 'Risk Culture Concepts in Firms and Society', strives to make links from the concepts presented in Part I to significant developments in society to date by appealing directly to history, regulatory practices and business case studies. This part presents a historical view of the development of the business model of UK banking and the inherent risk and risk culture implications; a close look at how UK regulations have addressed culture in the financial services and the complementary role of industry bodies; the ascendancy of risk culture in the aftermath of the GFC and whether this has informed the business value of risk culture in businesses; and how organisations assess their own risk culture in the context of their stated values and enterprise risk management processes.

### 0.3.1 Content Description and Overview

This volume endeavours to provide a multidisciplinary perspective on cultural issues informing the basic principles and foundations for better management of risk. Modern risk management goes beyond the credit, market and operational risk responsibilities typified in financial services and encompasses a broader set of issues. To address these, we have organised contributions into two parts. Both parts are summarised below, with a brief description of each individual chapter.

### 0.3.1.1   Part I: Risk Culture Conceptual Underpinnings

This part highlights thinking from several different disciplines providing foundations upon which culture is built, defined and better understood. From this broad view of cultural issues, risk management in organisations and its successes and failings can be assessed.

Jennifer Howard-Grenville places risk culture within organisational culture in 'Individual Agency and Collective Patterns of Action: Organisational Culture through the Lens of Organisational Theory' (Chapter 1). She reviews two prominent perspectives, that of Edgar Schein, which is popularised in three layers of organisational culture, beginning with espoused values – exemplified by 'tone from the top', which is omnipresent in discussion of UK financial services – then artefacts and finally the underlying assumptions or beliefs of members; and that of Ann Swidler, who coined the idea of 'culture as repertoire', which aims to extract the meaning of culture from the day-to-day actions, skills and habits of an organisation's people. While relating both individual agency and collective characteristics of an organisation to risk governance, the inherent resistance of culture to change is noted.

The prevailing idea of 'risk management of nothing' (Power, 2009), coined to describe the misguided focus of risk management on the audit function, is a backdrop for the conversation on 'Risk Culture and Information Culture: Why an 'Appetite for Knowledge' Matters' (Chapter 2). In this chapter, Michael Power highlights the relationship between risk information and risk management processes from an organisational perspective. This chapter posits that a focus on individual incentives and performance management has compromised a more nuanced understanding of group dynamics and has overlooked, amongst other things, that 'risk information production and flow is a fundamental feature of 'risk culture' and is itself constituted by an appetite for risk knowledge'. Three testable propositions on the role of information in risk culture are presented; these roughly align to the standard risk management structure of three lines of defence (mentioned above) and link information processes to organisational values.

Having seen the relevance of information processes to risk culture in Chapter 2, Michelle Tuveson and Daniel Ralph take a social network view of an organisation in 'A Network View of Tone at the Top and the Role of Opinion Leaders' (Chapter 3). Social networks are complementary to formal hierarchies such as lines of reporting and governance structures and arguably are under-studied within organisations. This chapter examines the role of individual staff, whether senior managers or not, in transmitting organisational culture across the firm through their social networks. The importance of the charisma and connectivity of individuals is modelled with agent-based simulation of communications within an organisation. The broad finding is that social networks may be critical to support tone from the top and may be an important complement to formal reporting or supervisory processes regarding maintenance and evolution of risk culture.

The ultimate value of any initiative to an organisation is the promise for a better future, and developing risk culture is no exception. This is explored through the relationship between innovative initiatives in an organisation and its culture in 'Rethinking Risk Management Cultures in Organisations: Insights from Innovation' (Chapter 4), by Stelios Kavadias and Kostas Ladas. Innovation is the subject of diverse management and sociological scholarship. Product portfolio management for a firm addresses its new offerings, which may be either novel products or entry to a new market. A related theme is that of firms adopting a 'strategic buckets' approach, allocating one bucket for incremental projects and another for radical experiments. This ring-fences opportunities in terms of both resourcing and within bucket management. Another strand of research from project management proposes that project planning should anticipate the emergence of unforeseen risks and hence focus on the ability to respond flexibly. The authors combine this wisdom by, first, distinguishing between radical innovation, which induces strategic risks, versus incremental innovation, which typically induces operational risks; and, second, by proposing a framework for innovation in an experimentation cycle – a process for balancing risk against reward by jointly managing evolution (exploration) and optimisation (exploitation).

### 0.3.1.2 Part II: A View of Risk Culture Concepts in Firms and Society

Following the concepts presented in the previous part, this part addresses the organisation as an entity and the dynamics of how the individuals, collective groups of individuals and external supervisors exist and engage within it. The concept of individual agency is explored within the context of how information is created and exchanged and where responsibility might lie within an organisation with respect to its governance structures. We focus on an important historical development in the banking sector, both in structure and oversight, that served to underpin modern culture issues.

How does risk culture evolve across an entire sector over nearly two centuries? 'The Changing Risk Culture of UK Banks', by Anthony Hotson and Duncan Needham (Chapter 5), charts the fundamental transformation in the business and risk culture of UK banking from the 1833 Bank Charter Act, which liberalised joint-stock banking in London, to the early 1900s, dominated by 'the Big Five', and continuing with the relative stability of the banking system and bank culture till after the Second World War, with big shifts in the 1970s and 1980s, eventually leading up to the GFC of 2008–9. This analysis looks at liability management and asset management as separate subsectors of the financial services, which have become combined under the heading of maturity transformation, e.g. mortgages. Viewing it through this historical lens, the GFC is described as being less about 'bad bankers' than a consequence of the transformation of commercial banks from being providers of short-term liquidity and payments services into residential property lenders.

Responding to the post-GFC wave of regulatory involvement covering risk culture, 'Regulating Agency Relationships and Risk Culture in Financial Institutions' (Chapter 6), by Kern Alexander, argues that the traditional understanding of agency problems in the

corporate governance literature cannot fully explain the risk management and operational failures of banks during the GFC. The chapter
suggests that human agency theory as it applies to the collective
efforts of individuals within an organisation can provide a fuller
understanding of how a weak risk culture can develop within banking
and financial institutions. The chapter reviews international regulatory developments in the area of risk culture and the main legal
and regulatory instruments adopted following the crisis to enhance
risk culture within financial institutions, including the UK Senior
Managers and Conduct Regime and how it attempts to address collective agency problems. The chapter concludes that the complexities
of regulating the collective activities of many individuals regarding
cultural standards and norms within large organisations can be more
effectively achieved through a balance between official sector regulation and self-regulatory initiatives that build on existing institutional
knowledge in the financial sector.

'What Does Risk Culture Mean to a Corporation? Evidence
for Business Value' (Chapter 7), by Andrew Freeman, offers a two-
part discussion. The first looks at the emergence of risk culture as a
focal regulatory theme in financial services starting from 2008. This
describes risk culture as a 'technocratic' child of financial regulation
rather than an element of broader sociological developments in management that relate to cultural studies and its impact on risk management and the writing of management gurus. This first part also
includes a de facto case study of the period 2008–12, following the
GFC, by identifying the ideas, institutions and key people in the
emergence of risk culture as a pillar of risk management in financial
services. A subliminal reading is that the importance of risk culture,
and later conduct risk, may be partially explained by the need for
financial services, regulators and firms to show to society and business
at large that some action was being taken by in response to the crisis.
Second, this chapter takes a sceptical view of the link between risk
culture and performance of firms. In that vein, Freeman predicts that
'much further study in the area of risk culture and performance

is likely to remain categorically confused' because the complexity of organisations, and in the environment generally, makes it hard to distinguish cause (here, the effort to improve risk culture) from effect (improving business value).

There is little distance between considerations of organisational culture and ethics, whether the latter concern individual behaviours or firm-level values and outcomes. In 'Values at Risk: Perspectives on the Ethical Turn in Risk Management' (Chapter 8), Anette Mikes places culture, as measured through an organisation's commitments, core values and priorities, within the context of ethics by asking whether those commitments and values are regularly compromised in practice. In two compelling case studies, Mikes explores how organisations constructively measure the gap between values espoused by their leaders and the concerns and activities of wider staff. The overarching proposal is the idea of 'values at risk' (VsR), together with identifying the demand, indeed need, for an ethical turn in risk management. Three areas of concern are used to highlight the potential for VsR to generate constructive debate and action: the incubation of man-made disasters, corporate failures due to conflicts of interest and large societal risks such as climate change.

These chapters broadly shed light on the thesis that risk is not solely due to chance and individual behaviours but that organisations play a vital role as both manufacturers and managers of risk. Additionally, many adjacent themes are worth exploring to further support the ideas presented. Further research is certainly warranted to verify and validate our thesis.

## 0.4 BEYOND THIS BOOK: BROADER THEMES RELEVANT TO RISK CULTURE

We are not suggesting or implying that the selection of chapter topics in this book represents the exhaustive set of subjects or even the most vital. Having outlined the motivation of the editors and authors in writing this book, we ask what other aspects of scholarship or practitioner attention could be brought to bear in a comprehensive study of risk culture. We outline additional themes that are not directly addressed in this book but may be important in further research on risk culture.

### 0.4.1   From Psychology to Sociology of Risk Culture

#### 0.4.1.1   Psychology of Individuals and Risk Culture

The need to better understand how and why organisations work in business has put focus on the fields of psychology and behavioural sciences. We start by noting several important areas of research on individual motivations and decision-making. Behavioural psychology (which addresses innate or unconsciously driven individual behaviour) and personality traits (psychometrics) are both well studied in psychology and partially adapted into corporate life via recruitment and staff development practices. Models for behaviour such as those based on Ajzen's (1991) theory of planned behaviour provide frameworks that tie beliefs and intentions to contingent behaviours. Neuropsychology studies the link between brain physiology and activity to a variety of behaviours and perceptions (including fairness, mentioned below). A little explored but fast-growing area is the relevance of human physiology, e.g. hormone levels, to decision-making (Coates, 2013). Nevertheless, there is a wealth of work on how individuals connect to what might be called organisational attributes, including organisational processes, and on team performance – though we bypass the latter.

We highlight three organisational themes: safety culture, psychological safety and fairness. Safety culture and safety climate are familiar terms in industries with high levels of physical risk, where evidence points to the effectiveness if not necessity of management attention, including training and monitoring, in organisational health and safety outcomes. Psychological safety, which addresses the level of risk perceived by an individual in interacting with others, has proven to be a link between managing risk culture in physically risky environments and how risk is recognised and managed in organisations generally. This topic is connected with oft-touted organisational values such as courage and integrity, feeding into considerations of risk culture, or, more subtly, creativity. Fairness in an organisation, as well as an aspect of individual perception, is linked to organisational actions and processes in the study of procedural justice. Both procedural justice and psychological safety have been studied in the context of stress and mental health in the workplace; arguably, procedural justice provides cultural artefacts in the organisation that influence psychological safety and risk culture.

### 0.4.1.2   Cultural Cognition and Professional Judgement

Cultural cognition describes the tendency of individuals to conform their beliefs about disputed matters of fact (e.g. whether humans are causing global warming, whether immigration is to blame for unemployment) to values that define their cultural identities. Its relevance to how people interpret, absorb or reject information is the focus of the Cultural Cognition Project (Yale Law School, n.d.), which has made substantive studies of how professional training or professional identity, indeed professional culture, interacts with cultural cognition (Kahan et al., 2016: 394). The role of cultural cognition in organisational (risk) culture is little studied, however.

### 0.4.1.3   The Sociology of Risk

This topic addresses the tacit and explicit recognition of risk, and the attribution of responsibility for managing it, within society. 'Risk society' is a prominent idea (Beck, 1992) that describes unintended and endemic consequences of transformation of society from industrial to modern, exemplified by climate change and also by the 9/11 terrorist attacks. Rather than advances in technology and society solving the problem of future uncertainty, the proposal is that these advances feed the complexity of 'modernity' that creates unknown unknowns. This framing of emerging risk as both material and ever-present has filtered into organisational and strategic thinking, suggesting that organisational risk culture reflects societal culture as it does internal culture and values.

### 0.4.1.4   Rogue Behaviours

Can risk culture thwart rogue behaviours by individuals? Risk culture is often cited as an explanation for actions and decisions by individuals. Recent years have brought many instances of ethical misbehaviour within corporations to the spotlight, such as insider trading, fraud and bribery, and served to make this association indelible. While these cases present outright criminality, speculations have been offered that culture may serve to thwart criminal tendencies or help in rehabilitating errant individuals. Putting aside causality, culture can serve to amplify or dampen an individual's actions. What may originate as an individual exercising independence to complete a job within scope could also result in escalating behaviours involving harassment, bullying and other predatory actions. A concern is that less desirable, unethical or even criminal behaviours can grow to become mainstream and endemic with an organisation. Indeed, a management conundrum is that growth of rules to guide behaviours in a complex working environment can promote rule-bending behaviour (Weinberg & Taylor, 2014). Another dimension of the gradual escalation of poor behaviour is the rogue individual who is rogue by nature or nurture and brings associated behaviours into a company. This situation, like an infectious virus, uses the immune system of the company's risk culture – risk culture as immunotherapy – to either kill off the virus or spread this behaviour. The literature suggests that contagion of one bad apple may not be to the whole barrel, however, but to the 'in-group' of staff who identify with the miscreant (Gino, Aval & Ariely, 2009).

### 0.4.2   Risk Subcultures

The notion of risk subcultures acknowledges that organisational culture is plural rather than uniform.

### 0.4.2.1   Organisational Subcultures

Perhaps the most obvious question is to ask what risk culture means in each division, or even team, of an organisation. The past and present – relating to staff, clients and business environments – may drive different manifestations of organisational culture, hence risk culture. For a division or business line, the question or risk culture addresses vertical structure and workflow, hence the transmission of risk culture from the top down, as well as the sensing and prioritisation of risk from the bottom up. Considerations of horizontal structure are natural when looking at corporate risk functions, e.g. in the financial services via the first, second and third lines of defence, which correspond roughly to risk management integral to business activities, risk oversight of business activities and independent assurance, also known as audit and compliance. On one hand, risk culture in the second and third lines of defence cuts horizontally across team and divisional boundaries. On the other, does risk culture in the first and second lines indeed exist independently of business activities, or, instead, is it inseparable from the way business is managed?

### 0.4.2.2 Geographical Impact on Culture

Globalisation has driven unprecedented growth in international trade but has also been credited to fuelling populist movements around the world. Greater interconnectivity exists throughout the world economies to support global markets via tactical components such as global value chains and broader socio-economic support networks. The impact of locale on risk culture of an organisation is highlighted in international management, e.g. country risk factors are relevant to both business prospects and the exposure of the organisation to bribery and corruption (Ministry of Justice, 2010). While tailoring global corporate practice to different locations increases the burden of management and oversight, bringing local knowledge and customs into that corporation may have resilience impacts on the wider organisation (Bunderson & Sutcliffe, 2002).

### 0.4.2.3 Overlapping Subcultures

A member of an organisation is a participant in several subcultures, including one for their professional identity within the organisation, perhaps as an engineer or executive (Schein, 1996), and another for their organisational silo, perhaps in a product division or a centralised function like human resources. Personal or political subcultures separate from the organisation may also be relevant. This raises questions about how individuals, and organisations, understand and react to multiple subcultures, particularly when they clash. Subculture scholars challenge organisational culture as a unitary entity.

### 0.4.2.4   Gender and Cultural Diversity

What are the implications to risk culture from increasing gender and cultural diversity within an organisation? The value of heterogeneity in improving resilience in many other regimes such as biological and ecological systems, species population and plant robustness has been well established and can serve as a reference point. Public knowledge of inequities associated with gender and diversity have highlighted the dark side of power structures in companies and the immutability of certain organisational and societal cultures. Gender and diversity risk encompass pay equality, creating a harassment-free workplace, safeguarding vulnerable employees and beneficiaries, fair hiring and gender balance. The business case for greater diversity has been made in the form of improved company governance – better practices in managing broader stakeholders by taking greater care in sustainable environmental practices, enhanced corporate social responsibility, organisational culture, recruitment and retention of talent (Page, 2007). Examples include the positive correlation between diversity at the executive level and profitability and value creation, and that companies in the top quartile for gender diversity are 27 per cent more likely to outperform their national industry average in terms of economic profit (Hunt, Prince, Dixon-Fyle & Yee, 2018).

### 0.4.3   Dynamics of Risk Culture

The way risk culture changes may relate to broader change in an organisation or its ecosystem. That is, organisational scholars study the dynamics of culture, including the potential for sudden shifts resulting from an internal jolt or external change. From a management perspective, the prospect of purposeful change of an organisation's culture suggests the potential for improving the performance of the organisation.

### 0.4.3.1 Drivers of Cultural Change

An understanding of evolving risk culture would be informed by a taxonomy of the drivers of change, internal or external. Potential influences on culture include (changes in) management of personnel (from recruitment and training through to incentives and promotions), leadership, governance and structure, regulation, market forces, consumer preferences and the broader economic and social setting.

Wider global forces like climate change and the fourth industrial revolution will bring macro-shifts and consequently challenge risk culture in organisations.

### 0.4.3.2 Complexity and Feedback in Organisations

Complexity is the subject of study and management insight across a variety of fields and scales (Helbing, 2008). With roots in control engineering models that incorporate feedback loops, this concept addresses the dynamics of change within organisations and other systems, explicitly accounting for multiple processes, formal and informal, at potentially different scales, each apparently following its own momentum while influencing and being influenced by other processes. Executive anecdotes aplenty inform this view, e.g. incentive schemes that inspire short-term mis-selling of products, leading to midterm legal and regulatory retribution and, in the longer term, reputational issues that harm commercial performance and also staff morale.

### 0.4.3.3 Measurement and Management of Risk Culture

To what extent is risk culture manageable, e.g. subject to controlled change that is effectively measurable? Hence, what is the benefit of such management? We note that Freeman, in Chapter 7, takes a sceptical view about how firm performance relates to risk culture, while Mikes, in Chapter 8, is more positive in showing how an organ-isation's values can be measured and linked to its risk culture.

### 0.4.4   Risk Culture and Risk Appetite regarding Value Creation and Innovation

The previous point, in Section 0.4.3.3, hints at the relationship between risk management and improved firm performance. A bolder aim is to understand the role of risk inherent in creating value within a firm, including innovation, which is discussed in Chapter 4, and at the firm level, how the implementation of strategy affects the risk of achieving the strategy. As noted in the literature (Tuveson & Ralph, 2016), risk that is attributed to organisational cultures that condone fraud and other bad behaviours should be distinguished from cultures that encourage decision makers to take on greater risks, exposing a firm to larger losses, provided these are within the firm's risk appetite. A separate point is that while risk appetite is standard lan-guage in banks, and even addresses non-financial concerns prevalent in operational risks, this terminology and perhaps this fundamental idea – of understanding the trade-off between the creation of value and the creation of risk – seems far from standard in the broader corporate setting.

REFERENCES

Ajzen, I., (1991). The theory of planned behavior. *Organizational Behavior and Human Decision Processes*, **50**(2), 179–211.

Ashby, S., Palermo, T. and Power, M. (2014). Risk culture: definitions, change practices and challenges for chief risk officers. In P. Jackson, ed., *Risk Culture Effective Risk Governance*. London: Risk Books., pp. 25–46.

Banks, E. (2012). *Risk Culture: A Practical Guide to Building and Strengthening the Fabric of Risk Management*. Basingstoke: Palgrave Macmillan.

Beck, U. (1992). *Risk Society: Towards a New Modernity*. London: SAGE Publica-tions Ltd.

Bunderson, J. S. and Sutcliffe, K. M. (2002). Comparing alternative conceptualiza-tions of functional diversity in management teams: process and performance effects. *The Academy of Management Journal*, **45**(5), 875–93.

Cambridge Judge Business School (2016). 7th Risk Summit. https://bit.ly/34aDIBi

Coates, J. (2013). *The Hour between the Dog and the Wolf*. New York: Penguin Books.

Gino, F., Aval, S. and Ariely, D. (2009). Contagion and differentiation in unethical behavior: the effect of one bad apple on the barrel. *Psychological Science*, **20**(3), 393–8.

Group of Thirty (G30) (July 2015). *Banking Conduct and Culture: A Call for Sustained and Comprehensive Reform*. Washington, DC: G30. https://bit.ly/32Uh27V

Helbing, D., ed. (2008). *Managing Complexity: Insights, Concepts, Application*. Berlin: Springer-Verlag.

Hunt, V., Prince, S., Dixon-Fyle, S. and Yee, L. (January 2018). *Delivering through Diversity*. London: McKinsey & Company. https://mck.co/2opBjmZ

International Institute of Finance (IIF) (2009). *Reform in the Financial Services Industry: Strengthening Practices for a More Stable System*. Washington, DC: IIF.

Kahan, D. M. et al. (2016). 'Ideology' or 'situation sense'? An experimental investigation of motivated reasoning and professional judgment. *University of Pennsylvania Law Review*, **164**(2), 349–440.

Ministry of Justice (2010). *The Bribery Act 2010: Quick Start Guide*. London: Ministry of Justice. https://bit.ly/34jtcYz

Page, S. (2007). *The Difference: How the Power of Diversity Creates Better Groups, Firms, Schools, and Societies*. Princeton, NJ: Princeton University Press.

Power, M. (2009). The risk management of nothing. *Accounting, Organizations and Society*, **34**(6–7), 849–55.

Power, M., Palermo, T. and Ashby, S. (2013). *Risk Culture in Financial Organisations: A Research Report*. London: Centre for Analysis of Risk and Regulation, London School of Economics.

Schein, E. H. (1996). Three cultures of management: the key to organizational learning. *Sloan Management Review*, **38**(1), 9–20.

Tuveson, M. and Ralph, D. (2016). Is regulation of risk culture the missing piece? Civil actions reconsidered. *Banking & Financial Services Policy Report*, **35**(1), 12–18.

Weinberg, M. and Taylor, S. (2014). 'Rogue' social workers: the problem with rules for ethical behaviour. *Critical Social Work*, **15**(1), 74–86.

Yale Law School (n.d.) *The Cultural Cognition Project*. www.culturalcognition.net

# PART I Risk Culture Conceptual Underpinnings

# 1 Individual Agency and Collective Patterns of Action

*Organisational Culture through the Lens of Organisational Theory*

Jennifer Howard-Grenville

In organisational life, the term 'culture' is frequently used to label the mundane and the quirky, to analyse battles won and lost, and to orient newcomers or dismiss the actions of veterans. At times, culture is offered as a scapegoat for wrongdoings and at other times celebrated as underpinning success. In short, culture is often invoked to explain the otherwise inexplicable. Scholarship on organisational culture has also tended to reinforce its mysterious quality, portraying culture as an organisation's 'deep structure', inhering in taken-for-granted assumptions or commitments, which rarely surface unless they are severely threatened (Schein, 1985, 1992; Canato, Ravasi & Phillips, 2013). At the same time, scholars portray culture as inhering in people's day-to-day actions, revealed through their skills and habits, or 'general way[s] of organizing action' (Swidler, 1986: 277). From this perspective, culture is highly accessible to members and observers, even if it still belies simple explanation. Each of these ways of seeing organisational culture is accurate and helpful, even if they appear initially at odds with each other. Further, by considering both, we can gain a richer and more nuanced understanding of this very important facet of organisational life.

In this chapter, I explore the ways in which organisational theorists conceptualise culture, foregrounding two distinct perspectives, which grant differing degrees of primacy to leaders, versus members, for the maintenance and change of culture. Each perspective has distinct implications for how we think about risk management and risk culture in firms. The chapter is structured as follows.

I first present a brief overview of the ways in which culture has been conceptualised since it first became a topic of interest to organisational scholars in the 1980s. I next explain the first predominant perspective on culture, that in which culture is regarded as inhering in shared values, largely established and changed through leaders' 'tone from the top', and explore its implications for cultural maintenance and change. I then explain a more recent perspective on culture, that in which culture is regarded as a repertoire of patterned actions, largely established and shaped through day-to-day actions of members, and similarly explore its implications for cultural maintenance and change. I conclude with reflecting on how each perspective brings forward different insights into the relationships between culture, risk and risk management.

## 1.1   ORIGINS OF ORGANISATIONAL CULTURE

Organisational scholars have long been interested in the study of culture in organisations, with significant attention beginning in earnest in the 1980s, alongside a broader 'cultural turn' in the social sciences (Weber & Dacin, 2011: 287). The publication of a 1983 special issue on organisational culture in *Administrative Science Quarterly*, a premier journal in the field of organisation studies, captured what was then a hot topic for scholars and business managers alike. The notion of organisational culture in the popular press was being used to illustrate the ways in which rituals and values could elicit employee engagement, creativity or commitment, and hence enable superior firm performance (e.g., Peters & Waterman, 1982). The scholarly literature had a similar focus, albeit with a more measured approach to questions of whether culture drove firm performance.

Informed by anthropological theories and approaches (Aten, Howard-Grenville & Ventresca, 2012), early organisational scholarship considered how rituals, symbols, shared beliefs, assumptions or narratives carried and conveyed culture (Kunda, 1992; Schein, 1992; Martin, 2002). Many scholars studied organisational cultures as anthropologists would study communities or tribes – through extended periods of ethnographic fieldwork, in which the researcher seeks to understand the norms and meaning systems in operation by living with and living like the 'locals' (Van Maanen, 1979; Barley, 1983; Kunda, 1992). As opposed to the popular press, which tended to portray culture as something that was amenable to managerial control, scholars informed by the anthropological tradition regarded culture as something an organisation 'is' rather than something it 'has' (Smircich, 1983).

Over the years, the study of culture by organisational scholars has also been characterised by plurality and debate over the exact nature of culture (Martin, 2002), the degree to which it is shared and coherent across an organisation (Howard-Grenville, 2006; Meyerson & Martin, 1987), the degree to which it actually guides behaviour (Chatman & Cha, 2003) and the importance of having a 'good' culture (Weeks, 2004). These debates, alongside broader shifts in how we conceive of the construction and spread of meaning in social life, have led to what has been termed the 'second wave' of cultural analysis in organisational scholarship (Weber & Dacin, 2011). These more recent studies posit a greater role for individual and organisational agency in using 'cultural materials as a pragmatic resource' and regard such processes as playing out on a broader stage, rather than being confined to 'private' interactions inside firms (Weber & Dacin, 2011: 288). The two perspectives I elaborate below have their origins in, respectively, the first wave of cultural analysis by organisational scholars, which tended to focus on cultural coherence and constraint, and the second wave, with its focus on cultural agency.

## 1.2   ORGANISATIONAL CULTURE AS SHARED VALUES

The perspective on culture most common in lay conversation is that which centres on the role of *shared values* in underpinning organisational members' actions. This has also been an enduring and predominant perspective in the scholarly literature, where the articulation of values is done by organisational leadership, and peoples' actions are then guided consciously and subconsciously by these values (Smircich, 1983; Ouchi & Wilkins, 1985; Martin, 2002). Accordingly, culture is viewed as a stabilising and unifying force, aligning what people do with the values organisational leaders espouse. Hence, it not only serves as the 'glue' of an organisation but also as an informal control mechanism.

Values are articulated and espoused, such that they are often disseminated in the organisation by leaders and included in mission statements, hiring criteria and behavioural and performance standards (Schein, 2010). However, the importance of values to culture lies in much more than their articulation. Values take hold when they become taken for granted 'assumptions' (Schein, 2010), which guide organisational members' actions even without their conscious attention. As Giorgi and colleagues, in their review of organisational scholarship on culture, explain, values work in concert with other elements to shape and sustain a culture:

> Once organisational values are validated – mostly as a result
> of organisational survival – they become taken for granted
> assumptions (Meyerson & Martin, 1987; Schein, 1985; Selznick,
> 1957) which are transferred to newcomers via socialization
> (Van Maanen, 1978). Rituals, practices, artifacts, and traditions play
> a significant role in reproducing existing values and socializing
> others (Alexander, 2004; Schein, 1985; Trice & Beyer, 1984).
> *(Giorgi, Lockwood & Glynn, 2015: 8)*

Ed Schein proposed a three-level model of culture that positioned values in relation to two other aspects, or levels, *artefacts* and *basic assumptions* (Schein, 2010). The artefacts of culture are its transparently observable manifestations. These include familiar aspects like physical layouts of office space (are there open, shared spaces or demarcated offices, open or closed doors, modern or stuffy furniture?), forms of dress (casual or formal, a uniform or not?), language used between members, and material artefacts like products or logos. As well, artefacts can include the stories and myths that circulate within an organisation. For example, I remember during my stint as a management consultant hearing from employees of a major global company that their CEO had a direct elevator shaft that led from the underground parking garage to his offices on the top floor of the building, bypassing all the floors in between. Whether it was actually true or not, that this story circulated among employees was somewhat telling about the relationship they saw their senior leadership as having with everyone else. However, as Schein warns, artefacts may be inaccurate signals of the organisation's real culture, for they are observable but not necessarily trustworthy. In an open-plan office, people may still not treat each other with collegiality. Even with a private elevator shaft, perhaps the CEO was a warm and personable man but had just inherited this building design feature from a prior holder of the office.

To learn the real values, and ideally, the deeper, basic assumptions, of an organisation's culture, one must use the artefacts as clues but look beyond them. Basic assumptions are 'unconscious, taken-for-granted beliefs and values' that 'determine behavior, perception, thought, and feeling' (Schein, 2010: 24). In other words, basic assumptions of a culture are those values that are so engrained in people's thoughts and actions that they no longer need to be articulated. To be treated as a basic assumption, something needs to have been deemed to work and stood the test of time. It is not enough that a leader express her or his ideals, goals, aspirations and rationalisations for the organisation. Members of the organisation must have taken these up in what they do and how they do it.

While there are others who foreground the importance of values to organisational culture, Schein's model is the most influential and also highlights this perspective's emphasis on how culture can create uniform behaviour. He writes, 'if a basic assumption comes to be strongly held ... members will find behavior based on any other premise inconceivable' (2010: 28). Clearly, when leaders aim to promote certain kinds of behaviour, be it around safety, risk or inclusion, it is not surprising that they regard the promotion of certain kinds of desired cultural values as important to this, given the grip such values apparently can have on behaviour. Frequently, organisational leaders create incentives, strategic goals and policies aimed at fostering behaviours aligned with desired cultural values (Schein, 2010; Howard-Grenville & Bertels, 2012). These moves work best when they amplify or reinforce already existing values and are supported by hiring individuals who align with the espoused values, socialising others and removing those whose behaviours do not align with the values. Internal consistency and reinforcement is critical when, as in this perspective, culture is held as a coherent and internally controlled system of meaning.

However, we risk oversimplifying this perspective if we regard the promotion of values as clearly and straightforwardly related to behaviour. Schein himself warns that organisational cultures are typically 'deep, pervasive, [and] complex' (Schein, 2010: 53), and the promotion of new values may be meaningless if they represent only desired aspirations or contradict other aspects of culture, which is frequently not uniform across an entire organisation. Many organisational cultures are, in reality, complex and differentiated, as occupational and geographical differences introduce perturbations (Schein, 2010) and some are more fully fragmented, better described as distinct subcultures with little that unites them (Meyerson & Martin, 1987). As well, taking values as the primary basis for culture can be misleading because manipulating values need not trigger the intended behaviours. Sometimes it can even produce the opposite effect. For instance, Gideon Kunda's study of a high-tech company's efforts to 'engineer' its culture to generate high commitment led to employee burnout and cynicism (Kunda, 1992). Relatedly, Cha and Edmondson (2006) found that charismatic leadership unintentionally produced employee disenchantment because employees perceived their leaders to be inauthentic.

When organisations serve as exemplars of the culture-as-shared-values perspective, they do carry some important lessons for how such cultures might be attained and sustained. Organisations that espouse common values, cultivate shared goals and enable some degree of employee autonomy in working towards these do exist. One exemplar is Nordstrom, a US-headquartered department store lauded for its culture emphasising customer service (Chatman & Cha, 2003). Nordstrom employees receive a single card titled 'Employee Handbook', which reads, 'We have only one rule ... use good judgment in all situations.' In so doing, Nordstrom sends the signal to employees that it trusts each one's autonomy and professionalism to serve the customer. Backed up by training and socialisation, the admonition to 'use good judgement' is also enforced by peers. For example, a salesperson was scolded by his peer for not working hard enough to source a customer's desired shoes from a competitor (which, while losing a sale for Nordstrom, would delight the customer and gain her ongoing loyalty). Other examples exist of organisational cultures that produce high levels of employee performance towards organisational goals and commensurately high levels of employee autonomy, creativity and peer sanction. Southwest Airlines long made news for its flamboyant CEO, exuberant celebrations and quirky employee practices (Bailey, 2008). It has been consistently profitable every year for the last forty-five (Schleckser, 2018), an impressive feat in the airline industry. Attaining this is only possible because Southwest's quirky culture supports its non-hierarchical and team-oriented approach, which helps it turn around aircraft at the gate faster than its competitors.

While the Nordstrom and Southwest examples point to customer-facing cultures that enable employees some discretion in the pursuit of organisational goals, many organisations in the energy and healthcare sectors have made investments in what have come to be called 'safety cultures' (International Nuclear Safety Advisory Group, 1991) or 'just cultures' (Reason, 1997). These aim to promote safety through employees being encouraged and even rewarded for error reporting and not punished for mistakes. However, this is done against a backdrop where serious negligence, deliberate violations and destructive acts are not tolerated because of the risks involved.

The lessons from these examples are that culture as promoted through shared values must be strongly tied to the actual work that employees are doing and the value of this work to the organisation and its strategy. Nordstrom needs to differentiate itself within the competitive retail sector, and be able to sustain higher pricing, by having intensely loyal customers who, in turn, come to rely on the unique and creative customer service experience employees offer. Organisations operating in environments where damage to human safety or ecosystem integrity are ever-present risks need to cultivate cultures where the shared expectation of employees is towards compliance – on certain matters at least – rather than creativity or autonomy (Bertels, Howard-Grenville & Pek, 2016).

In sum, perspectives on culture that foreground shared values draw attention to the role that commitment to certain values, and their taken-for-granted assumptions and associated behaviours, play in supporting associated organisational goals and strategies. Developing such a culture is easier when it originates with the founders of the organisation and the founding conditions, but even then it only becomes actually enacted as the culture when employees take it up and perpetuate it. When cultures are already deeply engrained and a shift is desired, for example, to create 'inclusivity' or 'diversity' within an existing culture, leaders often come up against the limits of regarding culture as shared values. This is because this perspective is particularly helpful and applicable when culture is regarded as internally consistent, relatively coherent and in alignment with organisational goals and strategies, and hence largely self-reinforcing and persistent. Next, we consider an alternative perspective that recognises that organisational cultures can equally be regarded as somewhat more malleable.

## I.3   CULTURE AS REPERTOIRE

The repertoire perspective on culture departs from much of the prior scholarly work on organisational culture, in that it emphasises, consistent with what Weber and Dacin (2011) label the 'second wave' of culture studies, that culture is produced by individual and organisational agency. In fact, much of the organisational literature from this perspective draws on the work of sociologist Anne Swidler (1986, 2001), who explicitly sought to counter a view of culture as depending on shared values. Swidler was concerned about culture at a broad, societal level rather than at the organisational level, but her work is highly consistent with a simultaneous swing in organisation studies towards more agentic explanations for organisational phenomenon.

Swidler (1986) emphasised that what might look like shared value commitments should in fact be regarded as shared 'strategies of action' – ways of acting that are socially recognised and validated. She argued that people might share certain values across society – such as valuing education – yet have different capacities to actually act in pursuit of these values. For example, those with limited economic means might have limited resources through which to pursue education, but that does not imply they don't value it. Conversely, Swidler argued, we often use similar strategies of action yet pursue somewhat different ends with them. She gives the example of Americans using a 'general way of organizing action (... [such as] relying on selling one's skills in a market)' (1986: 277) and points out that this individualistic approach allows people to reach many potential goals in American society. Her core argument, then, is that we should not mistake the pursuit of shared values as the 'end' of culture and hence its defining feature; rather, we should locate culture in the use of a shared set of 'means' (or strategies of action) and treat the ability to use these means as the defining feature of membership in a culture. Swidler's perspective on culture therefore suggests that organisational cultures hang together on the basis of their members' abilities to operate skilfully within them, not on the basis of shared commitments to values.

This perspective has a number of implications for how we understand organisational cultures and how they might be managed or changed. Before considering these, it is important to introduce a bit more of the language that is at the heart of this perspective.

In line with a focus on culture as a 'means' of organising social life and not 'ends' for it, the culture-as-repertoire perspective foregrounds actions, not values. People's use of culture emerges as sets of patterned behaviours, termed 'strategies of action' (Swidler, 1986). Strategies of action are 'general way[s] of organizing action' (Swidler 1986: 277), and they provide members of a culture with ways of 'construct[ing] chains of action beginning with at least some prefabricated links' (Swidler 1986: 277). In other words, strategies of action are recognisable and familiar patterns of acting that people learn to use as part of their socialisation to a culture. Because they are familiar to and valued by members of a culture, strategies of action tend to be drawn into use to accomplish a wide variety of specific tasks. For example, employees of 'Alpinista' (a pseudonym), a US-based a rock-climbing company, drew on the strategies of action of self-reliance and persistence in the face of failure, regardless of the exact work situations they faced (Harrison & Corley, 2011). One executive described the way employees worked to improve Alpinista's IT systems, saying: 'We've got grinder personalities: you give it your first shot, if that doesn't work you give it your second shot. If that doesn't work you go again' (Harrison & Corley 2011: 398). Importantly, this strategy of action of persisting in the face of failure applied not only to work within the firm but also reflected employees' experiences outside work as recreational rock climbers. Indeed, self-reliance and persistence are strategies learned and honed on a rock face that carry over, in this case, readily to a workplace that rewards and reinforces such patterns of action.

This example also highlights how the culture-as-repertoire perspective shifts from a focus on organisational culture as largely internally determined and hence a 'closed', or private, system (Weber & Dacin, 2011), understood and guided only by its members, and towards a focus on the interactions between organisational cultures and their broader contexts. Consistent with the second wave of cultural studies, regarding culture as an 'open system' (Harrison & Corley, 2011) draws attention to the potentially public nature of organisational culture and its permeable boundaries. Culture is open by virtue of the fact that employees operate in many domains of social life and learn and draw from varied strategies of action. As well, expectations and associated strategies of action, such as those for social and environmental responsibility, can be generated outside the firm and move within it through the help of regulation, industry or social norms (Howard-Grenville, 2007; Howard-Grenville, Golden-Biddle, Irwin & Mao, 2011). While some organisational cultures may encourage employees to check their strategies of action at the door, others will actively cultivate an internal culture that reflects aspects of external life. For example, Harrison and Corley (2011) describe Alpinista's intentional cultivation as an organisational culture infused with strategies of action drawn from the broader rock-climbing enthusiast community; conversely, Alpinista also seeded this external community with culture materials to influence its evolution. The cultivation of a culture that draws on strategies of action that span organisational boundaries may be particularly important for organisations that seek to reflect and guide customers, brand communities or other external stakeholders. Regardless of the nature of the organisation, the repertoire perspective alerts us to the fact that employees are important carriers of culture – via familiar strategies of action – from other domains of their lives.

A second key concept in Swidler's work is that of the actual repertoire of 'cultural resources' upon which people draw. Strategies of action must come from somewhere, and Swidler argues that strategies of action draw into use a set of *cultural resources* that reside in a broader cultural *repertoire*,[1] which might be held at the collective (group, society or organisational) level (1986). Cultural resources are both tacit and explicit carriers of cultural knowledge and can

---

[1] In her earliest work (1986), Swidler referred to the repertoire as a 'toolkit', and this terminology has taken hold among some authors. She later (2001) began referring to this as a repertoire because it implied greater flexibility of use.

include stories, symbols, roles, rituals and identities. So, for example, a company's founding story or iconic symbols from its history can serve as cultural resources that continue to inform employee's day-to-day strategies of action. The founding conditions of 'Oilco' (a pseudonym), which was established in the 1960s to extract oil from Canada's oil sands, a feat that was then deemed both technologically and economically infeasible, serve as the basis for stories that continue to inspire the company's current 'entrepreneurial spirit'. These resources manifest in contemporary employees' strategies of action, including that of 'get[ing] 'er done', or 'complet[ing] a task or achiev[ing]e a goal through sheer effort and pluck' (Bertels, Howard-Grenville & Pek, 2016: 580).

Because cultural resources are regarded as quite varied, values could be in fact be seen as one form of cultural resource. In fact, Swidler uses the term 'ideology' to refer to some cultural resources. The elements of her theorising might not therefore be regarded as so fundamentally different from those of Schein's, but their ordering and how they fit together is. The repertoire perspective takes a more dynamic and living view of organisational culture, viewing its members as skilled cultural actors, rather than guided by taken-for-granted values or assumptions (Martin, 2002; Howard-Grenville & Bertels, 2012). Hence, strategies of action take primacy, and culture inheres in their actual patterns of use, not in the values or beliefs one might infer to underpin them.

A major implication of the culture-as-repertoire perspective, beyond directing our attention to the open nature of culture, is for the role of individual agency in maintaining or redirecting culture. If the core of culture rests with the continued use of certain recognisable and valued strategies of action, then in order for culture to endure, these must be put to use on an ongoing basis. Therefore, even the persistence and maintenance of culture requires agency under this perspective. By contrast, persistence of a culture that rests on values or deep assumptions is more inertial. This does not mean that people use cultural strategies of action with explicit attention to them all the time – indeed, much of the time such strategies of action are largely habitual (Swidler, 1986). But by foregrounding how culture is 'done' by people in their day-to-day organisational lives, the culture-as-repertoire perspective carries the assumption that culture is only reproduced by people acting in a certain way. As well, it opens the possibility for culture to be changed when people either unintentionally or intentionally do different things. Adjustments to strategies of action are always possible because people might improvise, need to accommodate unusual circumstances or simply be too busy or lazy to do things as they typically would.

As well, consistent with the idea of a repertoire (e.g. as in dance or music), culture is broader than that which is performed in any given instance. That means that people have multiple strategies of action they *could* draw on and exhibit some degree of choice in what they *do* draw on and in what combinations they might string together several strategies of action. As Swidler asserts, people 'know more culture than they use' (Swidler 1986: 277). This is crucial to understanding the nature of individual agency that is exhibited in relation to culture. One the one hand, because people know more culture than they use, they are savvy users of culture, not 'cultural dopes' (Garfinkel, 1967, cited in Swidler, 1986: 277) who act only according to internalised taken-for-granted scripts. They know when and how to use certain strategies of action versus others. For example, when might persistence and self-reliance be most valued (e.g. when dealing with IT struggles at Alpinista) versus when is risk aversion most prudent (e.g. when dealing with accounting rules)? On the other hand, because people know more culture than they use, they may recombine strategies of action in novel ways or improvise within them, perhaps even importing strategies of action from other domains. Any of these moves could seed different ways of doing things with somewhat familiar cultural material. The answer to the question of whether such moves *change* the organisational culture resides with the degree to which these modifications spread to other people and other circumstances (Howard-Grenville et al., 2011). Finally, people are culturally savvy at using familiar strategies of action to block imposed change. For example, as Oilco executives worked to impose a major shift in how people would act in relation to environmental compliance, through systematising how compliance actions were undertaken and documented, some employees resisted by simply 'getting 'er done' by filling in *all* the year's compliance documentation on 1 January, as opposed to having it guide their actions throughout the year (Bertels, Howard-Grenville & Peck, 2016).

Finally, as suggested by this example, the role for leadership in directly shaping culture is subtler when culture is regarded as a repertoire than it is when culture is regarded as shared values. In each perspective, consistency between words and actions is essential, yet the culture-as-repertoire perspective foregrounds bottom-up (as opposed to top-down, leader-driven) processes. Just as members can resist efforts to change because they are comfortable with their familiar strategies of action, so too can they introduce variation within a culture because they may possess cultural resources from other settings. Middle managers, in particular, who know the existing cultural repertoire well but seek to change aspects of it, can be particularly effective at introducing and seeding variation within the repertoire by grafting new ideas on to existing strategies of action. In an athletic apparel company, middle managers worked to connect existing aspects of culture focused on innovation in product design with their concerns about sustainability by demonstrating how sustainability could be a pathway to and strongly connected with innovation; in this way, they used the culture itself and the space within the repertoire to fundamentally shift, over the span of a number of years, how the company acted on sustainability issues (Howard-Grenville et al., 2011). One concern with the culture-as-repertoire perspective is that it leaves culture as potentially too malleable and dispersed among diverse organisational actors, and the literature on it is often unclear about how members select certain resources over others and what might delimit these selections (Giorgi, Lockwood & Glynn, 2015).

In sum, perspectives on culture that posit it is a repertoire draw attention to the crucial role of members' actions in reproducing culture over time. Individual agency is central to this perspective because cultural strategies of action are the patterned behaviours performed by individuals. Further, people are culturally savvy enough to know when and how to enact certain strategies of action, capable of applying strategies of action from one setting to another and able to recombine them in potentially novel ways. This means that the opportunity for cultural change from the bottom up, through shifts in which strategies of action are used and how they are used, is ever-present. However, despite its emphasis on the 'means' (actions) of culture rather than its 'ends' (values or commitments), culture as a repertoire does not imply that 'anything goes'. Cultural change is constrained by virtue of the fact that people draw from a shared repertoire of cultural resources (stories, symbols, ideologies) in enacting strategies of action; further, these strategies of action must be valued by others to be effective. In essence then, despite its agentic and bottom-up nature, the culture as a repertoire preserves aspects of the social sanctioning that limits fundamental change, found also in the culture-as-values perspective. However, the culture-as-repertoire perspective does help us see how cultures can be malleable, and even at times internally inconsistent, because the resources from which people draw are not fully defined within the organisation nor primarily by its leadership.

## 1.4   IMPLICATIONS OF THE TWO PERSPECTIVES FOR RISK CULTURE AND RISK MANAGEMENT

The two perspectives on culture both have distinct implications for how one might think about generating a certain kind of culture, or cultivating certain orientations or behaviours within an existing culture. The management of risk is one important aspect of culture that has attracted increased attention and bears some resemblance to earlier attention to how organisations can orient their cultures and members' behaviours towards safety or compliance (Reason,

1997; Vogus, Sutcliffe & Weick, 2010). While other chapters in this volume go into much greater detail on the nature of risk management in particular settings, here I summarise the ways in which the two perspectives on culture presented can inform this conversation.

First, the culture-as-values perspective, with its attention to the important role of founders and organisational leaders in conveying the content of culture, suggests that the development of a culture more attuned to risk management demands a clear and consistent 'tone from the top' that sets out the core commitments and associated expected actions. These also have to have explicit and demonstrated connections to the organisation's overall goals and those of specific groups within the organisation in order for them to be considered meaningful to employees (Reason, 1997; Chatman & Cha, 2003) versus 'tacked on'. Cascading the message throughout the organisation and, critically, modelling it to employees by managers 'walking the talk' is essential since culture is transmitted and conveyed from the top down and new behaviours are soon rejected if they do not fit. Given the reinforcing nature of artefacts and symbols in conveying cultural values, it is important to draw on existing artefacts – such as symbols of the organisation's identity or stories of its founding conditions – that might reinforce the 'new' values. Finally, incentives that support behaviours in line with new values are critical in supporting cultural change from this perspective. Often overlooked but equally important is *removing* incentives (including informal supervisory support) for behaviours that reflect the *old* ways of working, and doing so in a manner that is consistent and visible to others. For example, we observed at Oilco that the one facility able to make a relatively quick and comprehensive cultural change was the one in which the senior leader visibly fired line managers who were continuing to model the 'get 'er done' behaviours, only paying lip service to the new compliance routines (Bertels, Howard-Grenville & Peck, 2016). While the emphasis in the culture-as-values perspective is on core commitments, day-to-day actions, rewards and sanctions must work with, not against, espousals of the culture, or else cynicism and confusion will quickly set in.

The culture-as-repertoire perspective suggests some additional and perhaps alternative ways of considering how a risk culture could be generated. First, since members of a culture can draw on a number of strategies of action, and do so skilfully to meet diverse demands, the first job for managers seeking to alter the cultural repertoire is to take careful inventory of its current state. What strategies of action – or patterned behaviours – are called on most reliably and frequently? How are strategies of action distributed in terms of their use across the organisation? In other words, do some groups use certain strategies of action more than others do? Are some strategies of action broadly shared while others are used by pockets of the organisation? This inventory will signal which cultural strategies of action are most relied upon and hence most valued. Effective ways to introduce change involve amplifying existing strategies of action by demonstrating their application towards new elements, in this way grafting on to these valued strategies and expanding from them (Howard-Grenville et al., 2011). Even when company members might resist new ways of working, being 'forced' at times to adopt new practices can help these become attached to already-valued strategies of action when members see how they can help them work more effectively (Canato, Ravasi & Phillips, 2013). While in the culture-as-values perspective, the tone from the top is very important as new commitments and associated practices are passed from the top down, in the culture-as-repertoire perspective, new practices may infuse laterally into the organisation, through middle and lower-level managers who knowingly or inadvertently use cultural strategies of action from other domains, including outside the organisation. This gives cultural change a middle-in or bottom-up character, and the role for senior management is to pick up and amplify productive changes and trends while quashing or redirecting those that are not productive or aligned with the desired direction of travel. As well, the middle-in character of cultural change implies that when trying to direct a culture, managers should identify cultural champions who are savvy users of existing strategies of action and well respected by their peers; their introduction of new strategies of action will be more likely mimicked and well received by others in the organisation.

The implications for changing culture – or curtailing its drift – under each perspective are not mutually incompatible. In fact, there is reason to see the two perspectives as consistent with one another, at least in some ways. For example, the culture-as-values perspective helps to draw attention to those aspects of organisational culture that are deeply held and inviolable, while the culture-as-repertoire perspective portrays some elements of culture as more malleable, and these might originate from a central set of core elements (Canato, Ravasi & Phillips, 2013). As well, the way in which aspects of culture are reproduced relies *both* on bottom-up processes (members putting to use strategies of action) and top-down processes (leaders articulating the set of cultural resources from which members draw in constructing their actions). Each perspective sheds light on different sides of the same coin – the 'ends' and the 'means' of culture – and gives primacy to one or the other. At times of crisis or when urgency is needed to shift a culture, it is inevitable that leaders are called on to articulate its central values and show how these are shifting to meet conditions or external demands. At other times, when culture is evolving or displays inertia, a culture-as-repertoire perspective might be more helpful in guiding inquiry into how strategies of action are reproducing the desired or undesired ways of working and how these can be nudged.

In closing, the organisational theory literature on culture has developed over time to capture greater nuance in how organisational culture is understood and to grant greater agency to individuals in reproducing and guiding culture. Both the culture-as-values and the culture-as-repertoire perspectives are helpful in guiding how culture might be managed and changed. If there is one thing that its anthropological roots remind us, however, it is that culture tends to be resistant to change, for it emerges out of the efforts of social groups to make sense of their worlds and to create norms for interaction. Hence any efforts to inculcate a certain type of organisational culture must take account of the culture already in use and plan for gradual change that will typically take far longer and require far more reinforcement than anticipated.

## REFERENCES

Aten, K., Howard-Grenville, J. and Ventresca, M. (2012). Organizational culture and institutional theory: a conversation at the border. *Journal of Management Inquiry*, **21**(1), 78–83. http://dx.doi.org/10.1177/1056492611419790

Bailey, J. (2008). Southwest. Way Southwest. *New York Times*, 13 February 2008. https://nyti.ms/2ooketu

Barley, S. R. (1983). Semiotics and the study of occupational and organizational cultures. *Administrative Science Quarterly*, **28**(3), 393–413.

Bertels, S., Howard-Grenville, J. and Pek, S. (2016). Cultural molding, shielding, and shoring at Oilco: the role of culture in the integration of routines. *Organization Science*, **27**(3), 573–93.

Canato, A., Ravasi, D. and Phillips, N. (2013). Coerced practice implementation in cases of low cultural fit: cultural change and practice adaptation during the implementation of Six Sigma at 3M. *Academy of Management Journal*, **56**(6), 1724–53.

Cha, S. E. and Edmondson, A. C. (2006). When values backfire: leadership, attribution, and disenchantment in a values-driven organization. *The Leadership Quarterly*, **17**(1), 57–78.

Chatman, J. A. and Cha, S. E. (2003). Leading by leveraging culture. *California Management Review*, **45**(4), 20–34.

Giorgi, S., Lockwood, C. and Glynn, M. A. (2015). The many faces of culture: making sense of 30 years of research on culture in organization science. *Academy of Management Annals*, **9**(1), 1–54. http://dx.doi.org/10.1080/19416520.2015.1007645

Harrison, S. H. and Corley, K. G. (2011). Clean climbing, carabiners, and cultural cultivation: developing an open-systems perspective of culture. *Organization Science*, **22**(2), 391–412.

Howard-Grenville, J. (2006). Inside the 'black box': how organizational culture and subcultures inform interpretations and actions on environmental issues. *Organization & Environment*, **19**(1), 46–73.

Howard-Grenville, J. (2007). *Corporate Culture and Environmental Practice: Making Change at a High-Technology Manufacturer.* Cheltenham, UK: Edward Elgar.

Howard-Grenville, J. and Bertels, S. (2012). Organizational culture and environmental action. In P. Bansal and A. J. Hoffman, eds., *Oxford Handbook of Business and the Natural Environment.* Oxford: Oxford University Press, pp. 194–210.

Howard-Grenville, J., Golden-Biddle, K., Irwin, J. and Mao, J. (2011). Liminality as a cultural process for cultural change. *Organization Science*, **22**(2), 522–39.

International Nuclear Safety Advisory Group (1991). *Safety Culture*, 75-INSAG-4, Vienna: International Atomic Energy Agency.

Jaskyte, K. (2004). Transformational leadership, organizational culture, and innovativeness in nonprofit organizations. *Nonprofit Management and Leadership*, **15**(2), 153–68.

Kellogg, K. C. (2011). Hot lights and cold steel: cultural and political toolkits for practice change in surgery. *Organization Science*, **22**(2), 482–502.

Kunda, G. (1992). *Engineering Culture: Control and Commitment in a High-Tech Corporation.* Philadelphia: Temple University Press.

Martin, J. (2002). *Organizational Culture: Mapping the Terrain.* Thousand Oaks, CA: Sage.

Martin, J., Feldman, M. S., Hatch, M. J. and Sitkin, S. B. (1983). The uniqueness paradox in organizational stories. *Administrative Science Quarterly*, **28**(3), 438–53.

Meyerson, D. and Martin, J. (1987). Cultural change: an integration of three different views. *Journal of Management Studies*, **24**(6), 623–47.

Ouchi, W. G. and Wilkins, A. L. (1985). Organizational culture. *Annual Review of Sociology*, **11**, 457–83.

Peters, T. J. and Waterman, R. H., Jr. (1982). How the best-run companies turn so-so performance into big winners. *Management Review*, **71**(11), 8–16.

Reason, J. T. (1997). *Managing the Risks of Organizational Accidents.* Vol. 6. Aldershot, UK: Ashgate.

Schein, E. H. (1985). *Organizational Culture and Leadership.* San Francisco: Jossey-Bass.

Schein, E. H. (1992). Corporate culture and performance. *Sloan Management Review*, **33**(3), 91–2.

Schein, E. H. (2010). *Organizational Culture and Leadership.* Vol. 2. Hoboken, NJ: John Wiley & Sons.

Schleckser, J. (2018). Why Southwest has been profitable 45 years in a row. *Inc.*, 28 August 2018. https://bit.ly/2JtHNZm

Smircich, L. (1983). Concepts of culture and organizational analysis. *Administrative Science Quarterly*, **28**(3), 339–58.

Swidler, A. (1986). Culture in action: symbols and strategies. *American Sociological Review*, **51**(2), 273–86.

Swidler, A. (2001). *Talk of Love: How Culture Matters*. Chicago: University of Chicago.

Van Maanen, J. (1979). The fact of fiction in organizational ethnography. *Administrative Science Quarterly*, **24**(4), 539–50.

Vogus, T. J., Sutcliffe, K. M. and Weick, K. E. (2010). Doing no harm: enabling, enacting, and elaborating a culture of safety in health care. *Academy of Management Perspectives*, **24**(4), 60–77.

Weber, K. and Dacin, M. T. (2011). The cultural construction of organizational life: introduction to the special issue. *Organization Science*, **22**(2), 287–98.

Weeks, J. (2004). *Unpopular Culture: The Ritual of Complaint in a British Bank*. Chicago: University of Chicago Press.

# 2 Risk Culture and Information Culture

*Why an 'Appetite for Knowledge' Matters*

Michael Power

This chapter explores a theme that has been surprisingly neglected in the risk culture debate, namely the centrality of information to both managerial agency and moral capability. The reasons for this neglect stem from a deep-seated 'individualism' in the approach to culture in general and risk culture specifically – the 'bad apples' bias. Ironically, this bias constitutes a distinctive culture of thinking about, and seeking to manage, culture in UK financial services that requires critical challenge. For example, surveys (completed by individuals) are evident in the emerging practice space of culture reform and shape a 'psycho-logistic' thought style at both policy and organisation levels. Despite the mantra of culture as 'how *we* do things around here' (Bower, 2003 – emphasis added), and despite recognising the significance of teams and groups in corporate misconduct (Greve, Palmer & Pozner, 2010), the analysis of culture by scholars and practitioners has tended to fall back on emphasising behaviour at the individual level.

The term 'groupthink' (Janis, 1982) has often been invoked to diagnose defective cultures, leading to calls for greater diversity in boardrooms and the workplace more generally. Furthermore, the importance of small, trans-organisational and deviant groups, as in the case of the LIBOR (London interbank offered rate) traders, has been noted and recognised (McConnell, 2013; Edmonds, 2014). Yet, reform processes (as opposed to disciplinary fines) have been shaped largely by a focus on the individual as the primary unit of regulation. This means that, again ironically, while the blame for the 2008 crisis has been placed on a culture of greed and individualism, the solutions remain epistemologically wedded to that individualism, despite wanting to break free from it. Indeed, for some financial organisations, the lever of cultural reform in the wake of the crisis has primarily involved adjustments to formal performance management systems for individuals.

What are the consequences of this apparent individualism and psychologism in the framing of the problem of culture in financial organisations? In this chapter, I argue that it leads to a significant underestimation of the cultural importance of knowledge production and of flows of knowledge in organisations in the form of information. Drawing on existing academic work, I argue that the general information environment is important in shaping organisational values and everyday control and performance narratives. Whatever 'doing the right thing' involves, it depends on a largely ignored collective capability grounded in the production and flow of information. Furthermore, I propose that this information flow is itself sustained by deeper organisational attitudes to knowledge production. It will be argued that organisations have, whether they are consciously aware of it or not, an 'appetite for knowledge', of which risk knowledge is a critical subset and which is revealed in the organisational life of their information systems.

That the dynamics of technical features of organisations, such as information systems, are intertwined with organisational culture and values is actually well known by organisational sociologists (e.g. Selznick, 1957; Besharov & Khurana, 2015) yet largely ignored in the financial services culture discussion for the reasons already noted. Commentators and policymakers have been quick to focus on values and on the need for ethical renewal but have failed to develop an understanding about how such a renewal may be deeply linked to the ecology of information technologies and the capabilities that they create and foster. Of course, this neglect is also understandable. Something like an organisational appetite for knowledge, and its implications for capability formation, is much less visible to the public and to policymakers than the deviant actions of individuals. It is much easier to hold individual people – rogue traders or directors – to account than intellectual systems and their assumptions.

This chapter challenges this deep-seated tendency to focus on individuals. It argues that the information environment, constituted by an appetite for knowledge production, shapes collective habits of risk identification, communication and mitigation. Studies show that warning signs of impending risk crystallisation cannot be acted upon unless the capability exists to produce and communicate them for attention. The root causes of individual bad behaviour do not simply lie in defective values, as if such values – good or bad – existed in an organisation independently of the technical tasks it performs. Rather, values are intertwined with the technical level, namely the information systems and the appetite for knowledge (or ignorance) that they exhibit.

By way of working definition, I take an 'appetite for knowledge' to be the empirical attitude of an organisation and its members to producing systematically (i.e. not informally or by gossip) facts about itself and its interface with its environment. This appetite expresses an important value of the organisation and is most likely shaped in large part by the institutional field within which it operates. 'Information' refers to the specific realisation of this appetite for knowledge in systems that distribute it as a flow within and beyond the organisation boundaries. These are idiosyncratic uses of these terms, but they enable the formulation of the core argument of the chapter: *risk information production and flow is a fundamental feature of 'risk culture' and is itself constituted by an appetite for risk knowledge.*

In the next section, the chapter develops the argument that capability is fundamental to organisational culture by adapting the philosopher Kant's famous and much debated argument that 'ought implies can'. This is followed by a brief review of the influential 'man-made disasters' thesis, which places ignored warnings at the centre of accident diagnosis and shows that important information existed in many cases but was not organised for attention and decision-making (Turner, 1976). The chapter then draws on further research to focus on three processes in which culture and information are intertwined: networking and interaction, technoculture and governance. Each discussion of these three processes is used to generate a testable proposition that could inform both policy thinking and further empirical investigation. The chapter shows how these processes and their respective propositions point to an underlying, but largely unproblematised, 'appetite for knowledge' in organisations, which is a critical element of risk culture and organisational culture more generally.

Finally, it is necessary to say a word about the terms 'culture' and 'risk culture', which will be used in close proximity to one another in this chapter. Their relationship has been a source of considerable debate and controversy – largely fruitless in my view and fuelled by confusion between nominalism and realism. Put simply, there is no doubt that the real empirical phenomena that we are trying to characterise with these terms are actually intertwined. We should not imagine therefore that tidy, mutually exclusive definitions of these terms are possible or even useful. However, it is still valuable to use the term 'risk culture' as a shorthand for those aspects of organisational culture that characterise the way organisations think about, know, process and act upon risks and uncertainties (Power, Palermo & Asby, 2013, chapter 1). What matters is not the label but the organisational features and practices to which it refers. Of course, nominalism and the power of words cannot be completely dismissed. We know that in some cases the more we use specific terms like 'risk culture', the more real they can become as organisational actors take them seriously (Ocasio, 2005).

## 2.1   FROM INFORMATION TO VALUE

Within moral philosophy there is an argument that individuals must have a capability to be held morally responsible for their actions. Kant famously and controversially established the principle of 'ought implies can' (Kekes, 1984). This principle is based on the plausible intuition that we cannot be held morally responsible if we genuinely lack the capability to be so. This is the reason that we do not normally judge the morality of actions by the humans we define as children, even though this intuition can be stretched to its breaking point by particularly repugnant actions. In essence, this means that our moral accountability is conditioned to a greater or lesser extent by a sense of our capabilities, including what we know or what others assume or think we know. For example, a chief risk officer (CRO) may only hear about a significant decision after it has been taken but may be judged *ex post* to have known about it in advance. Indeed, most legal systems embody the notion that we should judge the actions of individuals in terms of what it was reasonable to expect that they should have done or known in the light of their position and circumstances, subject to the caveat of wilful neglect and deliberate ignorance. In short, capacity, including knowledge, is therefore deeply important to morality and to accountability in general.

There are exceptions to this general conception. Lack of knowledge is a problematic defence for political and organisational leaders. First, we often take a view that they ought to have known something and did not take steps to do so. Second, we know that agency is 'distributed' (Enfield, 2017), meaning in part that it is impossible to understand the action of one human agent without reference to the actions of others. Societies design institutions to resist the fragmentation of responsibility that this distribution of agency implies and the excuse that 'I just did my job'. Thus, for leaders, if bad things happen 'on their watch', however distributed the agency of the situation, they can be held responsible. Indeed, laws and regulations often hold organisational agents responsible for matters that they cannot fully control or even know about. This principle seems unfair, but it also forces organisational leaders to recognise the risks associated with 'information silos', which may be tolerated because they allow them to be 'strategically ignorant' (McGoey, 2012) about deviant aspects of organisational practice.

The philosopher David Hume famously and controversially argued that one cannot derive an 'ought' from an 'is' and that the sphere of value, including morality, is entirely different from the way the world is according to science. But Kant's principle chips away at this dualism. If the way that the world is includes facts about our capabilities, then such facts provide at least an outer constraint to our moral responsibilities. We may value things and outcomes, but we have to be capable of responding to those values in order to be held responsible. Indeed, if we push this line of reasoning in a more socio-logical direction, then Kant's principle can be inverted and used to argue for the priority of capabilities in the formation of values. This means that before we can begin to think about what people ought to do – in society or in a specific organisation like a bank – we need to consider the routine settings in which, and through which, their organisationally valued capabilities are formed, a setting in which information flow is critical in the formation of agency. So, instead of 'ought implies can', this chapter argues for its inverse and also trans-forms it from a matter of logic into an empirical proposition, namely that 'information shapes values'.

This sociological shift in the philosophical argument matters to the debate about the renewal of values and ethics in financial services. In the first wave of reactions to the 2008 crisis, notions of 'doing the right thing' and 'tone from the top' were advanced as strong slogans that captured the essence of complex problems. However, not only did these and related ideas become increasingly empty, but the emphasis on values also presumed that they could be re-engineered in abstraction from other changes. Furthermore, values renewal in organ-isations was conceptualised predominantly as a matter of changing individuals – whether traders, CEOs or other board members.

This deep-seated diagnostic bias in the post-crisis period, des-pite appeals to non-individualistic notions like culture, reflected a moral panic triggered by the crisis and led to public critical narratives about individualism and greed. Indeed, it is argued that the 2008 crisis represented the logical playing out of the neo-liberal market impera-tive, with populist reaction as the inevitable result (Davies, 2018). To the trope of the 'rogue trader' in financial services, which reaches back to the collapse of Barings in the mid-1980s, was now added that of the CEO as narcissist or even 'psychopath' (Boddy, 2017). Hence the cultural turn in diagnosing the crisis was problematic from its very beginnings by having to accommodate a frenzied societal and popular media focus on individuals rather than the less visible determinants of collective behaviour, namely information structures and information flow. There was, and remains, little interest in a deeper diagnosis of what key actors, like CEOs, actually knew and why.

This constrained way of thinking about culture has been reinforced by oversight and advisory bodies, such as professional firms and self-regulatory entities like the Banking Standards Board in the United Kingdom, which came into existence in 2015. Firm-level cultural profiles and scores emerged as the aggregate outcomes of individually administered survey instruments. Indeed, surveys provided an attractive appearance of rationality and auditability for cultural reform processes. There was little or no place for the messier insights of organisational sociology or anthropology. Financial organisations had difficulties in digesting and operationalising sociological and anthropological approaches that could have radically reframed the culture problem (Power, Palermo & Ashby, 2013). Such 'soft' approaches produced too much complexity and were not readily 'actionable'. This was ironic given the difficulties that many firms experienced in using culture survey results, suggesting that such surveys were themselves more like 'rational myths' of good practice (Meyer & Rowan, 1977) than genuinely useful tools.

The urgency of value renewal in financial services also became translated into an increased emphasis on governance. Risk committees were normalised, and expectations of individual non-executive directors (NEDS) increased (Walker, 2009). At the centre of these changes, there was a new emphasis on the responsibility of directors to know and monitor their appetite for risk. A new kind of risk-based knowledge of the organisation was required, and demonstrating this knowledge to regulators became the new core skill set for boards in general and NEDs specifically.

I suggest that these reforms were largely acts of refining and making explicit existing modes of practical thought. This is not bad in itself, but it is not necessarily reform. In addition, the roll-out of the UK Senior Managers Regime from 2016 has formally reinforced a focus on individuals as units of both regulation and responsibility. The discourse of 'risky individuals' who were originally located in trading rooms has now shifted to the boardroom. As a corrective to this bias towards individuals and their perceptions, this chapter continues by focusing on the information environment that constitutes a risk culture and its values, and that shapes the individual perceptions of risk that feed surveys (Douglas & Wildavsky, 1983; Douglas, 2013). We begin by turning to the organisational sociology of risk.

## 2.2  MAN-MADE DISASTERS

Many accidents and disasters are not simply random natural events or bad luck but have their origins in the nature of organisations themselves and are 'man-made' (Turner, 1976; Turner & Pidgeon, 1997). Even an event like an earthquake, which is natural in its origins, may be exacerbated by failure to comply with building regulations. And, as we all know, the frequency of extreme weather is increasingly being attributed to the activities of mankind. At the heart of the man-made disaster concept is the idea of an 'incubation period', namely a period prior to a critical event like an accident in which, in retrospect, we can see that there were missed opportunities to act on warnings. These potential warnings were systematically nullified or somehow denied. A related but different foundational contribution to the organisational sociology of risk is that of the 'normal accident' (Perrow, 1984). Normal accidents characterise the risk of technological systems whose inherent complexity creates vulnerabilities. In 'tightly coupled' systems with insufficient redundancy, surprises are a normal outcome of the unknowable connectivity of risk. Yet critics of this notion of normal accident and its seeming technological fatalism have argued that the claimed paradigm case – the accident at Three Mile Island in 1979 – is more accurately analysed as a 'man-made disaster' in Turner's sense, since there had been specific warnings about the performance of the reactor type used there.

Vaughan (1996, 2005) builds on these analyses in the context of the *Challenger* launch disaster in 1986 and adds the notion of 'normalised deviance' to capture the sense in which entirely mundane and accepted management practices can incrementally give rise to failure. As small rules are broken without consequence and mistakes in the name of risk-taking and innovation become accepted, the standards against which deviance can be measured are progressively weakened leading to an increased likelihood of disaster, which is cumulatively unrecognised by organisational actors (Greve, Palmer & Pozner, 2010: 73).

These different analyses of the causes of accidents suggest that there is often prior information about relevant risks that eventually crystallised (Atkins, Fitzsimmons, Parsons & Punter, 2012). Fundamental epistemological ignorance of the kind attributed to Perrow's notion of the normal accident is rare. Rather, studies reveal widespread evidence of failure to assemble relevant information. Mundane compliance violations in the case of *Challenger* were normalised in such a way that they could not generate attention and questioning of existing ways of doing things and thereby inform mitigating or preventative action. Two further examples from financial services help to develop this insight a little further.

In 2007 and 2008, UBS made a number of announcements about losses in its trading and investment activities related to mortgage and asset-backed securities. In total, UBS reported net losses of \$18.7 billion for exposures to the US residential mortgage sector for the year ending 31 December 2007. One of the root causes of these losses was that UBS lacked both the data and the capability to perform a fundamental review of the exposure of its overall portfolio to asset-backed securities.[1] In effect, different divisions of UBS were trading in instruments that possessed similar risk characteristics, yet senior management lacked a consolidated picture of this distributed activity. Crucially, the risk function itself was fragmented across the

---

[1] See Haig Simonian, 'UBS details subprime losses', *Financial Times*, 21 April 2008.

group: there was either no or very limited central portfolio oversight capability. The organisation lacked the ability to trigger a corrective brake on the aggregate position even though there was information about the individual components. Management therefore lacked the capability to 'do the right thing', although we cannot know whether, had they had this capability, they would have acted on it.

In 2015, an extensive analysis of the collapse of HBOS in the United Kingdom was published by the Bank of England (PRA & FCA, 2015). It was reported that the bank operated de facto as a federation of businesses with their own plans. The report describes how the group strategy was in fact the outcome of a predominantly bottom-up planning process. This fragmentation affected the risk management at HBOS in two critical ways. First, the group 'risk appetite' was in effect merely an ad hoc composite of the many different bottom-up approaches. At the group level, it could not itself be changed or become an object of intervention by group board management. Second, as with UBS, the report finds no evidence of a rational risk aggregation process to understand how risks were distributed across, and concentrated within, divisions.

Along with the Royal Bank of Scotland (RBS), HBOS became a public emblem of what was wrong in banking. Like many financial organisations prior to 2009, it was seen in retrospect to have prioritised growth with little apparent sensitivity to risk. According to the report, this growth imperative led to the poor quality of risk information and the internal weakness of the 'voice of risk', dramatised by the case of an internal whistle-blower within the risk function whose representations were disputed. The HBOS report also draws particular attention to weaknesses in the presentation of risk management information. Issues with the quality of the underlying data were known in 2006 but there was no committed strategy to improve it (PRA & FCA, 2015, para. 896). It is argued that executives and group board members could have done better to challenge certain divisions, whose riskiness was known in general terms. However, like UBS, HBOS also lacked high-quality data about its real risk profile, and, without this information, meaningful challenge by the board would have been difficult. Furthermore, the report notes that risk and control information was rarely mentioned in the CEO monthly report. We can never know for sure whether more challenge would have been forthcoming had the risk data been stronger and more organised for oversight purposes. However, it is reasonable to conclude that its absence inhibited that challenge.

Both the UBS and HBOS cases support a general analysis in terms of incubation periods in which warning signs were ignored and normalised deviance in which risk acceptability was driven by risky practice rather than the other way around. Yet in these cases, it is also too simple to say that there was risk information that simply existed but was ignored by management or key operatives. While much has been made of the respective values and culture of HBOS and RBS – which were also shared by many financial organisations in the early 2000s – the problem of culture manifested itself primarily in a *failure to prioritise the primary assembly and aggregation of critical risk information as a necessary precondition for picking up signals of impending problems*. And, in both cases, the risk function seems to have been both distributed and fragmented. So while it is right to highlight lack of attention to information in the incubation period leading up to failure, these cases also suggest a different kind of failure, namely the non-production of the kind of information necessary for that capability.

In summary, many analyses of accidents and disasters have been drawn, explicitly and implicitly, to the theme of bad behaviour as a root cause. Turner's work, and that of other organisational sociologists, provides a different view. The root causes are to be found in fundamental weaknesses of information production and in defective routines for processing information, leading to collective failures of intelligence and poor responsiveness to the cues that were evident. Furthermore, this work suggests that we need to pay more attention to how the technical features of information systems are intertwined with values (Besharov & Khurani, 2015). Specifically, in thinking about the problem of risk culture, we need to focus more on the fundamental processes by which risk information is produced, assembled and repetitively flows within organisations to test the proposition that 'information shapes values'. Psychology and psychologists can inform us about the perceptions and attitudes of organisational actors at the end of this flow, but they tend to be silent on the social and organisational processes by which these perceptions and attitudes are formed (Douglas, 2013). In what follows, we focus on three such organisational processes in order to develop further the theme of information and values: networking, technology and governance.

## 2.3 NETWORKING AND INTERACTION

As noted earlier, policymakers, regulators and other commentators demanded value renewal in the financial sector after the 2008–9 crisis. The problem of so-called toxic cultures, which were allowed to thrive, was epitomised by insider revelations at Goldman Sachs that they had disrespected their clients and had taken positions that contradicted their advice.[2] Bad behaviour, individual and collective, was in the spotlight. Yet, for many organisations, there was little emphasis on values at the level of organisational practices and change programmes immediately following the crisis (Power, Palermo & Ashby, 2013). Rather, on the ground, many banks and insurers were taking a pragmatic approach to risk culture, emphasising structural change and the creation and strengthening of the kind of central risk oversight capability that had previously been weak or lacking. At this level of risk management reform, questions of ethics, values and behaviour, which were prominent in the public discourse, were much less evident.

This finding suggests that while many organisations were determined to solve the problems experienced by UBS, they did not see this initially as a task of re-engineering motives and behaviour, other than via the introduction of formal incentives for good compliance. Rather, they started by investing in changes to ensure that there would be no

[2] See Tom Braithwaite and Tracy Alloway, 'Goldman's 'muppet hunt' draws a blank', *Financial Times*, 10 October 2012.

invisible 'risk silos' and that there would be much stronger central control over the de facto organisational risk profile. Two factors were necessary for this to happen. First, senior management needed to empower the risk function and give it the status that it had lacked prior to the crisis in many banks. That was relatively easy. Second, this newly authorised risk centre needed to develop improved informational capability, in the form of high-quality data about trading and operational exposures across all product categories. Thus, while the public emphasis on culture gave rise to pressures for change, a central element of the risk culture reform process was a risk information quality enhancement process.

In parallel with this emphasis on improved information to support better decision-making, the 'three lines of defence' (TLD) model became institutionalised as a structural orthodoxy, despite criticism (Luburić, 2017). Regulators preferred this model because it categorised the risk function as 'second'-line oversight and advisory function, structurally independent from the business (the 'first' line). Yet, this idealised independence of the second line tended to downplay the informational *dependence* of centralised risk management functions and their need to embed risk managers within the first line (Power, Palermo & Ashby, 2013). Thus, while banks and other organisations represented pure TLD models in their annual reporting, organisational and informational realities necessitated blurring the distinction between the lines. And whereas regulators and policymakers placed great emphasis on 'independence' between the lines, organisations themselves were much more pragmatic, even though they saw the benefits of structural separation to avoid the UBS and HBOS problems. For many organisations, the rhetoric of TLD was useful support for strengthening central risk oversight and increasing the power of risk departments.

The manner in which risk managers occupied fluid and hybrid positions spanning second- and first-line functions was one feature of a more generally observable strategy of building networks of allies for risk information production and sharing across organisations.

Network building within organisations is hardly a very surprising phenomenon, but for risk managers it was crucial in securing flows of risk-relevant information to enable and refresh effective oversight and management. In other words, improving risk culture for many CROs began with improving data quality and flow. One CRO in a major insurer consciously constructed a network of allies across the organisation in different functional areas, including human resources and trading. She was primarily interested in creating a new kind of risk culture 'dashboard', using, and consolidating, existing information sets and key metrics in the wider organisation (Power, Palermo & Ashby, 2013). In this case, the project of increasing the status of the risk function and of building better risk information were one and the same: the network conferred both political and informational advantages for the CRO and her team (Hall, Mikes & Millo, 2013, 2015).

Another example in a non-financial setting involves a CRO involved in change programmes at a toy manufacturer (Mikes, 2016). This CRO decided to develop 'strategic risk' workshops as settings for risk identification and the determination of action. The workshops were characterised by efforts to avoid the specialist vocabulary of risk and thereby to democratise and pluralise the creation of risk information. They permitted and encouraged conflict and argument and always concluded with actions and linkages to business planning that were as natural as possible. The workshops were settings in which risk information was created collectively from asking 'what if' questions and by exploring related scenarios. The CRO saw himself only as a facilitator, a risk knowledge broker, who was humble and respected and operated with a light touch.

Improving risk culture has often been described as 'joining the dots' of existing capabilities.[3] Yet there is considerable work involved in dot joining. CROs and other groups who were initially tasked with improving risk culture had to work hard to create connections – firstly

---

[3] See Sara Silver, 'Joining the dots: risk management and regulation', *Financial Times*, 20 September 2011.

among people and then across data sets. There was a recognition at the practice level that information flow requires high interactivity and 'touch points' (Power, Palermo & Ashby, 2013) with the rest of the organisation such that information flows to and *through* the risk function, not just from it. I propose that this interactive risk management style builds the foundations for information flow, which enhances diagnosis and leads to further interaction in a positive feedback loop. In the examples described above, improving risk culture was not primarily or directly a project of creating better people and 'doing the right thing' but involved the less glamorous work of making connections and overcoming the information fragmentation that Turner places at the heart of man-made disasters. Creating shared commitments to risk information, its production, sharing and consolidation is the real currency of risk culture and is expressed in the first proposition:

**Proposition 1** Risk culture is stronger the more that risk managers engage with front-line and service departments and build information networks with them.

## 2.4   TECHNOCULTURE AND THE FLOW OF RISK INFORMATION

One of the consequences of framing culture and risk culture in terms of values and people is that the role of technology and information systems in their widest sense are often ignored or underestimated. However, a recent study emphasises the role of an airline safety management system (SMS) in the everyday work of identifying and recording risks (Palermo, 2016). It is well known from psychological studies that risk identification and assessment are laden with potential biases, which are further complicated by the organisational reporting climate for 'speaking up' about risk. In this airline setting, the value of a 'just culture' was internally promoted by senior management but was also combined with easy staff access to the SMS via apps on smartphones. The ease of reporting risk-relevant incidents and the idea of a just culture, in which individuals could be confident that they would not be 'unjustly' blamed, were mutually supportive and, in a practical way, overcame the traditional incentive problems that lead to under- or misreporting of incidents (Etienne, 2013, 2014). The 'just culture' was not only a widely touted motif and abstract value aspiration. It was also hardwired and operationalised by the SMS, and this generated a distinctive kind of culture of risk information production and flow within the airline (Palermo, 2016).

The airline example shows how, on the one hand, there is a concerted effort by management to promote an atmosphere of trust via the principle of a just culture in order to encourage and incentivise staff to be the front-line identifiers of safety risks. On the other hand, the SMS is designed to make the 'work' of this kind of self-reporting of risk as easy and attractive as possible for staff, via mobile technology and similar methods. This SMS is simultaneously democratic – all staff are empowered to use it – and forensic. For example, there is literally 'no hiding place' for pilots who are monitored both in real time as well as by incident recording and analysis. The SMS is a 'disciplinary' infrastructure in the sense that the commitment to use it is a commitment to the core value of safety and a necessary condition of being an organisational member of the airline. The SMS also contributes to a distinctive style of interactive control between staff and the technology that captures safety-relevant facts.

The SMS can be characterised as a 'technoculture' in which people, values and technology combine to produce information flows about risk (Palermo, 2016). The SMS is fed with raw live and reported incident data and applies advanced analytics to produce a continuous stream of safety risk event patterns for further processing and investigation. This technoculture grounds the social construction of a safety-conscious and compliant environment and is characterised by an alignment of self-motivation and external verification. This case also suggests that organisational values in abstraction are empty and must be embedded in concrete practices (Selznick, 1957; Besharov & Khurana, 2015). In this setting, the human–system interface is the place where the fundamental safety values of the organisation are repetitively produced and reproduced. From this technocultural perspective, the airline does not so much rely on 'good' people to do the 'right thing' as use the SMS to construct compliant organisational agents who execute good behaviour. Doing the right thing is defined, constituted and channelled by an information management system, which socialises organisational actors and generates both individual and collective agency.

These insights about technoculture can be extended to the analysis of more generic instruments of risk control, such as risk indicators (COSO, 2004; Beasley, Branson & Hancock, 2010) and risk maps (Jordan, Jørgensen & Mitterhofer, 2013). Even though they may be used mainly by the risk function in an organisation, the way that such embodiments and visualisations of risk are created, used, maintained and refreshed is an index of risk culture and of attitudes to risk information production more generally. Meaningful cultural questions about individual risk indicators might address the extent of consultation in their development and how tolerances and triggers ('risk appetite') are generated and reviewed.

Similarly, how 'risk maps' are developed and used by organisations also signifies the state of risk culture. A study of the everyday work of constructing, revising and drawing upon risk maps in an inter-organisational project in the Norwegian petroleum industry analyses the processes by which risk maps are developed and the issues and challenges that actors encounter when using them (Jørgensen & Jordan, 2016). In this setting, actors express concerns about the 'blinding' effect of the 'traffic light' grading of risks, the tendency to focus on short-term rather than longer-term objectives and the pseudo-commensuration of qualitatively different types of risk objects on risk maps. Yet, for all these difficulties, the risk map is also regarded as useful by project participants and something that facilitates inter-organisational collaboration and assurance, as well as supporting the execution of the project through its different phases.

Technocultures are not a panacea. There are well-known risks in excessive risk formalisation (Power, 2004, 2007). For example, on the one hand, key risk indicators and risk templates can provide helpful guidance and reassurance to operational staff and senior decision makers. On the other hand, they can also potentially displace meaningful action by being reified as instruments of technical compliance with mandated procedures (Hall & Fernando, 2016). More generally, there is a risk that technocultures generate their own bureaucratic imperatives and an autonomy that can lead to the well-known process-obsessed pathologies of the 'audit society' (Power, 1997). Leaders need technical practices like risk management to operationalise values but must equally be vigilant about the potential for 'value-subversion' (Selznick, 1957). In the case of both risk indicators and risk maps, the inculcation by leaders of more or less reflexive capacity in organisations to use these technologically embedded sources of information interactively and critically, and widening participation in their development and change, could be said to define the state of risk culture. This is captured in the second proposition of this chapter.

**Proposition 2** Risk culture is stronger the more that core values are embedded in risk information infrastructures.

## 2.5   RISK INFORMATION AND GOVERNANCE

The role of independent non-executive directors (NEDs) as 'gatekeepers' (Kirkbride & Letza, 2005; Coffee, 2006) has been a focus of diagnosis and reform in the decade since the financial crisis. Failures of risk governance have been at the very heart of the debate, and dedicated risk committees have been normalised in the United Kingdom (Walker, 2009). It is widely accepted that a flow of information is essential to the NED role and to the reality of the 'oversight' that they must execute. The key to effective governance is often framed in terms of how NEDs can mitigate and overcome the asymmetry that is grounded in executive control of information, as if this might be achieved by a shift in attitude, scepticism and challenge by NEDs themselves.

Once again, we see individualistic and psychologistic assumptions pervading debates about the NED role. I propose that we turn this emphasis on the character of the NED around and ask the following questions: 'How do organisations enable and support the oversight role of NEDs?' and 'How do organisations make themselves governable by enabling gatekeepers like NEDs to exercise effective oversight?' These questions locate key issues of risk culture not directly at the level of the behaviour of NEDs (or any other control agent), as if they were independent variables of governance, but in the collective organisational commitment to sustain infrastructure for the production and (vertical) flow of risk information to enable governance.

This emphasis on the organisational context of information production is not to say that individual motive and behaviour is irrelevant. A capable and experienced NED will of course seek information from many different sources. She will draw on her own networks and experience, such as other firms where she is, or has been, a NED. She must also negotiate the meaning of her independent oversight role in the face of its inherent ambiguity. For elite NEDs who chair risk committees, their independence is not an absolute quality but is a flexible attribute that is used strategically to manage complex relationships, both with regulators and with executive management (Zhivitskaya & Power, 2016). In constructing a working distinction between 'management' and 'oversight', independent directors engage in continuous and skilled 'boundary work', not only to maintain their identity and legitimacy at the management–oversight interface but also to facilitate information flow to themselves by accessing an autonomous 'exec network'. Sometimes they must be distant from management, more formal and regulation focused, and sometimes they choose to be close, supportive and collaborative. The regulatory emphasis on questions of independence, scepticism and critical challenge, not just for NEDs but for auditors and other gatekeepers too, ignores much of the lived reality and dynamics of their need to continuously negotiate ambiguous roles and to navigate a practical trade-off between proximity and distance. Formal regulation can interfere with this delicate trade-off and the governance-enabling, informal flow of information that it facilitates.

Yet, despite their networking activities, information flow for oversight is also largely out of the hands of NEDs. This means that we need to think harder about the nature of their *dependencies* rather than focus so much on a mythical concept of structural independence. The vertical information flow to NEDs in the form of a risk committee 'pack' does not just happen by accident; it is an organised form of truth production. In most organisations there are likely to be producers and editors of information for oversight purposes, yet we have little practitioner or scholarly insight into this process. While we expend diagnostic and regulatory energy focusing on boards and evaluating their intrinsic qualities, we may overlook the often humble organisational actors who enable the information flow and thereby construct the oversight capability of NEDs. These invisible editors are 'information intermediaries' (Zhivitskaya, 2015), and they have the power to make risk governance work or fail. I propose that policymakers could usefully focus more on these practices of information orchestration that support board oversight competence, in contrast to the present obsession with individual NED qualities. It is also in this mediating role that organisations reveal the nature of their appetite to allow themselves to be governed. Indeed, how executives think about and facilitate their governance by non-executives is a core feature of the 'tone at the top'. This notion informs our third proposition.

**Proposition 3** The more that organisations actively facilitate and enable their risk oversight by gatekeepers like NEDS, the stronger is the risk culture.

## 2.6   DISCUSSION: RISK CULTURE AND THE APPETITE FOR KNOWLEDGE

Previous sections have argued that information production and flow have been relatively under-discussed in the public debate about culture in financial services, despite the prominence of these issues in

sociological studies of organisations and risk (Short, 1984; March &
Shapira, 1987; Hilgartner, 1992; Short & Clarke, 1992; Clarke & Short,
1993; Weick, 1993; Gephart, Van Maanen & Oberlechner, 2009;
Power, 2014). Three processes have been discussed to show how information production plays a significant role in risk management: practitioner networking strategies, technology and infrastructure, and risk
governance facilitation. In addition, three indicative propositions have
been articulated that suggest how the quality of risk culture may
vary for each of these three processes. Combining these propositions,
we can say that 'weak' risk cultures are likely to be characterised by
some or all of the following information production defects: diminished interaction and networking, fragmented information infrastructures and collective indifference to the facilitation of risk governance.

To understand the significance of each theme and its respective
proposition, we must return Kant's principle of 'ought implies can'
and transform it from a logical claim to an empirical one. Thus we can
suggest that information capability, and the organisational vocabular-
ies and discourses that it generates (Ocasio, 2005; Maguire & Hardy,
2013), drive the organisational construction of values that orient
behaviour. In short, 'can constructs ought'. I propose that we can
think about the empirical dynamics of this reformulation in terms
of an 'appetite for knowledge'.

When we survey the landscape of financial services today, the
theme of risk appetite is prominent. Financial organisations are
required to have well-formulated risk appetites, codified in policies,
for all their major risk categories. Boards of directors – non-executive
and executive members alike – have a responsibility to articulate
and 'own' those risk appetite policies, making sure that they live in
the organisation via action-oriented risk indicators. Furthermore, an
important index of the quality of a risk culture is the extent to which
this embeddedness of risk appetite is realised. How organisations set
trigger thresholds for risk indicators and how responsive they are
when these triggers are breached are proxies for the quality of risk
culture. These tangible aspects of risk appetite have become accepted

as the everyday 'hygiene' of risk culture, and an industry of advisers has emerged to help organisations refine and improve their articulations of risk appetite.

Despite this focus on risk appetite, a more fundamental appetite for knowledge of risk has not itself been a focus of attention. Yet the existence of such an appetite potentially explains variation in the way that organisations produce and attend to information, as we saw in previous sections. The networking CRO wanted to know more about how risk was conceptualised and captured in other parts of the organisation; for the toy manufacturer CRO, the purpose of the workshops was not only to disseminate information but also to generate an appetite for knowing about risk by participating business leaders; the airline had an appetite to know about safety-relevant events in granular detail, investing in technology to support that appetite; and in the case of NEDs, organisations reveal an appetite for knowledge to the extent that they allow themselves to be known by these 'outsiders'.

This appetite for risk knowledge is only partially visible in the technical specifics of risk indicators and risk maps. An appetite for risk knowledge defines where an organisation sets the boundaries of the knowledge that it considers relevant and valuable to its purpose and is at best implicit in formal articulations of risk appetite. Thus, an airline with an advanced safety management system may have an ambition to know about the personal lives of pilots. The deliberate downing of a Germanwings aircraft in 2015 by one of its pilots shows how this ambition is itself bounded and imperfect. In contrast, despite the increased use of psychometric testing by financial services organisations, the need to know about the personal lives of staff is less evident in this field.

Thus, an appetite for risk knowledge is a value that can vary in nature across fields. But it implies a degree of respect for knowledge in general. An organisation that takes knowledge seriously, that has an empirical attitude to itself, encourages not just knowledge production and flow but also debate and interaction at key points across the organisation. If such a process nurtures capability and is value generative, as I suggest, then 'doing the right thing' is no longer anchored in individual psychology or looking to leaders to set the famous 'tone from the top'. It is grounded in the collective structures of an organisational appetite for knowledge.

There are barriers to the organisational development of an appetite for knowledge. For example, the bureaucratic form of organisation is not easily adapted to knowledge production. It tends to produce at best certainty and clarity of administrative function; organisations are known and know themselves through the observation of conformity to rules and procedures. Furthermore, we know that organisations are prone to excessive documentation, which 'crowds out' and suppresses knowledge production. Indeed, there is usually an appetite for opacity in cases of organisational misconduct (Greve, Palmer & Pozner, 2010). So issues of good risk culture also come down to complex questions about how to combine the procedural advantages of the bureaucratic form with a genuine appetite for knowledge about risk that is not subservient to this form. This combination is not an easy design or leadership issue, not least because organisations tend to generate risk bureaucracies and rule-based structures that stifle an appetite for knowledge. Two contemporary debates provide a potential platform and focus for organisational leaders to address and offset this tendency. These debates concern corporate purpose and the quality of decision-making.

### 2.6.1  *Knowledge and Corporate Purpose*

An appetite for risk knowledge is also, by implication, an appetite for ignorance (McGoey, 2012). Deliberately or unconsciously and habitually, organisations make decisions about what they do *not* need to know about themselves and their environments, what is considered *not* to be relevant to risk management. It follows that the risk function can be cut off from information simply by deep-seated assumptions about relevant knowledge rather than malign intent. Airlines are different from banks, and errors in the former are more consequential for human life. So it would be natural to expect different appetites for knowledge resulting in different investments in information gathering and flow. An investment in a system like the SMS at an airline is a choice about the kind of knowledge that defines the organisation. In this respect, this chapter proposes that financial organisations can address the problem of culture in part by becoming a little more like knowledge-based organisations. Indeed, they might in part become more like universities (despite the fact that universities are said to be more 'corporate' – in nature (Steck, 2003)).

Building on Turner and others, we can say that many of the high-profile accidents and disasters that have happened in recent years boil down to a culturally ingrained collective lack of curiosity in organisations coupled to pervasive individualism. The rogue trader and poor management are the visible signs of this failure, but the deeper causes lie, at least partly, in the absence of an appetite for knowledge, which would include cultural permission for scepticism and challenge. Indeed, the financial crisis could be said to be the result of 'strategic ignorance' by banks, regulators and society at large (Davies & McGoey, 2012).

This knowledge–ignorance dialectic is relevant to the larger post-crisis debate about corporate purpose in the United Kingdom, although it is not a new issue (Selznick, 1957; Bartlett & Ghoshal, 1994). Companies are being encouraged both by regulators and employees to ask themselves why they exist over and above making a profit (Mayer, 2018). This discourse is manifestly about values, but it is also profoundly to do with knowledge and capability. Organisations have become increasingly aware of their impact, both good and bad, on society at large. Risk is not a simple property of a situation – it is relational (Boholm & Corvellec, 2011). From this relational point of view, the core question is, 'Which values are at risk and for whom?' The appetite for risk knowledge is effectively an appetite to answer this larger question of purpose in terms of social impact. Wanting to know about impacts, good and bad, and regarding this knowledge as relevant is coextensive with defining organisational purpose: who are we, for whose benefit do we exist, and who do we put at risk?

An appetite for knowledge is not an absolute and may even be regarded as pathological in some cases. Digital information capabilities have created debates about the production and use of highly granular knowledge about individuals, their health, spending habits and lifestyles. Thus an appetite for knowledge may generate values in an organisation that conflict with other values in society, such as a right to privacy and to be forgotten. However, such a possible dynamic makes it more not less important for policymakers and organisational leaders to focus more on the underlying appetite for knowledge (or ignorance) and the organisational values that such an appetite may or may not generate.

### 2.6.2   *Risk Culture and Decision-Making*

Many commentators and advisers on culture and risk management have, very reasonably, placed the quality of decision-making at the centre of the cultural reform problem. However, I propose that we may need to step back from this notion of the 'good' decision. Contrary to many conceptualisations, the preceding arguments suggest that a decision is not simply an action by a single responsible individual at a discrete point in space and time. Decisions have their conditions of formation within a wider organisational environment – an 'ecology' of information (Miller & O'Leary, 2000; Miller, Kurunmaki & O'Leary, 2008). Agency and decision-making in complex organisations are also necessarily distributed (Enfield, 2017) both among people and also within the technocultures that shape their attention and action. It has been proposed that these systems instantiate an organisation's appetite for knowledge and generate implicit values that provide important boundary conditions for decision-making. Leaders and policymakers interested in addressing the quality of decision-making about risk could usefully 'map' these information infrastructures and their implied appetite for knowledge. This mapping process should begin by testing the three propositions proposed in this chapter about interactivity, technoculture and governance. The results of these tests would inform the development of benchmarks for 'healthy' risk cultures and their appetites for knowledge. Of course, the investigation of an organisation's appetite for knowledge itself requires an appetite for knowledge. Regulators and leaders may prefer to remain strategically ignorant.

## 2.7 CONCLUSIONS

In this chapter, I have argued that, despite the widespread interest in the culture of the financial services industry and in the behaviour of groups, there remains a strong bias towards the individual as a unit of analysis and accountability. I suggest that this bias has inhibited a more profound investigation of the value-generative role of information infrastructures within financial organisations. Examples have been discussed that suggest that the ways in which organisations create, gather and manage information, especially risk information for oversight purposes, are strongly indicative of culture. This suggests a culture reform process whose focus is not the ethics and self-respect of each individual member of an organisation. As laudable as such visions and missions for change may be, they often lose energy and are short-lived. Rather, it is a much more humble notion of cultural reform that is likely to be longer lived, namely change to the collective conditions under which organisational actors are enabled by information structures to be respectful of risk management and control processes.

The turn towards culture was attractive as an explanation of the crisis in various financial organisations, but then, as Freeman (Chapter 7, this volume) shows, it became contested as to what culture, and especially risk culture, meant and how to act upon it. Over time, the remedies for bad culture turned towards psychology and 'auditable' values at the individual level without an understanding of the processes – institutional and organisational – that generate them. There seemed to be no appetite for insights grounded in the well-established organisational sociology of risk begun by Turner, Perrow and others, or indeed in the work of anthropologists like Douglas. Consequently, culture and information systems have tended to be conceptualised and discussed by practitioners and regulators in isolation from one another.

Much has been written about the need for challenge by NEDs and for scepticism by auditors, as if these were properties of individual actors in isolation. Yet, if risk culture is about anything at all, it is surely about the organisational conditions supporting the risk information production that enables this challenge. This chapter has argued that this information production environment is itself a function of a deeper appetite for knowledge that shapes the individuals embedded in it and their moral capacity. This in turn means that a value like 'respect for control' or 'treating customers fairly' cannot simply be implanted in an organisation. It is necessarily an emergent property of infrastructure in which risk information, values and organisational capabilities are dynamically co-produced. The three propositions developed in this chapter provide an agenda for future work to explore these claims further.

## REFERENCES

Atkins, D., Fitzsimmons, A., Parsons, C. and Punter, A. (2012). *Roads to Ruin: A Study of Major Risk Events: Their Origins, Impact and Implications*. London: AIRMIC.

Bartlett, C. A. and Ghoshal, S. (1994). Changing the role of top management: beyond strategy to purpose. *Harvard Business Review*, **72**(6), 79–88.

Beasley, M., Branson, B. and Hancock, B. (2010). *Developing Key Risk Indicators to Strengthen Enterprise Risk Management*. New York: Committee of Sponsoring Organizations of the Treadway Commission.

Besharov, M. L. and Khurana, R. (2015). Leading amidst competing technical and institutional demands: revisiting Selznick's conception of leadership. In M. Kraatz, ed., *Institutions and Ideals: Philip Selznick's Legacy for Organizational Studies*. Emerald Group Publishing Limited, pp. 53–88.

Boddy, C. R. (2017). Psychopathic leadership: a case study of a corporate psychopath CEO. *Journal of Business Ethics*, 145(1), 141–56.

Boholm, Å. and Corvellec, H. (2011). A relational theory of risk. *Journal of Risk Research*, **14**, 175–90.

Bower, M. (2003). Company philosophy: 'the way we do things around here'. *McKinsey Quarterly*, no. 2, 110–17.

Clarke, L. and Short, J. (1993). Social organization and risk: some current controversies. *Annual Review of Sociology*, **19**(1), 375–99.

Coffee, J. (2006). *Gatekeepers: The Professions and Corporate Governance*. Oxford: Oxford University Press.

COSO (Committee of Sponsoring Organizations of the Treadway Commission) (2004). *Enterprise Risk Management – Integrated Framework: Application Techniques*. New York: COSO. https://bit.ly/2p9C2Jr

Davies, W. (2018). Sabotaging progress: the cultural economy of resentment in late neoliberalism. In J. Andersson and O. Godechot, eds., *Destabilizing Orders – Understanding the Consequences of Neoliberalism*. Proceedings of the MaxPo Fifth-Anniversary Conference, Paris, January 12–13, 2018. Paris: Max Planck Sciences Po Center on Coping with Instability in Market Societies, pp. 9–12.

Davies, W. and McGoey, L. (2012). Rationalities of ignorance: on financial crisis and the ambivalence of neo-liberal epistemology. *Economy and Society*, **41**(1), 64–83.

Douglas, M. and Wildavsky, A. (1983). *Risk and Culture*. Berkeley: University of California Press.

Douglas, M. (2013). *Essays on the Sociology of Perception*. London: Routledge.

Edmonds, T. (2014). *LIBOR, Public Inquiries & FCA Disciplinary Powers*. House of Commons Library Briefing Paper No. 6376.

Enfield, N. J. (2017). Distribution of agency. In N. J. Enfield and P. Kockelman, eds., *Distributed Agency*. Oxford: Oxford University Press, pp. 9–14.

Etienne, J. (2013). Ambiguity and relational signals in regulator–regulatee relationships. *Regulation & Governance*, **7**(1), 30–47.

Etienne, J. (2014). The politics of detection in business regulation. *Journal of Public Administration Research and Theory*, **25**(1), 257–84.

Gephart, R. P., Jr., Van Maanen, J. and Oberlechner, T. (2009). Organizations and risk in late modernity. *Organization Studies*, **30**(2–3), 141–55.

Greve, H. R., Palmer, D. and Pozner, J. E. (2010). Organizations gone wild: the causes, processes, and consequences of organizational misconduct. *The Academy of Management Annals*, **4**(1), 53–107.

Hall, M. and Fernando, R. (2016). Beyond the headlines: day-to-day practices of risk measurement and management in a non-governmental organization. In M. Power, ed., *Riskwork: Essays on the Organizational Life of Risk Management*. Oxford: Oxford University Press, pp. 72–90.

Hall, M., Mikes, A. and Millo, Y. (2013). How experts gain influence. *Harvard Business Review*, **91**(7), 70–4.

Hall, M., Mikes, A. and Millo, Y. (2015). How do risk managers become influential? A field study of toolmaking in two financial institutions. *Management Accounting Research*, **26**, 3–22.

Hilgartner, S. (1992). The social construction of risk objects: or, how to pry open networks of risk. In J. F. Short and L. Clarke, eds., *Organizations, Uncertainties and Risk*. Boulder, CO: Westview Press, pp. 39–53.

Janis, I. L. (1982). *Groupthink: Psychological Studies of Policy Decisions and Fiascoes*. Boston: Houghton Mifflin.

Jordan, S., Jørgensen, L. and Mitterhofer, H. (2013). Performing risk and the project: risk maps as mediating instruments. *Management Accounting Research*, **24**(2), 156–74.

Jørgensen, L. and Jordan, S. (2016). Day-to-day riskwork in inter-organizational project management. In M. Power, ed., *Riskwork: Essays on the Organizational Life of Risk Management*. Oxford: Oxford University Press, pp. 50–71.

Kekes, J. (1984). 'Ought implies can' and two kinds of morality. *The Philosophical Quarterly*, **34**(137), 459–67.

Kirkbride, J. and Letza, S. (2005). Can the non-executive director be an effective gatekeeper? The possible development of a legal framework of accountability. *Corporate Governance: An International Review*, **13**(4), 542–50.

Luburić, R. (2017). Strengthening the three lines of defence in terms of more efficient operational risk management in central banks. *Journal of Central Banking Theory and Practice*, **6**(1), 29–53.

Maguire, S. and Hardy, C. (2013). Organizing processes and the construction of risk: a discursive approach. *Academy of Management Journal*, **56**(1), 231–55.

March, J. G. and Shapira, Z. (1987). Managerial perspectives on risk and risk taking. *Management Science*, **33**(11), 1404–18.

Mayer, C. (2018). *Prosperity: Better Business makes the Greater Good*. Oxford: Oxford University Press.

McConnell, P. (2013). Systemic operational risk: the LIBOR manipulation scandal. *Journal of Operational Risk*, **8**(3), 59–99.

McGoey, L. (2012). Strategic unknowns: towards a sociology of ignorance. *Economy and Society*, **41**(1), 1–16.

Meyer, J. W. and Rowan, B. (1977). Institutionalized organizations: formal structure as myth and ceremony. *American Journal of Sociology*, **83**(2), 340–63.

Mikes, A. (2009). Risk management and calculative cultures. *Management Accounting Research*, **20**(1), 18–40.

Mikes, A. (2016). The triumph of the humble risk officer. In M. Power, ed., *Riskwork: Essays on the Organizational Life of Risk Management*. Oxford: Oxford University Press, pp. 253–73.

Miller, P., Kurunmaki, L. and O'Leary, T. (2008). Accounting, hybrids and the management of risk. *Accounting, Organizations and Society*, 33(7–8), 942–67.

Miller, P. and O'Leary, E. T. (2000). *Value Reporting and the Information Ecosystem*. London: PricewaterhouseCoopers.

Ocasio, W. (2005). The opacity of risk: language and the culture of safety in NASA's space shuttle program. In W. Starbuck and M. Farjoun, eds., *Organization at the Limit: Lessons from the Columbia Disaster*. Oxford: Blackwell, pp. 110–21.

Palermo, T. (2016). Technoculture: risk reporting and analysis at a large airline. In M. Power, ed., *Riskwork: Essays on the Organizational Life of Risk Management*. Oxford: Oxford University Press, pp. 150–71.

Perrow, C. (1984). *Normal Accidents: Living with High Risk Technologies*. New York: Basic Books.

Power, M. (1997). *The Audit Society*. Oxford: Oxford University Press.

Power, M. (2004). *The Risk Management of Everything*. London: Demos.

Power, M. (2007). *Organized Uncertainty: Designing a World of Risk Management*. Oxford: Oxford University Press.

Power, M. (2014). Risk, social theories and organizations. In P. Adler, P. du Gay, G. Morgan and M. Reed, eds., *The Oxford Handbook of Sociology, Social Theory and Organization Studies: Contemporary Currents*. Oxford: Oxford University Press, pp. 370–92.

Power, M., Palermo, T. and Ashby, S. (2013). *Risk Culture in Financial Organizations: A Research Report*. London: Centre for Analysis of Risk and Regulation, London School of Economics.

PRA and FCA (Prudential Regulation Authority and Financial Conduct Authority) (2015). *The Failure of HBOS plc (HBOS): A Report by the Financial Conduct Authority (FCA) and the Prudential Regulation Authority (PRA)*. London: Bank of England.

Selznick, P. (1957). *Leadership in Administration: A Sociological Interpretation*. New York: NY: Harper & Row.

Short, J. (1984). The social fabric of risk: toward the social transformation of risk analysis. *American Sociological Review*, 49(6), 711–25.

Short, J. and Clarke, L., eds. (1992). *Organizations, Uncertainties and Risks*. Boulder, CO: Westview Press.

Steck, H. (2003). Corporatization of the university: seeking conceptual clarity. *The Annals of the American Academy of Political and Social Science*, 585, 66–83.

Turner, B. (1976). The organizational and interorganizational development of disasters. *Administrative Science Quarterly*, 21(3), 378–97.

Turner, B. and Pidgeon, N. (1997). *Man-Made Disasters*, 2nd ed. London: Butterworth–Heinemann.

Vaughan, D. (1996). *The Challenger Launch Decision*. Chicago: University of Chicago Press.

Vaughan, D. (2005). Organizational rituals of risk and error. In B. Hutter and M. Power, eds., *Organizational Encounters with Risk*. Cambridge: Cambridge University Press, pp. 33–66.

Walker, D. (2009). *A Review of Corporate Governance in UK Banks and Other Financial Industry Entities*. London: HM Treasury.

Weick, K. E. (1993). The collapse of sensemaking in organizations: the Mann Gulch disaster. *Administrative Science Quarterly*, **38**(4), 628–52.

Zhivitskaya, M. (2015). The practice of risk oversight since the global financial crisis: closing the stable door? Unpublished PhD thesis, University of London.

Zhivitskaya, M. and Power, M. (2016). The work of risk oversight. In M. Power, ed., *Riskwork: Essays on the Organizational Life of Risk Management*. Oxford: Oxford University Press, pp. 91–109.

# 3 A Network View of Tone at the Top and the Role of Opinion Leaders

Michelle Tuveson and Daniel Ralph*

## 3.1 INTRODUCTION

Cultural backgrounds can cast long shadows on the perception, thinking and behaviour of an individual. Likewise, risk culture of an organisation is both pervasive and central in business execution. Sometimes culture is seen to be inextricable with the brand or identity of the organisation and may serve as a surrogate for its methods and processes.

Should risk culture and organisational structure in a firm be viewed in the same context? Structural formations within organisations such as size and scope have proven to matter in the functioning of a firm from the perspectives of transaction cost economics (Coase, 1937), network connectivity on communications and exchange (Powell, 1990), growth (McEvily, Jaffee & Tortoriello, 2012), innovation (Burt, 2004) and economic markets (Alonso, Bimpikis & Ozdaglar, 2008). We propose that organisational and social forms together provide an important backdrop for risk culture; we focus on the latter because it is under-studied.

Official communication of culture is espoused clearly and commonly in most global corporations through channels such as the human resources or corporate communications departments. They promote formal and carefully constructed messages regarding their core values and culture through mission, ethics and conduct standards.

* The authors thank Dr Ganchi Zhang for his modelling expertise, Jennifer Copic for her assistance in surveying the literature, Professor Stelios Kavadias and Professor Kishore Sengupta for their interest and insight, and Olivia Majumdar for her review of the characters from Victor Hugo's *Les misérables*.

These organisational artefacts convey a tone from the top regarding their moral and ethical positions. Phrases such as 'uncompromising principles', 'improving lives of consumers' and 'building long-term relationships based on trust and respect' make up the baseline messaging and underpinnings that pervade a firm's overall offerings of its products and services.

In reality, behavioural deviations from espoused norms occur despite clearly and unequivocally communicated aspects of organisational culture. This difference between reality and espoused values is a kind of cultural gap. Arguably, cultural gaps can take on contagion behavioural attributes and become endemic in an organisation. What are the conditions and contributors to such gaps and their spread? Looking ahead, we approach this somewhat from the opposite side by studying how charisma and connectivity of 'influencers' can close cultural gaps that might otherwise exist by default.

Unlike a simple transmission of information or a disease epidemic, the flow of culture can be expanded or diminished through the involvement of opinion leaders (Katz & Lazarsfeld, 2017). The Decatur study posits that the communication from person to person sets the norms within an organisation and thus provides the seeds for cultural development and sustainment. The study was based on voting decisions and found that informal 'opinion leaders' diffused media messages through their selection and interpretation of those messages. This view of the way media works is analogous to communications departments within corporations; the conclusion that the media have only 'limited effects' is likewise applicable to corporate communications within an organisation. Thus, the social network of opinion leaders, or influencers, within the social network affects the spread of culture.

Structures in organisations provide a framework for people to formally interact, highlight job roles and responsibilities and make associations with specific departments. Thus, structure sets procedural outlines for communications and, by guiding who communicates with whom, affects the culture of daily working practices.

In hierarchically organised firms with dominant formal structures of engagement, employee rank oftentimes determines influence. In less hierarchical structures, influence might be determined by other factors such as commonality (or homophily), bonds and charisma.

Individual agency is an important component for creating or reinforcing organisational culture. Organisational culture and individual agency are inextricably intertwined in forming the basis of moral values and behaviours in a firm. To be an agent is to intentionally influence one's functioning and life circumstances. This theory defines three different forms of human agency: personal agency, proxy agency and collective agency (Bandura, 2000). As reviewed by Alexander (see Chapter 6), a human agentic view of culture is balanced with the organisational view such that collective agency takes precedence when personal agency is weak, and vice versa. This suggests an equilibrium state that can be modelled by the counteraction between individual agency and group structure, e.g. a strong team is able to mitigate weaknesses amongst its members.

There is a further dimension of organisational scholarship that looks at the dynamic nature of culture in terms of selected characteristics such as rate of diffusion, openness to innovation, cultural conservatism and resistance to change (Hatch, 1993). As reviewed by Howard-Grenville (see Chapter 1), Schein's model of culture is still relevant today for framing organisational culture, and scholars have complemented his model in some cases by reformulating it to include elements of dynamics and movement.

## 3.2  REVIEWING RISK CULTURE AND TONE AT THE TOP

While the qualitative description of tone at the top provides a noble and virtuous vision for guiding or changing risk culture, the mechanisms for actualisation are less clear. Tone at the top became widely espoused after the global financial crisis as both an explanation and a solution for the crisis. Although its early roots stem from mainstream scholarship from the field of organisational behaviour, the terminology's concepts were widely applied to corporate discussions by scholars of business ethics as a result of corporate scandals and widespread governance failures, such as with Enron and WorldCom (Cohan, 2002; Daily, Dalton & Cannella, 2003; Schwartz, Dunfee & Kline, 2005). Internal control audit reports mandated by section 404 of the Sarbanes–Oxley Act require auditors to assess material weaknesses in internal control due to problems with senior management's tone, competence or reliability (Hermanson, Ivancevich & Ivancevich, 2008).

General supervisory guidance on risk culture has been outlined by regulators, advisory organisations and corporate boards to focus on tone at the top (Power, Palermo & Ashby, 2013; Financial Stability Board, 2014). The board and senior management at these entities are responsible for setting expectations for the risk culture of their institution as well as leading by example – 'walking the talk'. Emulation of their behaviours is expected to be adopted throughout the rest of their institutions. In addition to leading by example, characteristics of tone at the top include assessing espoused values, ensuring common understanding and awareness of risk, and learning from past experiences (Financial Stability Board, 2014).

The appropriate tone and standards of behaviour from the top is assumed to cascade from the top down within the institutions, with middle managers helping to transmit the culture (Financial Stability Board, 2014). Challenges of meeting corporate earnings expectations often put pressure on decision-making, especially in environments where there is heightened uncertainty, time pressures or competitive forces. What are the required parameters and structures within an organisation in order to realise tone at the top?

If tone at the top and healthy risk culture are to be synonymous in an organisation, then ample mechanisms for its diffusion within the organisation must exist. We hypothesise that the realisation of tone at the top requires 'opinion leaders' who have sufficient influence and connectivity to propagate the tone throughout the organisation. This new cultural tone is in effect a form of innovation that requires distribution or diffusion through the organisation.

We refer to the social and communication processes for spreading new ideas, technologies, processes and product adoption across members of a particular social system as diffusion (Kreps, 2017). The diffusion of innovations (DOI) model was first introduced in 1962 in the seminal volume *Diffusion of Innovations* (Rogers, 2003). It explains that people's exposure to innovations has a significant influence on the rate of overall adoption of the innovation and involves four interacting factors: innovation itself, its communication, context of social systems and time (Kreps, 2017).

Many campaigns direct messages en masse without factoring in internal structures of the receiving organisation, such as interpersonal communications networks. Other DOI models find that the spread of new ideas and practices can be accelerated using opinion leaders (Valente & Davis, 1999). Additionally, models of social networks show that charisma attributes of the opinion leaders significantly contribute to network effects of individuals who are part of the social structure (Pastor, Meindl & Mayo, 2002).

## 3.3   BACKGROUND ON ORGANISATIONAL STRUCTURES AND THEIR HIERARCHIES

In the highest form, organisations have both formal and informal elements. Formal aspects of organisations are described by some level of professional hierarchies that dictate rules of interaction, procedures and control, whereas informal elements in organisations are characterized by individually defined channels of communications and interactions outside of institutionally mandated structures. Informal structures in organisations are based on social and professional networks built on social and affinity relationships (Kilduff & Brass, 2010).

Centralisation and decentralisation have described the level of hierarchy in a firm. Centralisation refers to concentration of firm decisions by a small minority, usually by top management teams, and then filtered throughout the firm for execution. Decentralisation, on the other hand, supports firm decision-making performed in a more distributed fashion through varying hierarchical ranks, operating units or markets.

The history of corporate decisions presents the case for centralisation in support of strategies for increased efficiencies in operations and scaling (Carroll & Hannan, 2000). More specifically, it was long believed that 'the existence of a managerial hierarchy is a defining characteristic of the modern business enterprise' (Chandler, 1977).

By contrast, the literature shows that firms with decentralised structures realise greater effectiveness for reasons of performance, greater employee job satisfaction, participation, responsiveness to markets and intra-firm communications (Rapert & Wren, 1998; Alonso, Dessein & Matouschek, 2008).

A firm's structure is an important consideration when developing its strategy (Johnson, Scholes & Whittington, 2008). The modern global firm looks very different than its earlier predecessors. Globalisation of markets has moved many firms by default towards decentralised structures to support geographically distributed footprints. Starting in the 1960s, the US market became well known for the rise of the conglomerate business model, until the 1980s, when deregulation and the takeover strategies became pervasive. This change led to the growth of 'global corporations' and 'globalists'. Widespread globalisation activities of firms were embraced as they sought price efficiencies and proximity to their global marketplaces.

The context of risk culture given the multidimensional nature of a global corporation is much more amorphous than for a single entity firm. While the basic definition of a multinational corporation is controversial and ranges from having its facilities in more than one country to generating revenues from a non-parent country, the global corporation represents the global nature of exchanges, flows and connections. Despite the variety of businesses, publicly listed companies share common corporate codes.

Their regulatory requirements for reporting, organisational structures and mandates have shaped their foundations for risk management practices (Tuveson et al., 2018). As outlined by Alexander, regulatory changes can drive changes in risk culture (see Chapter 6). This brings to question how cultures evolve away from their historical precedents.

Geographically distributed footprints imply organisational decentralisation by the nature of their physical distribution and related separation of functions. Structural formations and organisational distance become important factors in actualising or hindering cultural change. Structure influences daily work processes, flow and frequency of communications, and level of employee engagement. For instance, co-location of employees promotes a different culture to the situation when many employees work virtually or across large geographical distances.

Intuition and research suggest that a strong organisational culture can contribute to the competitive advantage of a firm. The resource-based view of the firm (Barney, 1991) argues that competitive advantage derives from tangible and intangible assets such as a firm's organisational processes and routines. Strong cultures are associated with better performance over varying geographies and time horizons. A study of US insurance companies showed a correlation between a strong culture and premium growth rates (Gordon & DiTomaso, 1992). Strong cultures in tandem with performance measures lead to enhanced employee performance (Smith & England, 2019). Additional factors contributing to an organisation's success have been studied through the lens of structure, culture, power and political characteristics (Pettigrew, 1979). In a similar capacity, an organisation's structural, cultural and strategic characteristics support organisational effectiveness through knowledge management (Zheng, Yang & McLean, 2010). Knowledge in organisations is created throughout but maintained, shared or spread according to cultural norms and structures.

## 3.4    A SOCIAL NETWORK VIEW OF ORGANISATIONAL STRUCTURES

Both formal and informal structures provide the landscape within organisations on which members act. How dominant one form of structure is over the other, how these intertwine and how organisations function as a result depends on multiple factors (McEvily, Soda & Tortoriello, 2014). How risk culture features when superimposed on to these structures warrants additional research.

Network views of organisations have been studied extensively within the social network research literature (Bergenholtz & Walstrom, 2011) and sometimes provide contrasts to formalisms such as organisational charts. Analyses highlight the rise in relative frequency of the phrase 'social network' by comparison to organisation charts (McEvily, Soda & Tortoriello, 2014). We can see anecdotally that there has been relative growth in research incorporating social networks in the last decade within peer-reviewed journal papers.

We focus on how social network structure affects information flow and therefore the transmission and maintenance of culture within organisations. How do social networks shape the individual's experience of organisational culture and vice versa? There are various aspects of networks relating to how they function as carriers of information. Information diffusion, which is of special interest for this chapter, addresses questions such as which types of information or topics diffuse the most and which paths and individuals or nodes are most important to information diffusion (Guille, Hacid, Favre & Zighed, 2013).

Structure has been a favoured direction of mathematical research in the study of both real and theoretical networks (Newman, 2011). The core–periphery structure has been commonly observed in studies. This describes a densely connected central group of nodes, the core, surrounded by a cloud of nodes each connected to the core by a very small number of ties, even perhaps just one, the periphery. The core–periphery structure is frequently recognised in empirical settings such as friendship networks between members of community clubs, train stations in the public transportation network, collaboration between scientists in terms of co-authored publications and legislative voting similarity between members of the US Senate (Rombach,

Porter, Fowler & Mucha, 2017). The core–periphery is the selected reference network for this chapter.

The related literature of large-scale infrastructure networks such as telecommunications, electricity grids, public transportation and trade networks has identified some important network characteristics of resilience such as clustering, modularity and long path lengths (Ash & Newth, 2007). Core–periphery networks are observed to be efficient for the transfer of information, people and goods. In transportation, this structure is seen in the 'hub-and-spoke' networks used by airlines or delivery services, in which travel from one point on the periphery to another is via one link to a hub node, one or more hops between hub nodes and a final leg from the hub to the destination. (Verma et al., 2016). In the context of ideation in an organisation, core–periphery networks of individuals have been shown to be effective in facilitating communication (measured as number of communications per period) without increasing the amount of communication. (Lovejoy & Sinha, 2010).

In terms of organisations, we conjecture that core–periphery networks may also provide an efficient medium for transmission of culture. Anecdotally, for many international businesses with global headquarters, the formal and informal networks are partially aligned. The advice and friendship network of its staff, even those who work at the periphery of the firm, has a focal point in both communications and travel to the head office. In essence, the head office facilitates the development of a core global network.

More complex structures are also of interest. R&D collaborations give rise to what appear to be nested core–periphery structures (König, Battiston, Napoletano & Schweitzer, 2012). When the marginal cost of collaboration is at an intermediate level, efficient communication hierarchies are characterised by the degree of nodes, in which the neighbourhood of each node is contained in the neighbourhood of the next higher-degree nodes. 'Asymptotic learning' tries to measure the efficiency of communication as the number of network participants grows and is characterised in some cases by having many small social cliques connected in an informational ring (Acemoglu, Bimpikis & Ozdaglar, 2014).

Taking the network structure as given, the characteristics of nodes may relate to the functioning of the network as a whole or to the agency and incentives of each agent in finding its position in the network. Criticality is natural in discussions relating to the locations of nodes in infrastructure networks, for example, airport hubs are more important to an airline than peripheral destinations.

The power of social network research is the ability to marry both the network structure and characteristics of the nodes within the network to paint an integrated picture of the organisation. The next section will address the behavioural characteristics of the nodes and their contribution to transmitting risk culture.

## 3.5   CHARACTERISTICS OF INDIVIDUALS AND THEIR CONNECTIONS

What makes some messengers more effective than others in delivering a message? We argue that the spread of risk culture depends on the right sort of messengers – opinion leaders – having sufficient connectivity in the social network of firm. Risk culture is pervasive, and individuals have a role in its transmission.

Individuals learn and adopt their culture through interactions with their fellow colleagues. We believe that the stickiness of an interaction depends on additional factors beyond structure. Just because two individuals interact does not mean that culture will be shared; rather, the success of the interaction will depend on a number of individual factors. While the social network of an individual provides important pathways for spreading culture, an individual's attributes contribute to whether a transmission will be successful or not. We refer to the collection of these attributes of the opinion leaders as charisma (Pastor, Meindl & Mayo, 2002) and represent this by a parameter in our subsequent model for determining success in spreading tone from the top.

We highlight one behavioural characteristic of charisma associated with 'high self-monitors' (Mehra, Kilduff & Brass, 2001), individuals who tend to be 'chameleon-like' and adept at making the people with whom they interact identify them as allies. High self-monitors tend to ask more questions about other people than divulge about themselves and can adapt, relatively quickly, to their immediate social setting. Thus, they have aspects of charisma and are more likely to occupy and benefit from central positions in a social network than 'true-to-themselves low self-monitors'.

Centrality in a network is suggestive of greater access to influence on others, which can be further broken down into herd behaviour and information cascade (Guille et al., 2013). The former relates to the topic of homophily, which is the desire to conform to a social group. It also describes the tendency of people to be attracted to others who they see as similar to themselves. This is related to the self-monitoring personality trait; a high self-monitor can moderate their behaviour to elicit a better response from others in a social situation. Hence a high self-monitor can take advantage of homophily to exert influence over others. Interestingly, more than half of information cascading, or 'behavioural contagion', in some social networks is attributed not to the influence of specific high-status connections but to homophily (Aral, Muchnik & Sundararajan, 2009; Aral, 2010).

Status of individuals, beyond direct influence on information flow, plays a role in network structure. For example, high-status individuals may be particularly important as weak ties when seeking opportunities outside their social sphere (Lin, Ensel & Vaughn, 1981). The role of influencers is also recognised in studies of the growth of large-scale social networks in which those who project messages (information sources) are distinguished from those who absorb those messages (information sinks) (González-Bailón, Borge-Holthoefer, Rivero & Moreno, 2011). This model explores how information diffusion in a social network is mediated by the characteristics of the actors (nodes) in terms of their professional or organisational status. Finally, we mention that cohesion of individuals in a network, perhaps shared culture, is another factor in the effectiveness of information transmission (Sosa, 2011).

While it is not our intention to focus on relationships between two people, or dyad, in a social network, we again mention weak versus strong ties. A person's weak ties are relationships that are more distant, perhaps low trust, low familiarity or with relatively infrequent contact. While excessive dyadic cohesion in a social network is seen to be detrimental to creative idea generation, strong ties appear to be catalysts for actors who are intrinsically motivated to work. Network model formations of organisations have been studied from the perspective of multiple organisational attributes in reference to innovation and change management (Mihm, Loch, Wilkinson & Huberman, 2010). Network structures and linkages between the 'right people' highlight the exchange of 'local knowledge' in a decentralised setting. Examples of such dichotomies show relationships between excessive homogeneity and increased threats to stability (Mihm et al., 2010).

Weak ties are prominent in the finding (Burt, 1992) that social influence or importance of an actor in a network may be understood not by the size of their network but by the extent to which their weak ties provide novel information to other actors who are otherwise poorly connected, i.e. have 'structural holes' in their own networks. Social networks can be robust to the removal of strong ties; however, if the weak ties are removed, then they may cease to function following a shock event (Onnela et al., 2007). Intuitively, strong ties between individuals improve both transmission of information and creativity within a firm (Lovejoy & Sinha, 2010; Sosa, 2011). These differences between the value of weak ties and strong ties is an indication of the complexity of social networks and the need to consider local context carefully.

## 3.6 POWER AND INFLUENCE WITHIN A NETWORK

Power and influence are fundamental properties within social structures and thus are intrinsic to the understanding of risk culture. Power is deemed relational in the sense that individuals do not have power in the abstract but have power through their influence on others. Because power is relational, the amount of power and how it is distributed across actors can vary according to formal and social structures. Network analysis research has provided insights into social power and influence (Hanneman & Riddle, 2005).

We find the influence and power literature to be helpful in putting risk culture into perspective. Influence can be unpacked into some of its constituent components such as persuasion, imitation, manipulation and contagion. (Katz & Lazarsfeld, 2017). Measurement of influence is challenging as the process must first consider what influence is and then make a determination on whether influence has been transacted. Only then can quantitative measures of influence be determined.

We highlight 'selectivity' and 'interpersonal relations' as two intervening variables from the influence research (Katz & Lazarsfeld, 2017). Firstly, when selectivity is viewed from the perspective of reception research – the way that different 'readers' decode the 'same text' – the role of social influence becomes apparent. Knowledge gap studies indicate that those with prior cognitive structures affect the likelihood of absorbing information on a particular subject. Those who start with 'more' gain disproportionately. Secondly, interpersonal relations research shows that primary groups exert pressures on the opinions of other group members. The ability of opinion leaders to mediate and normalise a message is key to its stickiness.

We highlight a frequently cited example within the social networking literature that considers characters in Victor Hugo's *Les misérables*. See Figure 3.1. A history of character interactions is recorded and then grouped into communities (Humanities Commons, n.d.) using selected graph theory algorithms (Knuth, 1993).

Hugo's nineteenth-century opus is a fitting choice for this visualisation as it is a complicated novel teeming with characters and multiple, intersecting narratives. While Bishop Myriel, the judge and the minister of agriculture represent the formal power structure

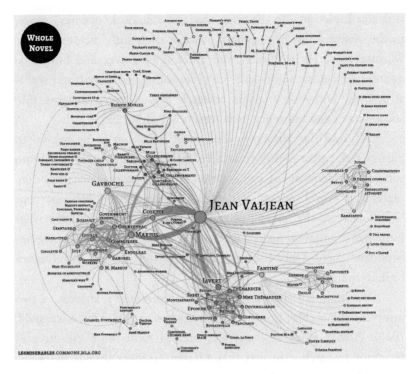

FIGURE 3.1 Character interactions in Victor Hugo's *Les misérables*.
Source: Humanities Commons, n.d.

within society, one can see from a network visualisation that they are
not as centrally connected to other general members of the society.
When their interactions are viewed from a network perspective,
the analysis highlights that Valjean and Marius have the greatest
centrality as measured by their influence and number of connections,
and thus they would be natural opinion leaders for transmitting societal innovations.

## 3.7   APPLICATION OF SYSTEMS MODELLING OF
FIRM STRUCTURES

### 3.7.1   *Background on Systems Modelling*

Dynamic aspects of network flow, and how these are mediated by
network structure, are of considerable interest to practitioner and

academics (Holme, 2015). Management and economics scholars have applied systems and dynamics control theories from the physical and biological disciplines to explain phenomena observed in organisations. Forrester is considered by many as developing the field of system dynamics modelling for corporate applications in understanding the long-term impacts of management policies (Forrester, 1968). Systems theory applied to organisations views individual organisational elements as part of a wider system, with each element having its own dynamics and interactions with other elements (O'Connor, 2008). Complexity theory extends the principles of systems theory by proposing that the interactions of the individual elements combine non-linearly to give a result that is more than the sum of its parts (Cachon, Zipkin & Anderson, 1999).

Small changes to system elements can cause significant changes to the overall system behaviour. In systems analysis, a fundamental premise is that every action triggers a reaction – this is called feedback. System dynamics further considers the influence of adaptive behaviours and feedback loops within the system (Forrester, 1994). Feedback loops when applied to management concepts within organisations encompass learning outcomes that warrant updates to a modelled system. The degree of motion, stiffness and compliance of elements within a physical system can rapidly adapt to changes in the external environment. Dynamic capabilities in systems can also be modelled to include an explicit role for management and leadership (Teece, 2018). Next, the concepts of system dynamics inform our model of how social networks relate to the spread of culture.

## 3.7.2 Conceptualising a Model of Risk Culture

Risk culture is intrinsic to an organisation as noted by Howard-Grenville (see Chapter 1), and it evolves and spreads depending on organisational factors such as tone from the top. This implies a top-down flow of attitudes and opinions from leadership associated with formal hierarchies.

We study the impact of charisma and strength of connections on transmission and persistence of culture in a given social network structure. We conjecture that a change in the values of the firm espoused at the board level can only be expected to change the values visible in the activities of its general staff if values are supported by influential staff throughout the organization. We study the effort to change culture in a firm by looking at communication effectiveness of influential staff throughout the firm, who are secondary to the board of the firm in that they act as 'repeater stations' in transmitting the tone from the top, which is set by the board. This is a refinement of the classical approach to culture (Schein, 1990), which tends to focus more on senior leaders, consistent with tone from the top but without accounting for the social network of the firm's staff.

We take inspiration from the study of information diffusion in social networks to model the propagation and maintenance of culture in an organisation. Our focus is on two aspects of the network constituents and how these affect the transmission of culture, taking the network topology as given. The first is charisma of an actor (Pastor, Meindl & Mayo, 2002), and the second is the strength in connectivity of the ties between individuals. The former relates to the characterisation of actors in a network as either information sources or information sinks (González-Bailón, et al., 2011). The latter relates to the closeness or coherence of the nodes, which are connected by social ties. Plausibly, higher-strength connections imply greater influence of one actor on another whether through persuasion or collaboration (Sosa, 2011). This analysis does not address the details of the network formation such as the observation that high self-monitors, who presumably are charismatic, find themselves more centrally located than other individuals (Mehra, Kilduff & Brass, 2001).

Our social network model has two kinds of agents, the first being influencers (opinion leaders), who propagate information about a cultural change that has, for example, originated at the board level, and the second called targets, who may accept or reject information that they receive from influencers. Influencers can communicate with all targets in their social networks. Targets with whom the influencers have a connection are called the contacts of the influencer and will aid in influencing interactions. That is, the social network is taken as fixed. We take a broad view of what constitutes information; for instance, it could be explicitly presented in the communications of influencers to targets or could be implicit in the behaviour of influencers that is observable by targets. This model could apply equally to the diffusion of a culture of innovation by Kavadias and Ladas (see Chapter 4) or another aspect of culture other than risk culture.

This set-up is illustrated in Figure 3.2, in which the small blue nodes represent influencers, and the large red nodes represent targets. The connecting lines between blue and red nodes indicate the ties between influencers and their contacts. We account for the strength of connections, which are shown in the figure as darker lines. The small number of nodes, twenty influencers and eight targets, is for simplicity. In fact, each target node may represent a subpopulation of the firm that is somewhat homogeneous with respect to the relationship with the influencer. For example, an influencer who has a certain level of formal (organisational) seniority will have strong ties to their

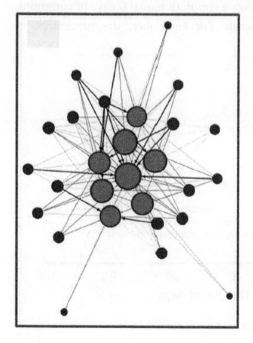

FIGURE 3.2 Network representation of strength of connectivity between opinion leaders and targets

subordinates, all of whom could be represented in one red group. Likewise, an influencer with charisma may be recognized as such due to a combination of behavioural or personality traits and measurable attributes. Such characteristics include professional experience or formal qualifications, which have the potential to provide weak ties to subgroups of staff with whom an influencer has no formal relationships. This snapshot is based on a survey administered to a subset of risk managers at a global financial institution.

### 3.7.3   Overview of Risk Culture Model Results

Even in the absence of a model, it seems intuitive that connectivity and influence ought to improve efficacy in transmitting any entity. We try to unpack that intuition to ask more nuanced questions. We use our risk culture model in the first instance to assess the survivability. We present results to highlight concepts of culture or information transmission rather than convey parameter values such as probability seeds, charismas and connectivity profiles, which have a significant effect on the model outcomes. Figure 3.3 shows how information is propagated over a simulation of 100 days of communication in the social network. For each day, the percentage of

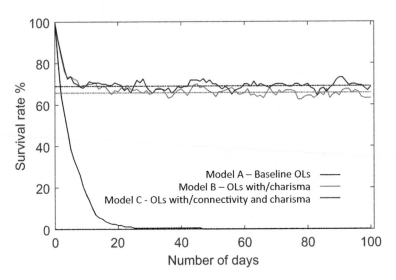

FIGURE 3.3 Message survival rates of opinion leaders

influencers whose motivation to transmit information survives that day is shown by the height of the curve on the vertical axis.

The baseline case (model A) shows information propagation dying off completely because all targets reject all communications, eventually discouraging all influencers from further communication. It is significant that in the situations with charismatic influencers (model B) and influencers with both charisma and strong connections (model C), the survival of information is prolonged indefinitely. All models also incorporate a random survival component to 'revive' an influencer who has 'died' (given up on further communication) because all of their contacts rejected their last message.

These results highlight the importance of having active cultural influencers in an organisation. The fact that information survives at a higher percentage in model C than model B is expected because there are more chances, via strong connections, for information to survive. If more of the links between influencers and their contacts are designated as strong connections, then the curve in model B would approach the curve in model C, reducing the gap between the two curves.

While an averaged view of data as displayed in Figure 3.3 is helpful in conveying behaviour of the network over a period of time, the view can miss or even obfuscate the general dynamics of the network. Additionally, the view allows multiple simulations with probabilistic seeds to be considered in the average. Stepping through a single simulation is not always reflective of the average, but it can display the nature of dynamic behaviour.

In our final output, Figure 3.4 uses a colour-based heat map to show which connections are alive on each day of the 100-day simulation when an influencer communicates with one of its contacts. The colour represents the cumulative number of days for which a connection is alive, where dark blue indicates near to 0 and dark red near to 100. The broad point is that the pattern of communications depends directly on the characteristics of the communicators, here the charisma of influencers, and the strength of their connections.

Figure 3.4a shows the baseline case, model A, in which all twenty influencers can connect with all eight targets, hence there

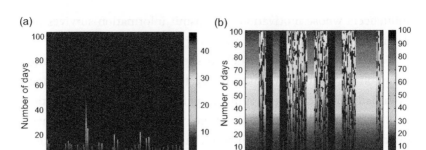

FIGURE 3.4 Message propagation by opinion leaders: (a) baseline OLs; (b) OLs with connectivity and charisma

are 160 connections; but every communication effectively kills the power of the influencer for future days, hence the graphic is dominated by dark blue. This shows that after approximately fifty days, there are only dead connections (no communication); red here designates cumulative number of days of activity.

Figure 3.4b corresponds to model C, in which there are charismatic influencers and strong connections between other influencers and their contacts. It is characterised by three kinds of vertical columns: rainbow-coloured columns, which are blue at the bottom (day 0) and progress vertically through the colour spectrum to be red at the top (day 100), show active communication through all 100 days; dark blue columns signify dead connections due to lack of both charisma and strong connections of influencers; and mottled columns show connections that are alive by rebirth after death. Non-charismatic influencers are discouraged by communication on weak connections but encouraged by communication on strong connections.

## 3.8   CONCLUSION AND FUTURE WORK

Networks can provide rich views into organisations. We believe network analyses complement other approaches to answer questions critical to risk culture, such as 'What does a 'good' organisation look like and what is its shape?', 'Where are the influential actors/nodes within the network, and what is their level of influence?' and 'How do ideas and local knowledge spread across the network and do they have staying power?'

With a network perspective, this chapter uses tone at the top to examine risk culture. Our analysis highlights the need and importance of opinion leaders to realise tone at the top. These influencers may provide critical roles in times of change, stress or great uncertainty. We highlight that self-monitoring and charisma characteristics are important traits in the influence exerted by opinion leaders. Further, an opinion leader's reach through their strong social ties may be essential in keeping a desired risk culture alive throughout an organisation.

We further conjecture that successful risk managers benefit more from having broader informal networks than other business leaders. In particular, behavioural or personality traits that enhance social influence would seem key to a risk manager's capacity to be an opinion leader.

Additional research is clearly required to provide specifics on the transmission of culture and the role of the opinion leaders and their value to creating or sustaining a good risk culture in an organisation. We believe the concepts and issues raised during our research provide an exemplar for a future research agenda addressing the contributions of the risk function to better functioning organisations. Below, we provide a short overview of our recommendations for future research on the following three key risk culture topics: (1) implications of structures and hierarchies in organisations; (2) trends in globalisation and de-globalisation strategies; (3) social networks and growth of artificial intelligence in changing and monitoring working practices in organisations.

## 3.9    IMPLICATIONS OF STRUCTURES AND HIERARCHIES IN ORGANISATIONS

Organisations have inherent structures and hierarchies whether they are formally or informally delineated. Without espousing a recommendation on the type of structure that a corporate should adopt, the study of its network topologies can help define such attributes as how many layers there are to an organisation, distance between members of the network and what level of agency anyone has. Social networks matter to culture, and thus it is natural to bring social network analysis to the forefront in cultural studies. A starting question is, 'How do network structures themselves mediate the flow of information?' And then, 'How related is information flow to culture flow in a network?' These questions both, of course, are linked the propositions of Powers (see Chapter 2) on the role of information in shaping and understanding organisational culture.

The presence of subcultures in organisations can be viewed through networks and subnetworks. Not having a monolithic culture is a reality in firms as different divisions often operate independently and might have quite different cultures from one another or the headquarters of the parent company.

## 3.10    TRENDS IN GLOBALISATION AND DE-GLOBALISATION STRATEGIES

As we noted in this chapter, the modern global firm's structure has evolved to support its changing strategy. Scholarship is warranted in further understanding how cultures spread and change in line with these structural and hierarchical changes. Global organisations have complex organisational structures within their hierarchies. This includes a firm's own operations as well as its global supply chains and customer bases. The overlaps in global governance and firm governance and their alignment in building a good risk culture are not well understood. Conversely, recent trends in nationalism have challenged the growth in globalisation for many firms. Supply chains have shortened through local sourcing and manufacturing. How such decisions and their respective transitions impact risk culture is an interesting question.

Many academic and practitioner studies have addressed the relevance of organisational structures on the performance of firms and individuals within those firms. A risk culture lens to the familiar question of whether structure matters would be a welcome addition to the risk culture literature.

## 3.11  SOCIAL NETWORKS AND GROWTH OF ARTIFICIAL INTELLIGENCE USE IN ORGANISATIONS

The acceleration and pervasiveness of technological advancement portends drastic changes to the future of work. Whether or not this hypothesis is vastly exaggerated, we can be sure that growth in social media adoption by organisations will change its business processes and thus have implications to its risk culture. At the moment, artificial intelligence implementations are not accurate or transparent (explainable) enough to completely displace many activities that seem ripe for automation, but the future may hold a place where error rates are within tolerance levels and artificial intelligence becomes endemic.

We see greater insertion of artificial intelligence through machine learning and automated algorithms to influence if not control important organisational decision-making. Defensive use of such systems to monitor employee traits and actions are already widely adopted by human resources departments and management, often with a focus on rooting out bad actors. Many firms keep records of employee email exchanges, phone calls and chat dialogues.

Our current business environment includes widespread practices of corporate monitoring, while the ethics of monitoring staff, and the impact on commitment and morale of staff of increasing levels of monitoring, is in an evolving space. For example, the ethics or lack thereof of automated data collection relating to an individual's psychometric traits challenge current social expectations for privacy. Additional research is needed to triangulate on risk culture, growth of technology adoption and people's understanding of and true attitudes towards a high-surveillance world.

## 3.12   CONCLUDING THOUGHTS

Whilst we have developed a social network view of risk culture through literature, intuition and conceptual modelling, we hope that additional research will bring greater insights and availability of empirical results. Maintenance and contagion of risk culture is evident in organisations, but the specifics of the conditions, mechanisms, triggers and actors are less clear; however, we conjecture that the role of networks in this is not marginal.

# Appendix    **Further Details of the Risk Culture Model**

The blue nodes represent managers, and the red nodes represent buckets of interactions with corporate entities or functions. Charisma and connectivity were derived from a corporate survey as characteristics of the blue nodes.

We measure an instance or time step of cultural change transmission as a single day. During a time step, influencers are provided the opportunity to communicate with their contacts (targets in their social network) in the firm. There is one possible communication between an influencer and each of its contacts per time step. An influencer whose information is rejected by all of its contacts on a given day may give up, i.e. not attempt to influence its contacts in all future time steps, in which case we say its influence dies. By the same token, an influencer whose message is accepted by one or more contacts will remain empowered to attempt influencing its contacts tomorrow; we say it survives.

The baseline or default response of a target is to reject a communication from an influencer; we use this simple mechanism to reflect the difficulty and complexity in managing cultural change (Schein, 1990). (The default of rejection is represented in our models by a 'predator' who kills the information; see Figure 3.5.) Nevertheless, all models have a random survival component, controlled by probability parameter, to revive an influencer who has 'died', i.e. given up on further communication, because all of their contacts rejected their last message.

In the baseline model, called model A, we ignore the social network in that each influencer is able to communicate with a target that is randomly chosen from all targets, rather than being restricted to its contacts. In models B and C, we introduce two factors that alleviate the rejection of information by targets.

In model B, some influencers are endowed with charisma; in this treatment, influencers still communicate with all targets; however, connected targets are seeded with a higher probability of accepting the information from an influencer with charisma.

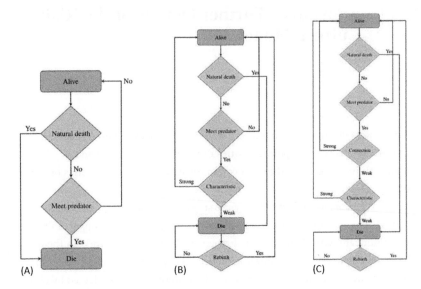

FIGURE 3.5 Schematic of risk culture model: (A) baseline OLs; (B) OLs with charisma; (C) OLs with connectivity and charisma

In model C, we retain the charismatic subpopulation of influencers set up in model B and, in addition, identify some strong connections between non-charismatic influencers and their contacts. In this treatment, contacts have a higher probability of accepting information that is received either from a charismatic influencer or via a strong connection. A minor feature of the model is that we allow any influencer whose influence has died to revive randomly, with small probability on any day, and resume information propagation to their contacts. Figure 3.5 gives schematic flow charts for each of the models.

Each of the three models is run over 100 days after initialisation. The baseline case, model A, is initialised with the list of influencers and targets, which remain fixed throughout. Model B is initialised with the influencers and targets, the connections or contacts of each influencer and the identification of a subset of the influencers with charisma, where this data remains fixed throughout. The initialisation of model C is like that of model B, with the additional identification of a subset of connections as strong connections.

REFERENCES

Acemoglu, D., Bimpikis, K. and Ozdaglar, A. (2014). Dynamics of information exchange in endogenous social networks. *Theoretical Economics*, **9**(1), 41–97.

Alonso, R., Dessein, W. and Matouschek, N. (2008). When does coordination require centralization? *American Economic Review*, **98**(1), 145–79.

Aral, S. (2011). Commentary – identifying social influence: a comment on opinion leadership and social contagion in new product diffusion. *Marketing Science*, **30**(2), 217–23.

Aral, S., Muchnik, L. and Sundararajan, A. (2009). Distinguishing influence-based contagion from homophily-driven diffusion in dynamic networks. *Proceedings of the National Academy of Sciences of the United States of America*, **10**(51), 21544–9.

Ash, J. and Newth, D. (2007). Optimizing complex networks for resilience against cascading failures. *Physica A*, **380**(C), 673–83.

Bandura, A. (2000). Exercise of human agency through collective efficacy. *Current Directions in Psychological Science*, **9**(3), 75–6.

Barney, J. (1991). Firm resources and sustained competitive advantage. *Journal of Management*, **17**(1), 99–120.

Bergenholtz, C. and Walstrom, C. (2011). Inter-organizational network studies – a literature review. *Industry and Innovation*, **18**(6), 539–62.

Burt, R. (2004). Structural holes and good ideas. *American Journal of Sociology*, **110**(2), 349–99.

Burt, R. S. (1992). *Structural Holes: The Social Structure of Competition*. Cambridge, MA: Harvard University Press.

Cachon, G. P., Zipkin, P. H. and Anderson, P. (1999). Complexity theory and organization science. *Organization Science*, **10**(3), 216–32.

Carroll, G. R. and Hannan, M. T. (2000). *The Demography of Corporations and Industries*. Princeton, NJ: Princeton University Press.

Chandler, A. D. (1977). *The Visible Hand: The Managerial Revolution in American Business*. Cambridge, MA: Belknap Press of Harvard University Press.

Coase, R. H. (1937). The nature of the firm. *Economica*, **4**(16), 386–405.

Cohan, J. (2002). 'I didn't know' and I was only doing my job': has corporate governance careened out of control? A case study of Enron's information myopia. *Journal of Business Ethics*, **40**(3), 275–99.

Daily, C., Dalton, D. and Cannella, A. (2003). Corporate governance: decades of dialogue and data. *Academy of Management Review*, **28**(477), 371–82.

Ethiraj, S. K. and Levinthal, D. (2004). Modularity and innovation in complex systems. *Management Science*, **50**(2), 159–73.

Financial Stability Board (FSB) (2014). *Guidance on Supervisory Interaction with Financial Institutions on Risk Culture: A Framework for Assessing Risk Culture.* London: FSB. www.fsb.org/wp-content/uploads/140407.pdf

Forrester, J. W. (1968). *Principles of Systems.* Waltham, MA: Pegasus Communications.

Forrester, J. W. (1994). System dynamics, systems thinking, and soft OR. *System Dynamics Review*, **10**(2–3), 245–56.

González-Bailón, S., Borge-Holthoefer, J., Rivero, A. and Moreno, Y. (2011). The dynamics of protest recruitment through an online network. *Nature Scientific Reports.*

Gordon, G. G. and DiTomaso, N. (1992). Predicting corporate performance from organizational culture. *Journal of Management Studies*, **29**(6), 783–98.

Guille, A., Hacid, H., Favre, C. and Zighed, D. (2013). Information diffusion in online social networks: a survey. *ACM SIGMOD Record*, **42**(2), 17–28.

Hanneman, R. and Riddle, M. (2005). *Introduction to Social Network Methods.* https://bit.ly/2JCXTjj

Hatch, M. J. (1993). The dynamics of organizational culture. *Academy of Management Review*, **18**(4), 65793.

Hermanson, D. R., Ivancevich, D. M. and Ivancevich, S. H. (2008). Tone at the top: insights from section 404. *Strategic Finance Magazine*, **90**(5), 39–45.

Holme, P. (2015). Modern temporal network theory: a colloquium. *The European Physical Journal B*, **88**(234).

Humanities Commons (n.d.). Visualizing *Les misérables.* Website. https://lesmiserables.mla.hcommons.org/

Johnson, G., Scholes, K. and Whittington, R. (2008). Organising for success. In *Exploring Corporate Strategy: Text & Cases*, 8th ed. Harlow: Financial Times/Prentice Hall.

Katz, E. and Lazarsfeld, P. F. (2017). *Personal Influence: The Part Played by People in the Flow of Mass Communications.* New York: Routledge.

Kilduff, M. and Brass, D. J. (2010). Organizational social network research: core ideas and key debates. *Academy of Management Annals*, **4**(1), 317–57.

Knuth, D. (1993). Coappearance weighted network of characters in the novel *Les misérables.* In *The Stanford GraphBase: A Platform for Combinatorial Computing.* Reading: Addison-Wesley.

König, M. D., Battiston, S., Napoletano, M. and Schweitzer, F. (2012). The efficiency and stability of R&D networks. *Games and Economic Behavior*, 75(2), 694–713.

Kreps, G. L. (2017). Diffusion theory in integrative approaches. In *Oxford Research Encyclopedia of Communication.* Oxford: Oxford University Press.

Lambiotte, R., Lefebvre, E., Blondel, V. D. and Guillaume, J.-L. (2008). Fast unfolding of communities in large networks. *Journal of Statistical Mechanics*.

Lin, N., Ensel, W. M. and Vaughn, J. C. (1981). Social resources and strength of ties: structural factors in occupational status attainment. *American Sociological Review*, **46**(4), 393–405.

Lovejoy, W. S. and Sinha, A. (2010). Efficient structures for innovative social networks. *Management Science*, **56**(7), 1127–45.

McEvily, B., Jaffee, J. and Tortoriello, M. (2012). Not all bridging ties are equal: network imprinting and firm growth in the Nashville legal industry, 1933–1978. *Organization Science*, **23**(2), 547–63.

McEvily, B., Soda, G. and Tortoriello, M. (2014). More formally: rediscovering the missing link between formal organization and informal social structure. *Academy of Management Annals*, **8**(1), 299–345.

Mehra, A., Kilduff, M. and Brass, D. J. (2001). The social networks of high and low self-monitors: implications for workplace performance. *Administrative Quarterly*, **46**(1), 121–46.

Mihm, J., Loch, C., Wilkinson, D. and Huberman, B. (2010). Hierarchical structure and search in complex organizations. *Management Science*, **56**(5), 831–48.

Newman, M. (2011). Communities, modules and large-scale structure in networks. *Nature Physics*, **8**(1), 25–31.

O'Connor, G. (2008). Major innovation as a dynamic capability: a systems approach. *Journal of Product Innovation Management*, **25**(4), 313–30.

Onnela, J. et al. (2007). Structure and tie strengths in mobile communication networks. *Proceedings of the National Academy of Sciences of the United States of America*, **194**(18), 7332–6.

Pastor, J.-C., Meindl, J. R. and Mayo, M. C. (2002). A network effects model of charisma attributions. *Academy of Management Journal*, **45**(2), 410–20.

Pettigrew, A. M. (1979). On studying organizational cultures. *Administrative Science Quarterly*, **24**(4), 570–81.

Powell, W. W. (1990). Neither market nor hierarchy: network forms of organization. *Research in Organizational Behavior*, **12**, 295–336.

Power, M., Palermo, T. and Ashby, S. (2013). *Risk Culture in Financial Organisations: A Research Report*. London: Centre for Analysis of Risk and Regulation, London School of Economics.

Rapert, M. I. and Wren, B. M. (1998). Reconsidering organizational structure: a dual perspective of frameworks and processes. *Journal of Managerial Issues*, **10**(3), 287–302.

Rogers, E. M. (2003). *Diffusion of Innovations*, 5th ed. New York: Free Press.

Rombach, P., Porter, M. A., Fowler, J. H. and Mucha, P. J. (2017). Core–periphery structure in networks (revisited). *Society for Industrial and Applied Mathematics*, **59**(3), 619–46.

Schein, E. (1990). Organizational culture. *American Psychologist*, **45**(2), 109–19.

Schwartz, M. S., Dunfee, T. W. and Kline, M. J. (2005). Tone at the top: an ethics code for directors. *Journal of Business Ethics*, **58**(1), 79–100.

Smith, J. A. and England, C. (2019). An ethnographic study of culture and performance in the UK lingerie industry. *The British Accounting Review*, **51**(3), 241–58.

Soda, G. and Zaheer, A. (2012). A network perspective on organizational architecture: performance effects of the interplay of formal and informal organization. *Strategic Management Journal*, **33**(6), 751–71.

Sosa, M. E. (2011). Where do creative interactions come from? The role of tie content and social networks. *Organization Science*, **22**(1), 1–21.

Sosa, M. E., Eppinger, S. D. and Rowles, C. M. (2004). The misalignment of product architecture and organizational structure in complex product development. *Management Science*, **50**(12), 674–89.

Teece, D. J. (2018). Dynamic capabilities as (workable) management systems theory. *Journal of Management & Organization*, **24**(3), 359–68.

Tuveson, M. et al. (2018). *Risk Management Perspectives of Global Corporations*, Cambridge: Cambridge Centre for Risk Studies. https://bit.ly/2BZNF8C

Valente, T. W. and Davis, R. L. (1999). Accelerating the diffusion of innovations using opinion leaders. *Annals of the American Academy of Political and Social Science*, **566**(1), 55–67.

Verma, T. et al. (2016). Emergence of core–peripheries in networks. *Nature Communications*, **7**(10441).

Zheng, W., Yang, B. and McLean, G. N. (2010). Linking organizational culture, structure, strategy, and organizational effectiveness: mediating role of knowledge management,. *Journal of Business Research*, **63**(7), 763–71.

# 4 Rethinking Risk Management Cultures in Organisations

*Insights from Innovation*

Stelios Kavadias and Kostas Ladas

## 4.1 INNOVATION AND RISK MANAGEMENT: A JIGSAW PUZZLE

The connection between innovation and economic growth is well established across different strands of the literature. The fundamental concepts find their origins in the early ideas presented by Schumpeter (1939) and then further established by neoclassical economists like Solow (1956) and Romer (1990), who challenged the traditional economic thinking that input, and in particular capital, is the major driver of growth. The overarching conceptual argument has been elegantly simple; for an economy to grow (i.e. produce more valuable output), there exist fundamentally two options: either to increase the number of inputs (whereby 'inputs' reflect the traditional economic classification into 'capital' and 'labour') or to find ways to produce more valuable output from the same input (economists have classified such new ways as another input called 'technology').

The fact that sourcing more traditional inputs runs into the problem of input sufficiency, but also the reality of inputs being sought from competitive agents at continuously higher prices, makes the first approach above a challenging one. Several studies (Abramovitz, 1956; Kendrick, 1956; Rosenberg, 2004) of the US economy (building up on Solow's exogenous growth model in 1956) have employed empirical methodologies across different industry sectors for the period 1870–1950 to indicate that only 15 per cent of the growth in the US economy is attributed to the increase of inputs. As such, the remaining 85 per cent has to come from the alternative option, which is the new ways[1] that produce more value from the same input; these new ways capture efforts to change the established production methods (Rosenberg, 2004) or to launch completely new offerings that appeal more to consumer markets.

Fast-forward to today; it is widely accepted by economists, management theorists and practitioners that innovation is the major driver of economic growth. A simple query in Amazon for the number of books that contain the term 'innovation' in their titles, returns over 50,000 findings. This indicates that innovation is well established as a key capability to be mastered by companies. However, by the same token, the amount of literature, and the persistence on the topic, gives rise to a simple question: why does innovation continue to be a relevant topic of discussion? Haven't we figured out how to develop innovation? Unfortunately, the answer is also a simple one: innovation is fraught with *risk* (Loch & Kavadias, 2008).

Indeed, it is readily observable from many anecdotal settings (Dillon & Lafley, 2011) that the likelihood to create value and deliver growth through new inputs or more efficient use of inputs, or even by creating different and better outputs, is admittedly small. Just as an example, in the pharmaceutical industry, the likelihood that a new discovered compound makes it into a drug prescribed to patients is less than one-fortieth (see Markou, Kavadias & Oraiopoulos, 2018 and references therein). To put this into perspective, the previous statistic translates into thirty-nine projects budgeted and resourced result in failure without producing tangible value! Thus, efforts to innovate appear to be questionably productive in economic terms. Instead, the positive impact of innovation on economic growth reflects an *average* effect (Aghion & Howitt, 1992; Pennetier, Girotra & Mihm, 2018). It applies at an economy level or across an industry sector as a whole, but it cannot translate into individual company effects. Instead, at

---

[1] Robert Solow has received the John Bates Clark Medal in 1961 and the Nobel Prize in the Economic Sciences in 1987 for showing an effect of what he termed 'technical progress' (his early attempt to characterise innovation) on growth.

the level of analysis of individual companies, the presence of risk makes it extremely difficult to establish a similar robust relationship between innovation efforts and value creation (Markou, Kavadias & Oraiopoulos, 2018).

If innovation is necessary but fraught with risk, and risk happens to be the core of expertise of risk management practices and methods, then naturally we should expect risk management experts to be core enablers of innovation within companies. However, among many others (see Koetzier & Alon, 2013), we observe that this is rarely the corporate reality. Quite the opposite; risk management, regulating or compliance functions often carry the identity of innovation 'killers' within companies as they try to limit the exposure of company assets, or efforts, to failure. If this is indeed the case, where is our aforementioned logic failing? Why does such a friction between risk management and innovation emerge? Do risk-aversion behaviours inhibit innovation?

The realisation that innovation and risk are two pieces of an organisational jigsaw puzzle motivates the discussion presented in this chapter. In this chapter we attempt to analyse the divide between the innovation and the risk management perspectives on value creation in order to understand whether, and how, risk management practices support or undermine innovation in organisations. Our thesis is that the misalignment between the two perspectives stems from the fundamentally different types of risk arising in different innovation activities. This distinction between the risks associated with innovation efforts reveals the important role that risk management practices might play in innovation within organisations. It highlights the limitations that certain (traditional) risk management toolboxes might impose on certain types of innovations.

We identify two major types of risk that arise during innovation efforts: first, the risk that innovation outcomes do not materialise despite the resources and efforts allocated to achieve them and the pre-existing knowledge regarding those outcomes, i.e. the risk of *known factors* leading to innovation failure; second, the risk that innovations fail due to lack of knowledge of the factors determining the outcome, i.e. the risk of *unknown factors* driving innovation failure. Whereas the former type of risk reflects the perils of project execution, the latter represents a higher-order challenge. It captures the concept of creative destruction also spelled out by the early works of Schumpeter (1939). Companies – even mighty ones – are vulnerable to the latter type of risk. Over the last fifty years, a great number of products have become virtually extinct (the rotary telephone, the photographic film, the tape player, etc.) and have been replaced with substitute offerings (products or services) that have led the original providers out of work. Almost none of the top ten performing companies fifty, or even thirty, years ago remain in the same list today.[2] These two types of risks map into a traditional classification of innovation efforts: *incremental* and *radical* (Ettlie, Bridges & O'Keefe, 1984).

This risk categorisation highlights an important implication for the respective risk mitigation: mitigation for known risks reflects practices that seek to choose either the best development actions (given all available information) to achieve the set objective or whether to 'pull the plug' in cases of clear failure signals. Such risk management practices reflect well-embedded mechanisms that risk management experts have codified and deployed robustly over the years. In other words, the predominant risk management practices described in the literature address effectively the circumstances of incremental innovation risks. However, mitigation for radical innovation risks is a more under-studied topic from a risk management perspective. The risk of the Schumpeterian creative destruction potentially reflects an organisational inability (or unwillingness) to pursue ambitious enough objectives; such avoidance of radical innovation, while harmless in the short term, eventually might result in

---

[2] In 1917 the top three US companies by valuation were US Steel, AT&T and Standard Oil. Fifty years later, in 1967, the top three companies were IBM, AT&T and Eastman Kodak. Another fifty years later, in 2017, the top three companies were Apple, Alphabet and Microsoft.

severe underperformance and, often enough, into complete destruction of a company. In fact, disruptive innovation theory (Christensen & Raynor, 2013) describes how this latter form of risk, and the lack of proper mitigation practices, leads to the dilution of entire industries.

Our discussion results in several insights: first, the fact that innovation efforts should not be at odds with risk management practices. Innovation implies an increase in the risk assumed by any organisation, and higher risk naturally calls for risk management. Yet, risk management practices without proper assessment of what type of innovation is pursued might result in hampering innovation. Practices that are often described in the literature under traditional risk management tend to serve better in cases of incremental (known) risks. However, the dominance of these practices in large organisations often take the form of institutionalised functions or even strong risk cultures and lead to non-desirable effects, namely the inability to pursue more radical innovation. Instead, we document a distinctively different set of risk management approaches that effectively address innovations that face unknown risks. This insight bears important managerial implications. Should organisations wish to pursue more radical innovations that challenge their existing business models, they need to adopt risk management approaches that are different from traditional practices. Such new approaches put into question the effectiveness of the existing risk culture and point to the need for a cultural change. Overall, we introduce a contingency framework that aligns risk management practices to different types of innovation efforts. We propose this framework as a tool for practitioners; the truly innovative capacity that different individual companies exhibit relies upon their ability to effectively implement these differentiated risk practices.

The chapter is structured as follows. In Section 4.2 we give a brief introduction to innovation management. We identify major typologies of innovation and discuss processes that make innovation happen both for radical and incremental innovation. We also discuss the necessary management mindset required to pursue either type of innovation. In Section 4.3 we present the current thinking of risk management in incremental innovation projects. Finally, in Section 4.4, we introduce a risk management framework capable of handling radical innovation efforts.

## 4.2   INNOVATION MANAGEMENT: A BRIEF OVERVIEW

### 4.2.1   Innovation: Definition and Typology

Innovation is so widely recognised as an activity in organisations that it naturally tends to succumb to multiple schools of thought and respective definitions. In that regard, any attempt to define innovation in detail might be deemed incomplete from the start, the reason being the multifaceted nature of the innovation activity: it involves multiple organisational stakeholders, requires different domains of technological and market expertise, and it is performed with incomplete knowledge and understanding of the underlying factors that drive its outcome. Despite the definitional diversity, though, it is always useful to identify boundaries on what an innovation activity is, or at least describe its key features, so that meaningful analysis and discussion happens by a common understanding of the concept of innovation.

In this chapter we adopt the following definition for 'innovation', which is motivated by definitions found in the literature (Trott, 2008) as well as cited in dictionaries.[3] Innovation represents the creation of something *novel*, that is *(economically) useful*, and it is *actually implemented in some form to deliver an outcome (e.g. process or artefact)* (Campbell, 1960; Simonton, 1998). In that regard, innovation is about economically rewarding changes, either in the type of output (e.g. a new product) or in the way inputs are transformed into outputs. For example, a company may use different raw materials or establish new structures by which the company engages with its supply chain through different partners. Equally, innovation

---

[3] The Cambridge dictionary defines innovation as 'the use of a new idea or method'.

may take place through new processes a company employs to develop their outputs, such as a new manufacturing or sales process.

This definition emphasises two important properties of innovation. First, the fact that innovation is a novel undertaking with an economic objective. Hence, its success (or failure) is eventually determined by a market of potential *customers*.[4] It is not sufficient to just exhibit a sophisticated or advanced scientific development or technology. What matters is that the output convinces customers that the proposed innovation offers sufficient *value* to them to either switch away from competitive offerings in an existing market or become an initial adopter in case of a new market segment (Rogers, 2010). The requirement of novelty and marketability points to the existence of *uncertainty* as to whether an innovation can achieve success. Innovation is subject to a number of sources of uncertainty: is the innovation objective unique enough with regards to competition? Can the technology, science or design be developed so as to perform successfully, on time and on budget? Will the customers perceive the value the innovation offers them? Questions as such indicate the variety of uncertainties that innovation efforts face.

Second, the definition accommodates the broad scope of innovation. Said differently, innovation can take place across any organisational activity. As firms transform inputs (raw materials, partnerships, technology or labour effort and knowledge) into outputs (distinct products or services offered through specific payment schemes) through processes that organise tasks, people and other assets (e.g. equipment), innovation can take place across any of the dimensions of such value creation (input, transformation, output). The literature has tried to capture possible dimensions of innovation

---

[4] We note here that we use the term 'customer' in a general manner, in order to encompass different business settings, such as other buying companies in business-to-business transactions, end-product users and consumers in business-to-customer settings, or adopters of new procedures and technologies in intra-organisational innovation circumstances.

through different studies (Sawhney, Wolcott & Arroniz, 2006): (i) the early distinction between product and process innovations (Utterback & Abernathy, 1975) is a subject of continuing study (Utterback, 1994; Cohen and Klepper, 1996); (ii) the classification in component versus architectural innovation (Henderson & Clark, 1990) has been developed to try to identify whether the change brought by the intended innovation is specified and contained within a special feature of the offering or whether it applies across multiple features and changes drastically the functionality (Baldwin & Clark, 1997); (iii) the distinction between competence-enhancing and competence-destroying innovation (Tushman & Anderson, 1986) has given rise to several similar typologies, all of them aiming to characterise the magnitude of impact on the focal company as well as the industry. Another such typology stemmed from Christensen's work on disruptive versus sustaining innovation (Christensen, 1997). This had led to a comprehensive approach to identifying the different typologies of innovation (Chandy & Prabhu, 2011).

Across all these typologies, an important common feature becomes apparent: innovation tends to range between small changes, similar to current offerings (e.g. addressing a close market segment, using similar technologies and processes), with limited given impact, all the way to larger changes through drastically new technologies or new market segments and entirely novel processes with sizeable possible impact. This observation helps us define the magnitude of innovation as the distance travelled from the current company position (captured by the inputs, transformation and outputs) to a new position with new inputs, transformation processes and/or outputs (Kavadias & Chao, 2007; Chao & Kavadias, 2008).

This general classification accommodates all the previous ones as these become special instances that focus on the particular dimensions of company's position that change. In addition, it maps effectively to the previous point we raised, namely the uncertainty experienced during innovation; the more dimensions that change, the higher the faced uncertainty. Therefore, for our subsequent discussion, we admit to the following distinction between types of innovation: *incremental* innovation, whereby changes are small to moderate and usually concentrated on well understood features of the current dimensions of business that a company performs; *radical* innovation, with significant changes in possibly multiple of the business parameters that determine company performance. For example, in the automotive industry models of cars undergo 'facelifts' every so often, i.e. small feature changes that provide a sense of freshness to customers without any major change. Such facelifts capture the concept of incremental innovation. At the same time, the introduction of a transportation service by car2go in 2008 enabled a complete change in the industry, through a fundamentally different business model – a type of change that adheres to radical innovation (Kavadias, Ladas & Loch, 2016). This distinction is not new (see, for example, Ettlie, Bridges & O'Keefe, 1984), but we believe it best captures the notion of magnitude of change, which is supported by empirical work (Chao & Loutskina, 2011).

The discussion above highlights the existence of different types of innovation. It is important to recognise that all innovations cannot be treated as identical efforts. Innovations that call for marginal departures from existing practices in an organisation, which we term *incremental*, might be managed differently than innovations that require fundamental changes in the activities of an organisation, which are *radical*. Such different management practices could include different risk management approaches as well. This distinction is motivated by the sheer amount of changes implied by the different types of innovation, and it is reflective of the uncertainty that governs the end result of the innovation efforts. It is also a distinction that has been particularly useful in the innovation literature as it has motivated the study of different management approaches to ensure innovation outcomes. At the same time, it has been advocated that companies benefit from a portfolio of incremental and radical efforts, i.e. from a mix of innovation projects that aim to support the overall strategic goals of the organisation (Kavadias & Chao, 2007).

## 4.2.2    *Making Innovation Happen: A Portfolio of Processes*

The typology of innovation efforts introduced above has informed an extensive literature in the domains of innovation management, the management of technological change and the management of new product development (Chao & Lenox, 2018). Over the years, both the academic community but also the extended practitioner enthusiasts have converged to a robust thesis: there seem to exist archetypal processes that correspond to the innovations of different type. These processes bear significantly different characteristics along multiple dimensions: from how they are structured, i.e. their workflow charts, all the way to how they are led, i.e. the attributes of the leaders that can effectively manage these processes (Chandrasekaran, Linderman & Schroeder, 2015).

Specifically, incremental innovation efforts are managed through processes that draw directly from, or are adaptations of, the original *phase gate*, or *waterfall*, approach, introduced in the 1950s by the Association of Cost Engineers and further popularised in the last three decades as *stage gates* by the work of Robert G. Cooper (Cooper, 1990). In contrast, since the late 1990s, and based upon the pioneering work of Clark and Fujimoto (1991), the processes that were found effective in supporting more radical innovation efforts have followed a different conceptual model: the 'build–test–analyse' development cycle originally described in Wheelwright and Clark (1992), which was later enriched as 'build–design–test–analyse' to explicitly account for learning (Thomke, 1998). Hereafter, we offer a concise description of the two different approaches with the objective to point out their key differences.

### 4.2.2.1    *Stage-Gate Processes*

Stage-gate processes have been built with a key premise in mind: the introduction of a disciplined way by which the development of innovations and new products takes place. There are great benefits from such a structural approach to innovation. The process breaks down any complex objective of transforming ideas into actual products or services into smaller and comprehensive *stages*. Within these stages, specific project activities and tasks are conducted. The key contribution of the stage-gate approach is manifested by the explicit institutionalisation of *decision gates*. It is within the context of such gates where detailed evaluations of the progress of an innovation project are conducted, with an objective to move forward, perform small adaptations[5] or terminate the project (go/kill decisions).

Stage-gate processes incorporate meaningfully the upfront pre-development activities (customer-driven business justification and preliminary technical feasibility), subsequent development activities (technical development and testing, marketing testing, and operations/manufacturing tasks) and commercialisation activities (market launch efforts, and post-launch assessment and learning) into one complete end-to-end business process. In that light, they exhibit certain key benefits for companies and managers: (i) they establish structure with respect to the workflow, as well as to the information exchange during the project; (ii) they allow for monitoring and accountability; (iii) they enable governance through explicitly informing as to the role of allocation and coordination across departments and functions; and (iv) they enable a *proactive* risk culture, whereby known uncertainties are a priori identified and then managed by the team. Along the lines of this last observation, a stage-gate process tries to minimise the exposure of the company to bad outcomes, i.e. outcomes that differ from the intended, preset objective, in innovation projects. Figure 4.1 depicts schematically a generic stage-gate process.

---

[5] In its traditional form, a waterfall approach does not theoretically enable repetitions and iterations. However, over the years stage-gate practitioners have advocated for either stage time reductions through concurrent task development (Terwiesch & Loch, 1999; Bendoly & Chao, 2016) or small iterations to take place in order to ensure improvement of the outcome of certain gates (Cooper, 1994; Rice, O'Connor & Pierantozzi, 2008)

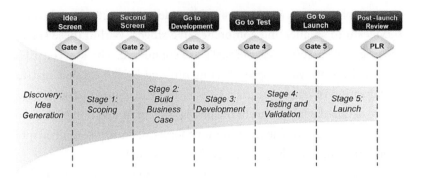

FIGURE 4.1 Adaptation of the stage-gate innovation process for six stages

### 4.2.2.2   Experimentation Processes (Build–Design–Test–Analyse)

The notion of developing innovation without explicit knowledge of the objective through a process has been first introduced by the 'build–design–test' cycle (Wheelwright & Clark, 1992). Wheelwright and Clark have posited that in order to solve problems where the end objective cannot be known in advance with certainty, teams would need to engage in an iterative process. They did not explicitly position their approach as a process for radical innovation, but they seeded the original idea. This idea eventually morphed into a structured experimentation process through the doctoral work and subsequent publications of Thomke (1995). The premise of his approach is as follows: in the presence of significant uncertainty, regarding the outcome of an innovation effort, the value of a priori planning diminishes. As the famous quote attributed to the German army general Helmuth von Moltke the Elder quips, 'No plan survives first contact with the enemy.' This happens because several possible outcomes are feasible and possibly successful, and it is unclear due to incomplete information which possible outcome is better to pursue (Krishnan, Eppinger & Whitney, 1997). In such a setting, this school of thought advocates that it is preferable to *test* the initial idea: either in the market or at the lab, depending on whether the lack of information stems from market or technical reasons, respectively. Such experimentation enables the measuring of adoption potential of the product/service in the market or an understanding of its technical limitations, and thus *learning* from the test results. Based on that learning, teams may pursue modifications, adaptations or even overhauls of the innovation objective. These changes become the starting point for a new version of a possible solution to the original innovation objective, which is then subjected to another experimental iteration.

Aligned with these guidelines, innovation projects progress through solutions that exhibit better fit to the original vision that initiated the efforts. Case studies illustrate very vividly the evolution of the concepts of Palm V (Thomke & Nimgade, 2000), a personal digital assistant device that presaged today's smartphones, where the original experiment of 3Com was done with a Palm V prototype made of wax! The effects of iteration and testing have also been showcased during software development (McCormack & Johnson, 2001) and adapted to also test business models for entrepreneurs (Ries, 2011), with a recommendation to build a *minimum viable product* as soon as possible in order to test the original venture idea and get market/technology feedback. Figure 4.2 depicts schematically the experimentation cycle process.

Experimentation cycles reduce the radical risk through learning – either through successes or failures – of what works and what doesn't. And they reduce the overall risk even if in some cases they temporarily increase the risk of pursuing objectives that have high probability of failure. Thus experimentation approaches require different risk management approach.

The two archetypal processes introduced represent the two notional ends of a spectrum of processes that practitioners have used. As expected, hybrid versions have been proposed (see, for example, Sommer, Hedegaard, Dukovska-Popovska & Steger-Jensen, 2015), but in most cases they end up being small departures from either the standard stage-gate process or the experimentation cycle. The reason for such a lack of an ideal process that serves all different types

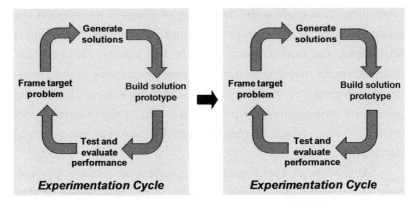

Experimentation Cycles (Build–Design–Test–Analyse)

- Based on *learning, redefine* the solution features, the goals or even the problem itself.
- *Iterate* until a satisfactory solution to the framed problem is found.

FIGURE 4.2 Experimentation cycle innovation process. Contrary to incremental innovation, radical innovation can be thought as a continuous cycle of product discovery

of innovation stems from the fundamentally different nature of the various innovation types; these require significantly different skills and capabilities to be managed. As a result, they might often be at odds with one another. We discuss this extensively in the next section, where we compare the necessary skills for each process, and we identify their differences as discussed across the literature.

### 4.2.3    Innovation Management: From Processes to Cultures

The different processes for executing innovation initiatives are insufficient by themselves to create successful outcomes. They require a set of organisational management structures, rules and norms to succeed. In other words, managers need to answer questions of the type, 'What are the broad characteristics of the associated organisations that can effective execute these processes?' 'What key performance indicators and metrics shall be used?' 'How should people and teams communicate during these initiatives?' 'What type of leaders can lead these processes effectively?' These questions are not arising out of sheer academic curiosity; they point to key complementary organisational dimensions that need to be defined and aligned to the processes in order for companies to systematically achieve their innovation goals. In other words, these questions seek to delineate the appropriate cultures that lead to innovation. Within the context of our discussion, we employ the term 'culture' as follows: the set of norms, beliefs, structures and routines (processes) that define operational patterns that social groups learn as they solve problems of external adaptation and internal integration. Under the assumption that these patterns have worked well enough to be considered valid, they are further disseminated to new members as the 'correct' way to perceive, think and feel in relation to the originally defined problems (Schein, 1992). Culture serves in meeting unforeseen contingencies as they arise, and it is the product of evolution inside any organisation; thus it is influenced by the organisational history (Hermalin, 2012). Culture has such a pervasive influence because it can reduce or even eliminate differences in objectives and thus mitigate the agency problem (Van den Steen, 2010).

Based on our definition of culture, and the previous discussion on different types of innovation and their respective processes, we posit that the successful development of incremental or radical innovation would require different cultures. Moreover, it remains an open question whether these different cultures can coexist under the same organisational hood. The coexistence of different processes and organisational rules under the common objective of innovation has been studied (Tushman & O'Reilly, 1996), and the value of coexistence of such incremental (exploitative) and radical (explorative) innovation cultures has been empirically validated (He & Wong, 2004). The need of such coexistence under a broad innovation *system* has been proposed (Loch, DeMeyer & Pich, 2006), leading to more operational views on *how* such coexistence might be achieved (Chandrasekaran, Linderman & Schroeder, 2015). We build on them and several case studies and anecdotal evidence to offer a summary of the key features of the two different innovation management cultures. We also discuss why these features make sense.

We identify six distinct dimensions that support these management cultures: the *scope* of the initiative; the *plan* and the *process* structure; the established *monitoring* mechanisms; the *evaluation* and *incentive* procedures employed; the organisational *coordination* and *communication* practices; and finally the *leadership* attributes that align with the two different processes. These together offer a complete description of the distinct archetypal innovation approaches within organisations. Figure 4.3 outlines these differences that support the two different types of innovation.

With respect to the scope, it stems directly from the definition of the two types of innovation that incremental efforts tend to address, small and well-understood changes in the existing offerings (solutions) to company challenges. Hence, their scope is relatively well defined and broadly understood by all engaged stakeholders in

| | Incremental Innovation<br>Scope: usually well defined; small departure from existing offerings | Radical Innovation<br>Scope: relatively undefined; sizeable departure from existing offerings |
|---|---|---|
| Plan and Process | • Plan tasks and targets<br>• Plan backwards from targets<br>• Waterfall process<br>• Assess uncertainty and determine mitigation actions<br>• Decide stop 'trigger' outcomes | • Set overall vision<br>• Ideate initial set of different solutions (under same vision)<br>• Plan (parallel or sequential) round of experiments |
| Monitoring | • % of target achievement<br>• Progress tracking<br>• Key uncertainty monitoring | • Uncertainty resolution: what has been learned? Learning indicators<br>• Define and adapt stopping criteria<br>• Process quality monitoring |
| Evaluation/<br>Incentives | • Measurement of output<br>• Plan adherence<br>• Risk avoidance | • Upward incentives (improvement?)<br>• Tolerance 'window' for failure<br>• Shared incentives (collective effort)<br>• Process quality |
| Organizational<br>Coordination/<br>Communication | • Hierarchy important<br>• Top-down direction<br>• Efficient information exchange: progress and deliverables status | • Diverse problem-solving capabilities<br>• Flat(ter) structure, bottom-up initiative necessary<br>• Share information across experiments, relative comparison |
| Leadership | • Efficient communicator<br>• Command and control oriented<br>• Plan owner | • Team motivator<br>• Effective synthesiser of diverse inputs<br>• Vision owner |

FIGURE 4.3 Incremental versus radical innovation

the effort – often enough without explicit communication. In contrast, radical efforts suffer from a lack of predefined scope; companies often seek to address broad and complex challenges (e.g. 'Can we develop an automobile with a hybrid source of energy generation?'), where the exact solution is hard to describe *ex ante*. Starting from this key difference in their scope, different management approaches are required to deliver effective outcomes. At a planning and process level, for incremental innovation projects, such management approaches call for determining the tasks to be executed by plotting 'backwards' from the objective; thus, by identifying the sequence of tasks and the associated responsible teams and resources. Given the past knowledge and experience that incremental changes imply, an overall metric of success can relate to efficiency and/or productivity measures, e.g. 'Can we introduce the new product version at a given budget and within the fastest development time?' Radical innovation projects, on the other hand, call for searching the product/market 'landscape' for possible solutions to the challenge and for authorising a set of experiments that will determine which of the solutions addresses the challenge and supports the vision more preferably.

These different approaches in planning and structuring the innovation process naturally translate into distinctively different rules for monitoring the execution and evaluating the success. Specifically, during incremental innovation, management benefits from controlling the execution through, for example, tracking the percentage of targets achieved as a function of time and cost/budget, and/or through assuming corrective actions depending on the deviations from the predefined objective. Instead, during radical innovations, the reduction of the overall system *entropy* (Loch, Terwiesch & Thomke, 2001) is the true underlying objective; targets are 'fuzzy' and possibly even unknown upfront. Thus, management has to assure that their experimental cycles are able to reduce the uncertainty around which outcome fulfils the broad vision and challenge. Moreover, any new experiments should build upon the knowledge gained in previous iterations. In fact, the choice of experiments, determines how management can maximise the *signal-to-noise ratio*[6] (SNR), which fulfils the entropy reduction objective. This calls for indicators of learning and improvement but also for the capacity to redefine and adapt the stopping criteria for the experiments. Moreover, management benefits from monitoring the process quality as opposed to the outcome. These measures cascade similarly to individual and team incentives.

Finally, from an organisational structure and management viewpoint, the two different approaches to innovation exhibit, again, fundamental differences (see Chandrasekaran, Linderman & Schroeder, 2015, and references therein). Incremental innovation projects benefit from hierarchical (top-down) approaches, since tasks are well defined and the capacity to achieve a successful outcome depends critically on the controlled and timely executed tasks that might span multiple departments in a company. In contrast, a flatter, more flexible and fluid organisational structure suits better radical innovation because it is a priori unknown which tasks need to be performed and what departments need to be involved. During radical innovation efforts, information sharing across all relevant stakeholders about the experiments, and their results, facilitates learning and leads to improved solutions. Given the different organisational structures, it is expected that different leadership approaches are necessary to orchestrate these efforts. Whereas leadership for incremental innovation efforts should focus on command and control in order to ensure efficient communication and plan adherence, leaders would not benefit from the same approach. Instead, the risk of incompatible knowledge that characterises radical innovation efforts demands from leaders strong motivating skills (to keep their teams going under adversity), as well as the capability to synthesise the diverse inputs

---

[6] A theoretical model approach (Loch, Terwiesch & Thomke, 2001) to how project teams should select experiments based on the experiments' *fidelity*, an equivalent term to SNR (Shannon, 1948).

and ensure adherence to the overall vision; their challenge is to combine vision adherence with project adaptability.

This short comparison reveals an important insight: the different processes that are set up to serve different innovation objectives also demand fundamentally distinct organisations and cultures so that they are effectively conducted. Said differently, it is insufficient to expect that the management mechanisms instituted for incremental innovation are able to address radical innovation challenges. Unfortunately, companies need to think in different terms to address radical innovation. This would possibly result in the creation of different entities to ensure their cultures are different (Tushman & O'Reilly, 1996; Christensen, 1997).

## 4.3 RISK MANAGEMENT IN (INNOVATION) PROJECTS

Any human endeavour faces to a smaller or larger extent unforeseen factors that affect its eventual outcomes in a positive or a negative way. Risk management is defined as the 'identification, evaluation and prioritisation of risks[7] followed by coordinated and economical application of resources to minimise, monitor and control the probability or impact of unfortunate events, or maximise the realisation of opportunities'. This definition comes as an adaptation of several definitions found in the literature over time, including the early and oft-mentioned work of Knight (1921). It captures the essence of risk management practice: the systematic effort to identify, evaluate and control uncertain factors in order to avoid or mitigate potential negative effects and exploit arising opportunities (Wideman, 1992; Kliem & Ludin, 1997).

In general, projects are endeavours that harbour novelty and uncertainty. Innovation projects, in particular, have been viewed as essential contexts for the application of risk management practices. In fact, since early on, the economics and management literature have analysed optimal decision-making in the presence of risk. This

[7] Risk is defined as the effect of uncertainty on objectives (Knight, 1921).

includes rigorous treatment of risk management in projects, identifying the necessity to update the available information, and the identification and evaluation of actions that should be contingent on the realisation of risk (Roberts & Weitzman, 1981). Albeit a stylised normative approximation of reality, their study, together with the mechanics of financial options (Black and Scholes, 1973), has been at the origin of an entire stream of research studies on investment and decision-making under uncertainty (Dixit, 1993; Pindyck, 1993; Trigeorgis, 1996). The main thesis of this extensive literature has been the optimisation of managerial actions undertaken depending on the risk realisation. In that regard, this literature has had a valuable impact on strategic thinking. It has highlighted the value of managerial flexibility (see Luehrman, 1998; Kogut & Kulatilaka, 2001; Kulatilaka & Trigeorgis, 2004, and references therein). Moreover, it has offered a strong indication that risk management approaches can carry strategic impact. Estimating the value of flexibility in the outcome of innovation projects is also the subject of research (Huchzermeier & Loch, 2001; Santiago & Vakili, 2005).

The aforementioned literature establishes a strong theoretical support for the risk management approaches advocated in practice. In addition, business cases are used as illustrative examples of these approaches (Loch, DeMeyer & Pich, 2006). In Figure 4.4, we capture the essential features of what risk management approaches have been advocated with respect to projects.

Any risk management approach starts with the *identification* of the possible risks. Depending on the nature of the undertaken project activity, such risks may span across different categories, and they may reflect the existence of new technologies (e.g. the possibility of unsuccessful application of a new insulation material during the development of a real estate project) or new markets and customer behaviours (e.g. the event of a lukewarm response to a new series of cosmetics from the APAC region customers) or even new competitive regulations (e.g. the marketing communication complications from the introduction of GDPR regulation in the European continent).

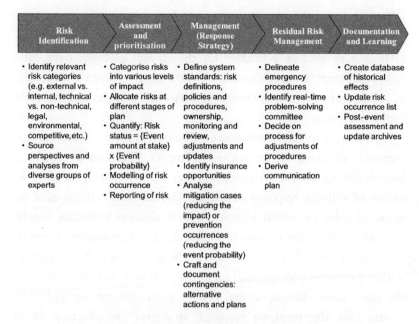

| Risk Identification | Assessment and prioritisation | Management (Response Strategy) | Residual Risk Management | Documentation and Learning |
|---|---|---|---|---|
| • Identify relevant risk categories (e.g. external vs. internal, technical vs. non-technical, legal, environmental, competitive, etc.)<br>• Source perspectives and analyses from diverse groups of experts | • Categorise risks into various levels of impact<br>• Allocate risks at different stages of plan<br>• Quantify: Risk status = {Event amount at stake} x {Event probability}<br>• Modelling of risk occurrence<br>• Reporting of risk | • Define system standards: risk definitions, policies and procedures, ownership, monitoring and review, adjustments and updates<br>• Identify insurance opportunities<br>• Analyse mitigation cases (reducing the impact) or prevention occurrences (reducing the event probability)<br>• Craft and document contingencies: alternative actions and plans | • Delineate emergency procedures<br>• Identify real-time problem-solving committee<br>• Decide on process for adjustments of procedures<br>• Derive communication plan | • Create database of historical effects<br>• Update risk occurrence list<br>• Post-event assessment and update archives |

FIGURE 4.4  Risk management in projects: a framework

A crucial capability for successful risk identification is the organisational access to a diverse set of experts that can cover multiple perspectives and viewpoints as well as the effective codification of past risk realisations, which allows for a broad upfront mapping of negative occurrences and possibly opportunities.

While identification is a critical first step in effective risk management, it is the second step that has received most of the attention from risk experts: the *evaluation* of risk and its impact. This translates into a reliable assignment of the probabilities of occurrence to the identified risks and into a robust estimate of the impact on the business (usually in monetary terms). As one might expect, there exist no standardised theories around probability estimation for uncertain events. Unfortunately, behavioural scientists have shown that decision makers tend to exhibit biased perspectives in the presence of uncertainty (e.g. Tversky & Kahneman, 1974). In that context, risk experts try to ensure as much as possible statistically unbiased estimates through a variety of methods, e.g. scenario analysis or decision trees (Schoemaker, 1995). The overall effort is to provide risk estimates as well as estimates for the impact of these risks. The risk assessment and prioritisation efforts have received a great deal of attention from the risk experts as they enable the largest technical sophistication.

Yet, risk management's core value does not lie within the estimation of the event occurrence and its impact. This is simply the basis for calculating relative priorities. The key value lies with the identification of suitable *response strategies*. Unfortunately, there exist no standard rules by which response and mitigation strategies can be identified during the process of deploying a risk management effort. As someone would expect, the idiosyncrasies of the risk occurrences within particular contexts call for equally idiosyncratic responses. At the same time, though, several generic principles can be applied to ensure that the resulting response strategies are effective. Good response strategies benefit from a clearly set-up system of standards. What is considered to be risk in different circumstances? Who owns different types of risk within an organisation? Who is responsible for assessing, evaluating and monitoring risks and eventually activating the response to risk? The process of assessing different types of risk reveals cases where insurance policies would act as effective response mechanisms. Such circumstances apply in situations where uncertainties are outside of any mitigation control. For example, the delaying of a project and the introduction of an insurance mechanism, which effectively offers an additional buffer of time, can prove successful enough. Beyond such cases, risk management teams can try to develop mitigating responses through their analysis of how to reduce the impact of certain risk realisations or how to decrease the probability of the actual negative event occurrence. Such analyses open up the risk management team to alternative actions and plans that can be formally documented as contingencies of the overall risk management plan.

However, despite all efforts to identify a complete set of risks, practice often proves that it is impossible to produce a complete list.

There are always events that might take place, and the organisation would not have accounted for them. These events are often called *unknown unknowns*, given the fact that they are occurrences of whose existence the risk management team was unaware. The general admission – in traditional risk management approaches – is that such events shall be rare, given a proper upfront exploration and assessment of the possible risks by the team. In that regard, they represent *residual risks* that must be managed in real time upon their occurrence as opposed to being a priori mitigated through a crafted plan. In such circumstances, instead of plotting case-specific idiosyncratic response plans, an organisation should shift their mindset away from particular responses to specific risks and towards key actions that are necessary to manage risk occurrence. Such actions include the delineation of when such an emergency procedure is enacted, how the procedure is governed (e.g. setting up a committee of experienced members to problem-solve in real time), what the communication plan should be to the rest of the organisation and external stakeholders, etc. In other words, the management of residual unexpected risks focuses on the procedural knowledge of what to do to plot a plan *when* bad things happen, as opposed to plotting a plan *before* things happen.

A final step in any risk management approach relates to the build-up of experience in the type of risks that might emerge again in future projects as well as the possible approaches to mitigate these risks. Said differently, effective risk management is heavily guided by the past knowledge that has been codified at the overall organisational level with respect to negative events and the capability to deter them or manage them. As such, it is imperative for any organisation to build up such a repository in the form of an accessible database that allows future project management teams to source information as to broader risk lists or diverse response strategies. Moreover, the occurrence of unforeseen risks allows the addition to the database of new possible risks, which greatly facilitates the first step of the risk management process listed earlier.

The aforementioned description of the risk management process reveals the essential logic of such a process: managing risks usually implies either avoiding them by taking preventing actions, using buffers (often time or budget) to contain small variations of risk factors or creating contingency plans to address the risk effects in the most promising way in case these risks materialise (De Meyer, Loch & Pich, 2002).

Yet, it is fair to question under what premises this approach faces challenges. The risk management steps introduced above are effective when the set of risks, their likelihood of occurrence and the capacity to either mitigate their occurrence or their effects are reliably known. In other words, the traditional approach delivers successful outcomes when there is already enough knowledge prior to the execution of the project, which limits the possibility of unexpected events.

Interestingly, these are premises that coincide with the circumstances of incremental innovation, whereby stage-gate processes allow the project management teams to contain the evolution of the different risks between the gates. Recall from Section 4.3.2 that in incremental innovation the goal and the steps required to achieve results are pretty much well understood. What often remains unknown is the time it takes to perform the tasks and, in most cases, the cost required (as a deviation from the originally set budget). Traditional risk management enables managers to estimate the deviation from the upfront targets and to take corrective action that is contingent on the size of the deviation. Therefore, risk management, as conducted by the traditional approach, can be instrumental for incremental innovation endeavours. Such a risk management mindset propagates a *proactive* culture that may present benefits but also limitations. The benefits materialise under the conditions cited above. Limitations manifest themselves in the context of many unknown unknowns similar to radical innovation. In radical innovation efforts, the risk circumstances are significantly different because radical innovation faces a fundamentally different type of uncertainty, as we have argued.

## 4.4 RISK MANAGEMENT RETHOUGHT: LEARNING FROM RADICAL INNOVATION AND CONCLUDING REMARKS

We have argued so far that innovation activities capture major uncertain undertakings within organisations. The literature in innovation has pointed out two different types of uncertainty: uncertainty that comes from *known unknown* factors, and uncertainty that comes from *unknown unknown* factors.

The known unknown factors range from the myriad of small-noise sources that can shift schedules or change the cost of activities during innovation projects to distinguishable events that upon occurrence bear serious impact on the developmental path of an innovation project, factors whose realisation leads to different critical paths for the remaining part of the project. The former category of factors introduces variance in the performance of an innovation project with respect to the completion time and cost, but usually they do not put in question the detailed activities and tasks identified for achieving the project goal. The latter category introduces risks that may lead to different tasks depending on the realisation of these risks. These circumstances are usually mitigated through contingency plans (Pich, Loch & De Meyer, 2002).

Instead, the unknown unknown factors emerge in circumstances when the technology envelope is pushed further or new customer needs are revealed. In these cases, the fact of the matter is that managers are faced with situations in which they have limited or no experience. As such, it is impossible to foresee the target output. As a consequence, there is no capacity to fully define a path to the target; the target may shift.

Depending on the type of uncertainty that dominates, different efforts require distinctly different management approaches. Since these two types of uncertainty represent differences in the detailed risks faced by the organisation, they are expected to benefit from different risk management approaches and cultures. Yet, the literature in project risk management demonstrates that the existing toolbox and frameworks in risk management tend to align primarily with incremental innovation efforts. Risk management practices based on risk lists have little to offer to radical innovation cases, since it is not known a priori which events may occur.

This leaves open-ended questions regarding effective risk management approaches for radical innovation efforts and the role that risk management experts can play in such strategically important endeavours. In Section 4.2, we have shown that radical innovation benefits from parallel and iterative experimentation approaches, where the objective is initially to understand the complex and unknown market-technology landscape, before launching towards a specific goal. This approaches is characterised by a sequence of actions that fall into the following pattern: (i) generate alternative solutions to the problem or challenge posed; (ii) based on the actual performance of tests conducted for these (imperfect) solutions, select the ones that are aligned with the overarching vision and seem promising for further development; and finally (iii) identify what works and what does not work in the prior solutions in order to build upon that learning and move to the next iteration (where new improved alternative solutions are generated, etc.).

The aforementioned pattern bears close similarity to the basic evolution cycle as introduced by Darwin in 1859, whereby *variation* of alternative organisms is subjected to *selection* based on their fit to the environment and the *retention* of key fitness factors to the next generation of offspring. In that regard, evolutionary biology offers the right theoretical lenses to cope with high levels of uncertainty, as the latter is experienced by organisms trying to survive within an unknown landscape.[8] Despite its simple structure, the repetitive cycle of evolution has led to robust solutions for many difficult

---

[8] While at first glance it may seem provocative to parallel complex human decision-making with the automaton behaviour of simpler types of life, e.g., amoeba, earlier studies have argued for similarities due to the existence of bounded rationality (see Newell & Simon, 1972; Levinthal & March, 1981, 1993).

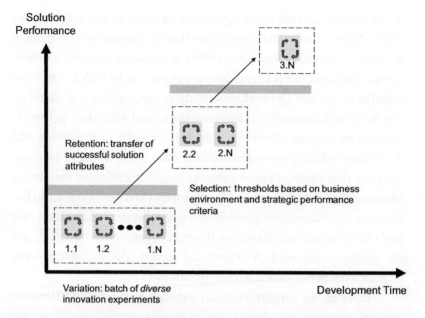

FIGURE 4.5 An evolutionary analogue for the radical innovation process

problems, including, among many others, locomotion, vision, flight, magnetic navigation and echolocation (Valiant, 2013). Moreover, it has provided an unparalleled 'database' of strategies that cope with unforeseen uncertainty and complexity (Simonton, 1999) during the last 3 billion years. Figure 4.5 illustrates an adaptation of the evolutionary process for the context of radical innovation, and it is straight borrowing from the literature discussion of Section 4.2.

In each experimentation cycle, a company commissions a set of diverse experiments that aim to test the feasibility of new applications and the willingness of the market to entertain them and perhaps accept them as new standard ways of satisfying a particular consumer need. It is important that each experiment differs from the others along a set of technological or market-related attributes, e.g. changing the size of a product, the duration of the service or the definition of who the particular offering is intended for. Not all experiments will be successful, but, if chosen properly, all experiments must identify or negate directions along which the company could pursue further development of the offering. Hence, it is imperative that all experiments bring some *learning outcome*. In that light, failure is no longer a negative experimental outcome, but it becomes synonymous to the inability to learn from the outcomes. The evaluation of these experiments, and therefore the associated capacity to learn what works and what does not work, stems from a *fitness* threshold, which is external to the efforts and determines which experimental efforts bear the promise to perform; the ones that perform better than the others are selected for further improvement. The technology/design/market attributes that fit to the business landscape, and possibly drive the better performance that leads to selection, are retained in the next experimentation cycle, and the process is repeated. As Figure 4.5 depicts, the iterative process increases the performance in each iteration.

In order to support such an experimentation-based iterative process, organisations should aim to develop capabilities along the lines of the right column presented in Figure 4.6. Experimentation through different approaches (in series or in parallel) is required because the goal cannot be articulated upfront, and all that matters

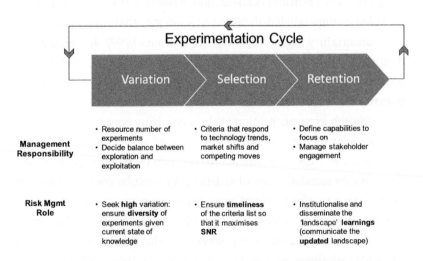

FIGURE 4.6 The role of senior management and risk experts for radical innovation

is whether each new version of the offering copes 'better' with the environment (technology-market landscape) than the previous one. The breadth and speed of each experimentation cycle is an essential managerial decision because of the limited resources. The tension between speedy and high-breadth experimentation versus slower and focused iterations is a point of consideration (Loch & Sommer, 2005), ensuring the learning from the current iteration is important because the next iteration builds on the knowledge gained in the previous one. The adoption of such a paradigm is necessary to pursue transformative business changes, but it bears implications for both the roles and objectives of senior management and risk management experts in organisations. Hereafter, we attempt a delineation of these role implications, and we view this as a contribution of the chapter.

During each variation phase, the goal is to maximise the coverage of the unknown landscape and therefore minimise the possibility that good solutions to the challenge go unnoticed; given that, senior management has to decide on the number of experiments to resource and the experimental mix between the exploration of new original solutions, and further exploitation of prior considered solutions. These decisions have to be taken with the existing resource constraints in mind; therefore, senior management needs to consider how to allocate resources between different options. To support these tasks, risk management experts should ensure sufficient *diversity* amongst the conducted experiments in order to realise enough variation. This is a major departure from the traditional processes of risk management whereby the objective is to identify what can go wrong in order to minimise the assumed risk; here, risk management seeks more risk through diverse experiments that by definition will result in several failures and negative outcomes. Said differently, risk management trades off the higher risk assumed during the experimentation phase for the lower overall risk of failure of the whole cycle.

For the selection phase, management is responsible for defining the *fitness* threshold. This is slightly different from traditional biology and Darwinian evolution, where fitness is a measure of the benefits that an agent (species, organism) enjoys within the premises of a specific environment.[9] Therefore, in these cases selection happens *naturally*, as Darwin has argued in his *Origin of Species* oeuvre. However, in economic contexts, selection is not solely natural. Whereas there exist external to the organisation factors that shape the fitness of a particular solution (e.g. a test revealing that consumers like a particular offering, and they would be willing to purchase it), there are also multiple combinations of factors that may lead to well-performing solutions.[10] In other words, there is no unique solution; instead, the solution reflects also internal organisational factors, i.e. capabilities and managerial strategic choices and beliefs. Therefore, selection is also a (strategic) choice by senior management. In that regard, management has to identify what constitutes success with respect to the results of the experiments (Kovach & Kavadias, 2014). Given that senior management defines the set of criteria that will determine the successful and unsuccessful experiments, the role of risk management morphs into ensuring that these criteria reflect the up-to-date contextual reality. As technology shifts along trends, consumer behaviours change over time because new functionality is introduced through substitute offerings; and as competition changes organisation's market strategies, the fitness threshold changes. Risk management should ensure that the determinants of the fitness threshold remain current in order to avoid an even greater risk: steering the possible solutions to low-performing strategic directions. Said differently, risk management prevents the undertaking of the 'wrong' path.

Finally, for the retention (or learning) phase, senior management has to define and invest in expanding through (or creating from

---

[9] Selection directs evolution to favour entities with higher fitness.

[10] Profit might be a good overall proxy for fitness in economics, but it captures multiple confounding drivers; technical functionality of the offering, design aesthetics, utility curves, customer willingness to pay and similarities with competitive offerings can be some of the parameters of the fitness function.

scratch) the organisational necessary capabilities to learn from the experimental results. Much like in biological contexts, where learning is the mechanism by which any entity extracts information from the environment, retention allows companies to create an operational map of the attributes that drive success within their business landscape. Given that mental map, senior management should ensure that all relevant external stakeholders are engaged in the delivery of the intended value (through contractual or relational mechanisms). In that context, risk management experts become responsible for institutionalising and codifying the learning that has been realised; this also implies that this learning is communicated to all stakeholders through the right channels. Then, the next cycle of iteration takes into account the learnings accumulated so far. Figure 4.6 maps the senior management and risk management's role during the evolutionary cycle of radical innovation changes.

Overall, we advocate that the role of risk management in the context of ambiguity (i.e. high unknown unknowns) emerges to be that of a guardian of the proper functioning of an evolutionary process. In order for such evolutionary process to deliver results, certain premises must fall in place: the upfront diversity of solutions, the reliable selection based on fitness in the contemporary business environment and the effective transfer of learning between consecutive iterations. A successful evolutionary process leads to higher fitness and lower entropy, and risk management can ensure that the key inputs for this to happen, as described above, are present. This role comes into stark contrast with the role of traditional risk management experts. Yet both roles are necessary, as both types of strategic efforts are necessary (incremental and radical changes). Known risk efforts and the traditional risk management approaches ensure the current viability. But competition forces companies to delve into unknown unknowns, and radical innovation approaches are then needed together with a new risk management culture. As such, we call for senior managers to identify how these different risk management approaches can coexist under the same organisational roof, in the same way that different innovation processes should coexist within an organisation. Future research could shed more light into this direction as well as into the detailed mechanisms by which risk management experts can support their role for radical innovation efforts.

REFERENCES

Abramovitz, M. (1956). Resource and output trends in the United States since 1870. *American Economic Review*, **46**, 5–23.

Aghion, P. and Howitt, P. (1992). A model of growth through creative destruction. *Econometrica*, **60**(2), 323–51.

Baldwin, C. Y. and Clark, K. B. (1997). Managing in an age of modularity. *Harvard Business Review*, **75**(5), 84–93.

Bendoly, E. and Chao, R. O. (2016). How excessive stage time reduction in NPD negatively impacts market value. *Production and Operations Management*, **25**(5), 812–32.

Black, F. and Scholes, M. (1973). The pricing of options and corporate liabilities. *Journal of Political Economy*, **81**(3), 637–54.

Campbell, D. T. (1960). Blind variation and selective retentions in creative thought as in other knowledge processes. *Psychological Review*, **67**(6), 380.

Chandrasekaran, A., Linderman, K. and Schroeder, R. (2015). The role of project and organizational context in managing high-tech R&D projects. *Production and Operations Management*, **24**(4), 560–86.

Chandy, R. K. and Prabhu, J. C. (2011). Innovation typologies. In B. Bayus, ed., *Wiley International Encyclopedia of Marketing*. Hoboken, NJ: John Wiley & Sons, pp. 96–100.

Chao, R. and Kavadias, S. (2008). A theoretical framework for managing the new product development portfolio: when and how to use strategic buckets. *Management Science*, **54**(5), 907–21.

Chao, R. and Lenox, M. (2018). Towards a unified model of innovation and technological change. *Journal of Enterprise Transformation*. https://doi.org/10.1080/19488289.2018.1424060

Chao, R. and Loutskina, E. (2011). How complexity impacts R&D portfolio decisions and technological search distance. *SSRN Electronic Journal*. Darden School of Business Working Paper. DOI: 10.2139/ssrn.1917607

Christensen, C. (1997). *The Innovator's Dilemma: When New Technologies Cause Great Firms to Fail*. Cambridge, MA: Harvard Business School Press.

Christensen, C. and Raynor, M. (2013). *The Innovator's Solution: Creating and Sustaining Successful Growth*. Cambridge, MA: Harvard Business Review Press.

Clark, K. and Fujimoto, T. (1991). *Product Development Performance: Strategy, Organization, and Management in the World Auto Industry*. Cambridge, MA: Harvard Business School Press.

Cohen, W. M. and Klepper, S. (1996). Firm size and the nature of innovation within industries: the case of process and product R&D. *Review of Economics and Statistics*, 78(2), 232–43.

Cooper, R. G. (1990). Stage-gate systems: a new tool for managing new products. *Business Horizons*, 33(3), 44–54.

Cooper, R. G. (1994). New products: the factors that drive success. *International Marketing Review*, 11(1), 60–76.

De Meyer, A. C. L., Loch, C. H. and Pich, M. T. (2002). Managing project uncertainty: from variation to chaos. *MIT Sloan Management Review*, 43(2), 60.

Dillon, K. and Lafley, A. (2011). I think of my failures as a gift. *Harvard Business Review*, 89(4), 86–9.

Dixit, A. (1993). Choosing among alternative discrete investment projects under uncertainty. *Economics Letters*, 41(3), 265–8.

Ettlie, J. E., Bridges, W. P. and O'Keefe, R. D. (1984). Organization strategy and structural differences for radical versus incremental innovation. *Management Science*, 30(6), 682–95.

He, Z.-L. and Wong, P.-K. (2004). Exploration vs. exploitation: An empirical test of the ambidexterity hypothesis. *Organization Science*, 15(4), 481–94.

Henderson, R. M. and Clark, K. B. (1990). Architectural innovation: the reconfiguration of existing product technologies and the failure of established firms. *Administrative Science Quarterly*, 35(1), 9–30.

Hermalin, B. E. (2012). Leadership and corporate culture. In R. S. Gibbons and J. Roberts, eds., *The Handbook of Organizational Economics*. Princeton, NJ: Princeton University Press, pp. 432–78.

Huchzermeier, A. and Loch, C. H. (2001). Project management under risk: using the real options approach to evaluate flexibility in R&D. *Management Science*, 47(1), 85–101.

Kavadias, S. and Chao, R. (2007). Resource allocation and new product development portfolio management. In C. H. Loch and S. Kavadias, eds., *Handbook of New Product Development Management*. London: Routledge, pp. 135–63.

Kavadias, S., Ladas, K. and Loch, C. (2016). The transformative business model. *Harvard Business Review*, 94(10), 91–8.

Kendrick, J. (1956). *Productivity Trends: Capital and Labor*. Washington, DC: National Bureau of Economic Research, pp. 3–23.

Kliem, R. L. and Ludin, I. S. (1997). *Reducing Project Risk*. Aldershot: Gower.

Knight, F. H. (1921). *Risk, Uncertainty and Profit*. Boston: Houghton Mifflin.

Koetzier, W. and Alon, A. (2013). Why 'low risk' innovation is costly. Accenture. https://bit.ly/36ueW0I

Kogut, B. and Kulatilaka, N. (2001). Capabilities as real options. *Organization Science*, **12**(6), 744–58.

Kovach, J. and Kavadias, S. (2014). Focused or flexible targets? How organizational design influences the definition of success for strategic initiatives. http://dx.doi.org/10.2139/ssrn.2444444

Krishnan, V., Eppinger, S. D. and Whitney, D. E. (1997). A model-based framework to overlap product development activities. *Management Science*, **43**(4), 437–51.

Kulatilaka, N. and Trigeorgis, L. (2004). The general flexibility to switch: Real options revisited. In E. Schwarz and L. Trigeorgis, eds., *Real Options and Investment under Uncertainty: Classical Readings and Recent Contributions*. Cambridge, MA: MIT Press, pp. 179–98.

Levinthal, D. and March, J. G. (1981). A model of adaptive organizational search. *Journal of Economic Behavior & Organization*, **2**(4), 307–33.

Levinthal, D. A. and March, J. G. (1993). The myopia of learning. *Strategic Management Journal*, **14**(S2), 95–112.

Loch, C., DeMeyer, A. and Pich, M. T. (2006). *Managing the Unknown: A New Approach to Managing High Uncertainty and Risks in Projects*. Hoboken, NJ: John Wiley.

Loch, C. and Kavadias, S. (2008). *Handbook of New Product Development Management*. London: Routledge.

Loch, C. and Sommer, S. (2005). *Vol de nuit*: the dream of flying car at Lemond Automobiles SA. INSEAD Case Study.

Loch, C. H., Terwiesch, C. and Thomke, S. (2001). Parallel and sequential testing of design alternatives. *Management Science*, **47**(5), 663–78.

Luehrman, T. A. (1998). Strategy as a portfolio of real options. *Harvard Business Review*, **76**(5), 89–101.

Markou, P., Kavadias, S. and Oraiopoulos, N. (2018). Project selection and success: Insights from the drug discovery process. http://dx.doi.org/10.2139/ssrn.3225056.

McCormack, K. P. and Johnson, W. C. (2001). *Business Process Orientation: Gaining the E-business Competitive Advantage*. Boca Raton, FL: CRC Press.

Newell, A. and Simon, H. A. (1972). *Human Problem Solving*. Englewood Cliffs, NJ: Prentice-Hall.

Pennetier, C., Girotra, K. and Mihm, J. (2018). R&D spending: dynamic or persistent? Working Paper.

Pich, M. T., Loch, C. H. and De Meyer, A. (2002). On uncertainty, ambiguity, and complexity in project management. *Management Science*, 48(8), 1008–23.

Pindyck, R. S. (1993). A note on competitive investment under uncertainty. *The American Economic Review*, 83(1), 273–7.

Rice, M. P., O'Connor, G. C. and Pierantozzi, R. (2008). Implementing a learning plan to counter project uncertainty. *MIT Sloan Management Review*, 49(2), 54.

Ries, E. (2011). *The Lean Startup: How Today's Entrepreneurs Use Continuous Innovation to Create Radically Successful Businesses*. New York: Crown Books.

Roberts, K. and Weitzman, M. L. (1981). Funding criteria for research, development, and exploration projects. *Econometrica*, 49(5), 1261–88.

Rogers, E. M. (2003). *Diffusion of Innovations*, 5th ed. New York: Free Press.

Romer, P. M. (1990). Endogenous technological change. *Journal of Political Economy*, 98(5), 71–102.

Rosenberg, N. (2006). Innovation and economic growth. In *Innovation and Growth in Tourism*. Paris: OECD, pp. 43–52.

Santiago, L. P. and Vakili, P. (2005). On the value of flexibility in R&D projects. *Management Science*, 51(8), 1206–18.

Sawhney, M., Wolcott, R. C. and Arroniz, I. (2006). The 12 different ways for companies to innovate. *MIT Sloan Management Review*, 47(3), 75.

Schein, E. H. (1992). *Organizational Culture and Leadership*, 2nd ed. San Francisco: Jossey–Bass.

Schoemaker, P. J. (1995). Scenario planning: a tool for strategic thinking. *Sloan Management Review*, 36(2), 25–50.

Schumpeter, J. A. (1939). *Business Cycles: A Theoretical, Historical and Statistical Analysis of the Capitalist Process*, vol. 1. New York: McGraw–Hill.

Shannon, C. E. (1948). A mathematical theory of communication. *Bell System Technical Journal*, 27(3), 379–423.

Simonton, D. K. (1998). Donald Campbell's model of the creative process: creativity as blind variation and selective retention. *The Journal of Creative Behavior*, 32(3), 153–8.

Simonton, D. K. (1999). *Origins of Genius: Darwinian Perspectives on Creativity*. Oxford: Oxford University Press.

Solow, R. M. (1956). A contribution to the theory of economic growth. *The Quarterly Journal of Economics*, 70(1), 65–94.

Sommer, A. F., Hedegaard, C., Dukovska-Popovska, I. and Steger-Jensen, K. (2015). Improved product development performance through agile/stage-gate hybrids: the next-generation stage-gate process? *Research–Technology Management*, 58(1), 34–45.

Terwiesch, C. and Loch, C. H. (1999). Measuring the effectiveness of overlapping development activities. *Management Science,* **45**(4), 455–65.

Thomke, S. (1998). Managing experimentation in the design of new products. *Management Science,* **44**(6), 743–62.

Thomke, S. and Nimgade, A. (2000). *IDEO Product Development.* Cambridge, MA: Harvard Business School Press.

Thomke, S. H. (1995). *The economics of experimentation in the design of new products and processes.* Unpublished PhD thesis, Massachusetts Institute of Technology.

Trigeorgis, L. (1996). *Real Options: Managerial Flexibility and Strategy in Resource Allocation.* Cambridge, MA: MIT Press.

Trott, P. (2008). *Innovation Management and New Product Development.* Harlow: Pearson.

Tushman, M. L. and Anderson, P. (1986). Technological discontinuities and organizational environments. *Administrative Science Quarterly,* **31**(3), 439–65.

Tushman, M. L. and O'Reilly, C. A. (1996). Ambidextrous organizations: managing evolutionary and revolutionary change. *California Management Review,* **38**(4), 8–29.

Tversky, A. and Kahneman, D. (1974). Judgment under uncertainty: heuristics and biases. *Science,* **185**(4157), 1124–31.

Utterback, J. M. (1994). Radical innovation and corporate regeneration. *Research-Technology Management,* **37**(4), 10.

Utterback, J. M. and Abernathy, W. J. (1975). A dynamic model of process and product innovation. *Omega,* 3(6), 639–56.

Valiant, L. (2013). *Probably Approximately Correct: Nature's Algorithms for Learning and Prospering in a Complex World.* New York: Basic Books.

Van den Steen, E. (2010). On the origin of shared beliefs (and corporate culture). *The RAND Journal of Economics,* **41**(4), 617–48.

Wheelwright, S. C. and Clark, K. B. (1992). *Revolutionizing Product Development: Quantum Leaps in Speed, Efficiency, and Quality.* New York: Free Press.

Wideman, R. M. (1992). *Project and Program Risk Management: A Guide to Managing Project Risks and Opportunities.* Drexel Hill, PA: Project Management Institute.

# PART II A View of Risk Culture Concepts in Firms and Society

# 5 The Changing Risk Culture of UK Banks

## Duncan Needham and Anthony Hotson

Victorian bankers rarely wrote mortgages. As George Rae, author of a widely read bankers' manual, explained, 'house or shop property, even of a superior class, is not a desirable security ... on the grounds of its uncertainty of sale' (Rae, 1885).[1] Until the 1970s, clearing bank assets mainly comprised commercial bills of three months' maturity or less, short-term advances and short-dated British government securities (Hotson, 2017).[2] Mortgages were largely the preserve of private investors and the building societies (Offer, 1981, 2014). Clearing bank liabilities were dominated by retail deposits, mostly interest free and mostly payable on demand (Goodhart & Needham, 2017).[3] Short-term assets were therefore 'matched' against short-term liabilities.[4] Nor did the banks compete on deposit rates or borrow materially from each other. From the mid- nineteenth century, London's leading banks paid no interest on current accounts (payable on demand), and they paid similar rates on deposit accounts (payable after a specified term). In 2007, however, on the eve of the global financial crisis, mortgages comprised around two-thirds of UK clearing bank assets. These long-term assets were funded increasingly in wholesale markets, with

---

[1] George Rae was chairman of the North and South Wales Bank, later incorporated into the Midland Bank. His manual went through six editions between 1885 and 1976.

[2] A typical commercial bill was 'drawn' when the seller of a consignment of goods (the 'drawer') presented their signed bill to the buyer of the goods (the 'drawee'), specifying the amount to be paid, the timing of the payment and the party to whom payment should be made. The drawee 'accepted' the bill by signing it. The drawer could hold the bill to maturity or 'endorse' (promise to pay) the bill themselves and sell it at a discount (bills paid no interest) to a third party, often a specialist financial institution or 'discount house'.

[3] The divide between current and deposit accounts was porous, with customers usually able to withdraw time deposits immediately for a fee.

[4] Cash and liquidity reserves make exact matching unnecessary.

Northern Rock, for instance, sourcing just 22 per cent of its total liabilities from retail depositors in 2006 shortly before it was taken into public ownership (House of Commons Treasury Committee, 2008).[5]

This chapter charts the changing risk culture within UK banking by analysing the changing balance sheet structure of the London clearing banks.[6] We describe a shift that began with the dismantling of wartime regulations in the 1950s and accelerated through the 1970s and 1980s, to the current situation in which UK clearing banks use wholesale funding to write mortgages on a scale that would have had their Victorian forebears reaching for the smelling salts.

## 5.1  LIABILITY MANAGEMENT

The London clearing banks emerged after the 1833 Bank Charter Act explicitly removed the monopoly on joint-stock banking within a sixty-five-mile radius of London enjoyed by the Bank of England (the 'Bank') since the early eighteenth century (Needham, 2018).[7] After an early period of intense rate competition for deposits, the new joint-stock banks fell in with the long-standing private bank practice of paying zero interest on current accounts.[8] They continued to pay interest on deposit accounts but from the 1850s increasingly observed the 'town deposit rate', which fluctuated with Bank rate (usually 1 per cent, later 2 per cent, below).[9] The banks did compete on the size of their balance sheets, the convenience of their branch networks and the provision of trustee and execution services and foreign exchange, but it was considered 'bad form' for one clearing

[5] Retail deposits comprised 63 per cent of Northern Rock's liabilities when it was demutualised in 1997.
[6] The London clearing banks held equity stakes in the Scottish and Northern Irish clearing banks, which displayed similar risk behaviour.
[7] Scotland had multiple joint-stock banks from the mid-eighteenth century and English provincial joint-stock banks were permitted from 1826.
[8] Private banks were limited to 6 or fewer partners. Provincial banks continued to pay interest on current accounts (Nevin & Davis, 1970).
[9] Provincial banks tended to observe a fixed 2½ per cent deposit rate (Sayers, 1967; Nevin & Davis, 1970).

bank to solicit customers from another (Hotson, 2017). A wave of amalgamations in the late nineteenth and early twentieth centuries left the 'big five' (Barclays, Lloyds, Midland, National Provincial and Westminster) dominant, further reducing the competitive pressure on deposit rates. In any event, as Rae pointed out, a bank that had to compete on deposit rates was unlikely to last long:

> Your fear that the newcomer will offer more than the market rate of interest, and this will drain away thousands of your deposits, may be equally groundless. The Bolchester Bank is a respectable institution, and it is unlikely to give more than the current rate for deposits: but, if otherwise, and its rates are what you are informed and believe them to be, the Bolchester Bank will not trouble Oxborough or any other place for long. The first money panic will bring it to book.
>
> *(Rae, 1885)*[10]

With a cartel in operation on the one hand, and no further clearing bank mergers until 1968 on the other, the structure of British banking remained stable (Needham, 2018).[11] As former Bank Chief Cashier John Fforde pointed out, 'our banking system in 1955 was not very different from what it had been fifty years before, in respect of the range of facilities offered and the way in which they were provided. By 1983 it had become a lot different' (Fforde, 1983).

The catalysts for change were innovation within the banking system and deregulation. In 1953 UK local authorities were freed from the requirement, in place since the Second World War, that borrowing should come almost exclusively from the Exchequer via the Public Works Loan Board (Needham, 2018).[12] They entered the growing

---

[10] Nearly a century later, Einzig warned new entrants that bidding above market rates for interbank deposits would 'convey the impression that they badly needed the cash' (Einzig, 1971).

[11] This was despite an official enquiry appointed in 1929 'to inquire into banking, finance and credit' (Macmillan, 1931).

[12] Local authorities could finance capital expenditure 'to a very limited extent' from local tax revenue, stock issues, mortgages and bank lending (Radcliffe, 1959).

'parallel' money markets where holders of large deposits could obtain higher rates than the clearing banks could pay, constrained as they were to offer the cartelised seven-day rate (regardless of maturity) (Einzig, 1971). The local authorities were joined by the burgeoning hire purchase companies, themselves freed from controls in 1958 and seeking to finance loans to increasingly affluent consumers on instalment terms for products such as motor cars and televisions (Dow, 1970).

In 1971, Paul Einzig summarised the key differences between the parallel and traditional money markets dominated by the discount houses:

1. In the traditional markets loans must be fully secured, while in the parallel markets they are unsecured.
2. In the traditional markets loans are supposed to be self-liquidating, while in the parallel markets they need not be self-liquidating.
3. In the traditional markets there is a lender of last resort – the Bank of England – while in the parallel markets there is no such lender.
4. In the traditional markets the authorities often take the initiative to regulate the flow of funds, while the parallel markets are left to their own devices.
5. In the traditional markets the need for conforming to well-established rules slows down business to some extent, while in the parallel markets business is more informal and therefore more expeditious.
6. In the traditional market it is sought to uphold the traditional method of transacting business through personal calls – even if only in the mornings – while most business in the parallel market is transacted by telephone.

*(Einzig, 1971)*[13]

---

[13] Einzig recognised this schema was oversimplified.

In 1958 another wartime control was loosened with the abolition of the Capital Issues Committee, which had regulated sales of new public securities since 1939. While the Bank continued to monitor the timing of new issues, larger borrowers were free to access debt markets without prior official approval. Finally, in 1958 the ceiling on bank lending imposed in 1955 was lifted, with qualitative guidance withdrawn a year later (Montgomery, 1977).

Accompanying these domestic developments was the growth of the Eurocurrency, principally Eurodollar, markets. Eurodollars are wholesale dollar-denominated time deposits held with banks outside the USA.[14] With Regulation Q capping the rates US banks could pay on domestic dollars, and persistent US current account deficits increasing their international supply, London bankers seized the opportunity to borrow offshore dollars (Needham, 2018).[15] They were encouraged by the Bank, keen to maintain the City as the leading entrepôt market for international capital as sterling declined in importance as a reserve and international trading currency, especially after 1957, when the authorities restricted the use of sterling acceptance credits for trade between non-sterling countries.[16] The wholesale markets became even more attractive after 1966, when the Bank sanctioned another American innovation, the negotiable certificate of deposit (CD) (Needham, 2018). CDs enabled borrowers to access medium-term funding while at the same time offering lenders the opportunity to monetise those deposits in the secondary market prior to maturity.[17]

[14] By extension, Eurocurrencies are 'time deposits denominated in a given currency and held with banks outside that currency's country' (Battilossi, 2000).

[15] Introduced in 1933, Regulation Q prohibited interest on demand deposits and capped rates on savings deposits. Borrowers could hedge currency risk with forward exchange contracts.

[16] There had been US dollar deposits in London since at least the 1920s. The market was boosted by Chinese and Soviet depositors' fears of US sequestration during the Korean and Cold Wars (Battilossi, 2000; Kim, 2017).

[17] Negotiable dollar certificates of deposit were introduced by First National City Bank of New York (later 'Citibank') in 1961. Sterling certificates of deposit were authorised in 1968.

In 1951 non-clearing bank deposits equalled just over 10 per cent of clearing bank deposits.[18] By 1966, having increased around eight-fold, they amounted to nearly two-thirds as the clearers chafed under the balance sheet restrictions imposed by the authorities, often at the behest of the International Monetary Fund (IMF), as a condition of financial assistance.[19] With increasingly stringent ceilings on the growth of bank lending, there was little incentive to bid aggressively for deposits, and the clearing banks relied on their less-regulated finance subsidiaries to capture new business. The cartel attracted the ire of the Prices and Incomes Board, which recommended its dissolution in 1967 – 'to sharpen the competitive pressures on the banks' – and the Monopolies Commission, which criticised the 'soporific nature' of British banking in 1968 (National Board for Prices and Incomes, 1967; Monopolies Commission, 1968). These recommendations came to naught so long as the clearing banks were required to constrain lending as a requirement for continued IMF assistance, particularly after sterling was devalued from \$2.80 to \$2.40 in November 1967 (Needham, 2014).

If the IMF's insistence on controls applied to the clearing banks was partly responsible for their losing market share, so the IMF was (indirectly) responsible for the controls being removed in 1971. In October 1968, in anticipation of stricter conditionality for yet another IMF loan, the Bank undertook a thorough investigation into the latest developments in monetary theory and practice. Its final report, 'The Importance of Money', underpinned what one official Bank historian refers to as 'the biggest change in monetary policy since the Second World War', Competition and Credit Control (CCC), in 1971 (Capie, 2010).

---

[18] This included the deposits of overseas, principally American, banks in London (Revell, 1972).

[19] The IMF was instrumental in the non-specific request for lending restraint in 1961 and the reintroduction of lending ceilings in 1965 (Goodhart & Needham, 2017).

Bank officials believed they had isolated a robust causal link from the growth of the broad money supply (M3) to nominal GDP growth and that bank lending, the largest component of M3, could be regulated with the 'interest rate weapon' – more active use of Bank rate.[20] As one of the authors of 'The Importance of Money' wrote shortly afterwards: 'The demand-for-money functions appeared to promise that credit and money could be controlled by price (interest rates), so that [lending] ceilings could be abandoned. Although some older and more experienced officials doubted all the econometrics (quite rightly as it happened), they wished to embrace this latter message' (Goodhart, 1984). In September 1971 the authorities removed lending ceilings, abolished the liquidity requirement on foreign currency deposits and replaced the 28 per cent liquidity ratio with a 12.5 per cent reserve asset ratio.[21] Shortly afterwards, the clearing bank cartel was dissolved 'at official request' (Fforde, 1983).[22] Credit rationing 'by cost' replaced credit rationing 'by control'. There followed a fundamental transformation in the way British banks managed their risk.

With the abolition of the cartel, officials anticipated that more frequent changes in Bank rate would prompt the banks to vary their deposit rates and lending rates while leaving margins fairly stable (Needham, 2014). They had not anticipated that banks, competing for market share, would allow their lending rates to become 'sticky' while actively managing their liabilities in the wholesale markets. Sterling interbank deposits increased from £2 billion (15 per cent of

---

[20] M3 comprised currency in circulation with the public (excluding cash in banks' vaults but including non-UK residents' currency holdings) and (sterling and foreign currency) deposits of UK (public and private) residents with UK banks (Goodhart & Crockett, 1970).

[21] The new ratio comprised a narrower range of assets, so the banks were then holding about 16.5 per cent of eligible reserves (under the new definition). While they were left with spare lending capacity that the authorities hoped they would direct towards industry, excess liquidity was 'mopped up' with a three-tranche jumbo gilt issue (London Clearing Banks, 1977; Capie, 2010).

[22] Barclays was first to break with the clearing bank cartel when it lowered its base rate on 14 October 1971 (Times, 15 October 1971).

total sterling bank deposits) in December 1970 to £7.7 billion (33 per cent of sterling bank deposits) in December 1973 (*Financial Statistics*, 1975). Clearing bank sterling CD issuance went from practically nil in June 1971 to £1.7 billion by March 1973 (*BEQB*, 1971; Fletcher, 1976).

The official response to the credit explosion that followed the introduction of CCC was to reintroduce qualitative lending guidance, cap the rate paid on deposit liabilities below £10,000 (to safeguard building society deposits) and impose the supplementary special deposit scheme (the 'corset') in 1973.[23] The corset recognised the transition towards liability management by imposing progressively tougher reserve requirements on banks that increased their interest-bearing deposits above specified limits.[24] As the corset's designer, Charles Goodhart, points out, this was to ensure that 'the punishment fitted the crime' by penalising institutions that drew heavily from the wholesale markets (Goodhart, 2015). The corset did exert some control over interest-bearing bank liabilities, but this was largely cosmetic and worked by encouraging precisely the disintermediation to the secondary markets that had been a driver of CCC in the first place.

The corset was discarded in 1980 (having been removed twice during the 1970s). It had been rendered obsolete by the abolition, in 1979, of the exchange controls imposed as a wartime expedient forty years earlier. Buoyed by North Sea oil and high interest rates, sterling had risen from a 1976 IMF crisis low of $1.55 to $2.11. The Thatcher government hoped that dismantling exchange controls would increase capital outflows, bring down the currency and increase net exports (Needham, 2014).[25] If banks were brushing up against the corset, they could now circumvent liability controls by directing borrowers to their overseas branches.

---

[23] The rate payable on deposits was capped at 9.5 per cent from September 1973 to February 1975 (London Clearing Banks, 1977).

[24] There were no limits on non-interest-bearing deposits since banks have less control over their sight deposits (London Clearing Banks, 1977; Battilossi, 2002).

[25] Exchange controls were also at variance with the monetary targets then in vogue.

Since 1981 there have been few restrictions on liability management. This is perhaps surprising given the financial turmoil that has
usually followed their removal. The rapid growth of the wholesale
markets under CCC was followed by the secondary banking crisis
of the mid 1970s. Petrodollar recycling through the Euromarkets
after the oil shocks was followed by the Latin American debt crisis,
starting with the Mexican debt moratorium in 1982. This left at least
one London clearer technically insolvent (alongside a number of New
York money centre banks). And of course, the rapid growth of securitisation and the shadow banking market precipitated the global financial crisis.

## 5.2    ASSET MANAGEMENT

Bank assets sit on a liquidity spectrum, with cash at one end and
longer-term investments such as mortgages at the other. Since depositors can demand their money back immediately, usually even for
time deposits in the United Kingdom, banks have to keep enough
cash on hand to meet withdrawals and drawings on agreed loan
facilities. In 1861, Walter Bagehot explained that different types of
bank required different levels of prudential cash on hand (*Economist*,
6 April 1861). Nonetheless, following an 1891 appeal by Chancellor
Goschen for greater banking transparency in the wake of the Baring's
rescue, the industry moved towards a position of greater uniformity
(Hotson, 2017). By the time of the Macmillan Committee's 1931
report on finance and industry, the 10–11 per cent ratio of cash against
total deposits was a 'bedrock' (Balogh, 1950).[26] The cash ratio was
formalised in 1946 when the clearing banks were required to hold
8 per cent of their total deposit liabilities in notes, coin and balances
at the Bank. From 1971 to 1980, the clearing banks held 1.5 per cent

---

[26] Cash comprised till money and bankers' balances at the Bank of England. Since
the clearing banks reported on different days, cash could be moved around the
system to 'window dress' reserves.

of eligible liabilities in non-interest-bearing accounts at the Bank in addition to their own till money.

As custodians of the payments system, the clearing banks also held liquidity reserves of assets that could be quickly monetised in the discount market, with the Bank acting as lender of last resort. These mainly comprised Treasury bills, commercial bills, and money at call with the discount houses.[27] By the 1930s, the clearers were working to 'well established' ratios of liquid assets to total deposits (BEQB, 1962). These were formalised in 1951, when the Bank 'indicated' that a 28–32 per cent liquidity ratio would be 'regarded as normal', with less than 25 per cent 'undesirable'.[28] In 1957 this was narrowed to 30 per cent. This remained the norm until 1963 when, to encourage lending in a slack economy, the minimum was lowered to 28 per cent, where it remained until 1971, when the liquidity ratio was replaced by the reserve asset ratio.

Before the First World War, the principal reserve asset was the prime commercial bill, discountable at the Bank. With the government budget generally in balance, there was little need to issue short-term debt, and Treasury bills, introduced in 1877, comprised just 1 per cent of the discount market in 1913 (King, 1936). About 15 per cent of the British First World War effort was financed with short-term borrowing, however, so by 1919 Treasury bills had displaced commercial bills as the principle short-term asset (Broadberry & Howlett, 2005). Commercial bill issuance fell during the 1930s slump, recovering only during the 1960s as the wartime monetary overhang was finally dissipated.[29]

---

[27] Liquid assets also included tax reserve certificates, certain loans to stockbrokers, re-financeable export and shipbuilding credits.

[28] This figure included the cash ratio (BEQB, 1962).

[29] There was a brief technical revival of bill finance in the 1980s, when, to offset the impact of increased bank credit on broad monetary growth, the authorities 'overfunded' the budget deficit with gilt sales. This created a shortage of Treasury bills, so the Bank used commercial bill operations to retain control over the money markets (Allen, 2012).

The next category of assets on the liquidity spectrum is 'investments'. These comprised British government and government-guaranteed securities, including those issued by colonial governments, municipalities and the nationalised industries.[30] As with Treasury bills, holdings were driven by the exigencies of war, with gilt-edged comprising two-thirds of clearing bank balance sheets in 1950.

The traditional business of banking, however, is the short-term advance of working capital to the commercial sector. In the early twentieth century, the preferred instrument was the 'seasonal advance', usually of six months or less to finance, for example, stock building ahead of Christmas, or for farmers between planting and harvesting (Nevin & Davis, 1970). In the provinces, and increasingly in London, lending took the form of overdraft facilities.[31] While overdrafts are legally repayable on demand, thus conforming to the short-term nature of clearing bank balance sheets, they tended to be rolled over for long periods, thus taking on the appearance, if not the legal reality, of medium- to long-term finance. The key, for the banks, was to avoid locking up financial resources (Needham, 2018).

Term loans provide borrowers with longer investment horizons with greater certainty and flexibility, effectively shifting the duration mismatch from borrowers to the banks. They are offered on the basis of the client's creditworthiness as a 'going concern', rather than the value of secured assets. Developed in the USA during the Great Depression, term loan issuance accelerated during the 1950s as the American money centre banks responded to client disintermediation by extending medium-term loans to corporations.[32] In 1959 the

---

[30] Gilts with less than twelve months to maturity counted as liquid assets alongside Treasury bills.

[31] In peacetime, holdings of government securities tended to be the residual after customer demand for advances and liquidity requirements were satisfied.

[32] Reasons included slack demand for short-term loans during the Depression; the search for alternative revenue streams after the Glass–Steagall Act restricted commercial bank business in securities markets; the advent of deposit insurance; changes in the eligibility of longer-term assets at the Fed discount window; more lenient treatment of term loans by bank examiners; and more widespread amortisation (Merris, 1979).

Radcliffe report noted that, while 'no longer completely alien to British banking practice', term loans had not yet 'found favour with banks in this country' (Radcliffe, 1959). The report recommended that they be offered as an alternative to overdrafts 'within reasonable limits' and 'with due regard to their liquidity requirements'. Term loans received cautious official blessing from the UK authorities with guarantees from the Export Credits Guarantee Department, but ratio controls and lending ceilings on the clearing banks restricted their supply, as the clearing banks preferred to keep their resources available for the short-term needs of their customers (Montgomery, 1977). However, ceilings increased customer demand for term loans, which provided insurance against the withdrawal of shorter-term facilities in the event of a government-imposed credit squeeze (Einzig, 1971).

Just as the dissolution of the clearing bank cartel in 1971 ushered in more active liability management, so CCC sparked a transformation on the asset side of clearing bank balance sheets. As Figure 5.1 shows, as well as through increased retail deposits, the banks funded the post-war growth in advances to the private sector

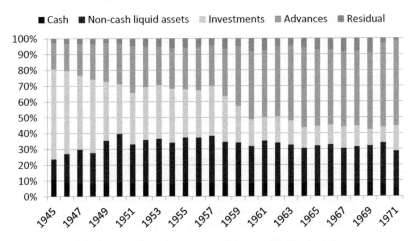

FIGURE 5.1 London clearing bank assets, 1945–71.
Source: *Bank of England Statistical Abstract*, no. 1 (1970), table 9(1), no. 2 (1975), table 8/2

by running down their holdings of longer-dated British government securities.[33] From 1971, however, with no quantitative restrictions on their lending volumes (other than their own prudential require- ments) and no qualitative guidance against lending to property companies, for instance, they could become increasingly 'advance driven' – capturing lending business and *then* sourcing the deposits in the wholesale and Eurodollar markets.[34] This fuelled rapid credit growth. Bank lending to the private sector grew by 121 per cent between May 1971 and August 1973, with loans to the financial sector (including the secondary banks) rising by 280 per cent and loans to the personal sector increasing by 209 per cent.[35] Prime Minister Heath had hoped the banks would fund his 'dash for growth' with increased industrial investment. They instead financed a property boom that crashed in 1973–4, bringing down eight secondary banks and forcing many more to clamber aboard the 'lifeboat' launched by the Bank at the end of the year (Reid, 1982).

Another consequence of the changes introduced in 1971 was increased maturity transformation. As the London clearing banks (1977) explained in their evidence to the Wilson Committee: 'Before Competition and Credit Control the banks' subsidiaries had started to make contractual medium-term loans in a modest way. The ending of quantitative restrictions in 1971, and the greater degree of operational flexibility obtained through access to wholesale deposits, provided the opening for the clearing banks themselves to market such loans.' By 1976, nearly half of all clearing bank advances had an original matur- ity of more than two years (London Clearing Banks, 1977). But more

---

[33] The pre-war ratio of advances to deposits was regained in 1960 (London Clearing Banks, 1977).

[34] Foreign currency deposits no longer counted as eligible liabilities after 1971 so required fewer reserves.

[35] Interest payments became tax deductible for individuals in 1972. For a basic rate taxpayer, the cost of servicing a loan was immediately reduced by 30 per cent. For the highest-rate taxpayer, it was reduced by 90 per cent (Needham, 2014).

than three-quarters of clearing bank liabilities still matured in seven days or less.[36]

## 5.3   DEREGULATION IN THE 1980S

As we have seen, the Thatcher government moved swiftly to abolish exchange controls in 1979. With the subsequent abolition of the corset, the banks could bid more aggressively for wholesale term deposits, thereby increasing their capacity to make longer-term loans (Fforde, 1983). The mortgage market therefore became another candidate for deregulation, with the long-standing 'gentlemen's agreement' that the banks would not compete for first mortgage business lapsing towards the end of 1980.[37] The clearers remained wary of the mainstream mortgage market, however. They expected the building societies would defend their market share, taking advantage of their lower cost ratios and mutual status that allowed them to accept lower returns on capital. Interest margins were already competitive, with societies relying on fee income, notably commissions received from insurance companies for the sale of endowment policies, alongside mortgage loans. Endowment mortgages allowed borrowers to maximise tax relief on both interest payments (mortgage interest relief at source – MIRAS) and life assurance premiums (life assurance premium relief – LAPR), by repaying the mortgage at the end of its term from the proceeds of their endowment policy. This type of loan also maximised the interest income and fees arising for lenders and insurers. Despite the abolition of both MIRAS and LAPR in the mid 1980s, it was not obvious that the clearers would launch themselves into the mortgage market, and, for many, the securities market seemed more attractive with the Big Bang reforms of 1986 clearing

[36] Absent a crisis, the 'stickiness' of some deposits meant their de facto maturity was longer.
[37] The banks' self-denying ordinance also conflicted with the Thatcher government's promotion of home ownership.

the way for banks to purchase stockbrokers, and jobbers, to offer a wider range of services under one roof.[38]

After a foray into the securities market, Lloyds followed a different, 'bancassurance' strategy, directing its attention towards retail customers by focusing on savings, mortgage loans and related insurance products (Rogers, 1999; Hotson, 2017). Under Chief Executive Brian Pitman, Lloyds acquired the life assurer Abbey Life, in 1988, and the Trustee Savings Bank, in 1995, to form Lloyds TSB. Contrary to many expectations, housing finance proved to be an attractive market. Notwithstanding the abolition of MIRAS and LAPR, the endowment mortgage remained a staple of the sector throughout the 1990s, with margins remaining intact.

With cross-border lending, international acquisitions and entry into the securities market all failing to match expectations, the Lloyds approach became the orthodoxy for all the High Street banks.[39] The big four no longer constituted a distinct group, however (Ackrill & Hannah, 2001). The Building Societies Act 1986 triggered consolidation amongst the building societies, while also presenting the opportunity for mergers between societies and the banks.[40] Abbey National, the second-largest building society, was first to use the new powers granted by the 1986 Act to demutualise and became a bank in 1989.[41] The largest society, Halifax, converted in 1997 and

---

[38] Barclays acquired the largest stock jobber, Wedd Durlacher, and the stockbroker de Zoete & Bevan, forming the broker–dealer Barclays de Zoete Wedd. Midland already had an interest in the merchant bank Samuel Montagu and acquired two stockbrokers, Greenwell's and Simon & Coates. NatWest assembled a new firm, County Bank, and the recently floated TSB Group acquired the merchant bank Hill Samuel (Hotson, 2017).

[39] The banks all suffered losses during the Latin American debt crisis; Midland was weakened by its ill-fated purchase of Crocker Bank in California, and Barclays was the only clearer to succeed in the securities market.

[40] Cheltenham & Gloucester Building Society (C&G) grew to be the sixth-largest society by acquiring a raft of smaller societies, before itself being acquired by Lloyds in 1995. Life assurer Scottish Widows was acquired by Lloyds in 1999 (Boleat, 1985; Rogers, 1999).

[41] The only large society not to convert was the previous number three, Nationwide.

merged with Bank of Scotland in 2001.[42] The line-up of High Street banks therefore became Halifax/Bank of Scotland, HSBC/Midland, Lloyds TSB, Royal Bank of Scotland/NatWest and Santander/Abbey National, followed by Alliance & Leicester and Bradford & Bingley. The remaining sixty or so building societies continued to be represented by the Building Societies Association, and the Council of Mortgage Lenders was formed to represent providers of home finance, be they banks, building societies or specialist lenders. Nonetheless, power gravitated towards the major institutions, with government-sponsored regulators superseding self-regulation. The markets were overseen by a succession of statutory bodies: the Securities and Investment Board, the Financial Services Authority and then the Financial Conduct Authority, together with the Prudential Regulation Authority.

The 2008 collapse called into question the deregulated mortgage banking model, but it did not usher in a regulatory counter-revolution. There was no attempt to rebuild the model that had provided London's international banking market its century of stability from the 1870s until 1971. Despite superficial similarities, the proposals of the Independent Commission on Banking (the Vickers Report) were not about recreating pre-1971 banking structures. Vickers did not consider curbing liability management, and side-stepped any assessment of money market issues (Vickers, 2011a). Although the ring-fenced banks are called retail banks, they provide money transmission and plain vanilla lending facilities to major corporations as well as personal customers and small businesses. Despite being an amalgam of clearing banks and building societies, they lack the traditional protections that characterised the pre-1971 regime.

---

[42] Northern Rock and Alliance & Leicester were demutualised and floated in 1997, as was Bradford & Bingley in 2000. Like C&G, Woolwich and Bristol & West converted with a view to becoming part of larger banking groups.

## 5.4 MATURITY TRANSFORMATION

The Victorian principle that short-term deposits should be matched against short-term assets, undermined by the growth of the parallel and Eurocurrency markets, was destroyed by the mortgage market revolution (Collins, 1990). Previously, if the clearers suffered an out-flow of short-term deposits or a sudden loss of capital, they could contract their balance sheets by running off short-term assets. It was taken for granted that they should not tolerate significant maturity mismatching. Wilfred King, author of the main interwar book on London's discount market, declaimed the 'cardinal principle that to lend 'long' one must also borrow 'long'' (King, 1936). In the absence of longer-term funding, he suggested that it was the banker's duty to hold 'virtually all his assets in liquid form, and part of them in highly liquid form'. It was the job of the banker 'to tide over temporary lack of ready money, not to provide capital on which the customer carries on his business' (Sykes, 1947). These views were still held in the 1960s and 1970s by many practitioners who regarded borrowing short and lending long as a 'classic error' (Gordon, 1993).

In contrast, the deregulated clearing banks became property lenders. Short-term bank deposits predominantly funded multi-year loans secured on real property, and shadow banks funded investment assets with relatively short-term repos, assuming these could be rolled over.[43] The political drive for wider home ownership, and the contingent necessity for home finance, helped to fashion an argument that banks' long-term property lending could be justified if they held sufficient capital to cover the risks. Macro-prudential measures were put in place in case property prices looked like getting out of hand (Calomiris & Haber, 2014; Wolf, 2014).

---

[43] Mortgagors often repay a traditional twenty-five-year mortgage before final maturity as they move home. Nonetheless, funding the resulting five-to-eight-year-average loans with short-term deposits still generates a significant mismatch with considerable rollover risk, notwithstanding the 'stickiness' of some retail deposits.

Maturity mismatching was given a more respectable title – maturity transformation – and is now regarded as a key component of socially useful banking. As the final report of the Vickers' Commission outlined: 'Banks are able to fund illiquid assets with short-term, liquid liabilities ... The production of liquidity in this fashion is socially valuable because it allows savers to withdraw funds when they want, rather than when the investments they ultimately fund pay off (Diamond and Dybvig (1983))' (Vickers, 2011a).[44]

Diamond and Dybvig outlined the theoretical case for maturity transformation in the 1980s, and the Vickers Commission endorsed their view, citing their 1983 article, 'Bank Runs, Deposit Insurance, and Liquidity', in its final report (Diamond & Dybvig, 1983). Diamond and Dybvig (1983) argue that callable deposits provide bank customers with liquidity in a world where it is not practical to write insurance policies offering pay-offs covering a wide range of spending contingencies. To use Keynes' (1936) terminology, individuals hold precautionary balances to cover uncertain spending requirements that are not covered by insurance. In contrast, producers create illiquid investments, giving rise to a mismatch between the needs of households and firms. If banks intermediate between the two – accepting short-term deposits and lending long – they bear the liquidity risk.

Diamond and Dybvig suggest that the problem of maturity mismatching can be overcome if depositors' cash needs are asynchronous, since this allows the banks to pool withdrawal risk. The banks can therefore allocate resources more efficiently, with liquid deposits funding illiquid assets. The authors confront the problem of depositor runs, which might be prompted by fears of others making withdrawals, by recommending deposit insurance, provided by the state if necessary. Additional liquidity insurance can be provided in the form of market assistance and lender of last resort facilities at the central bank. They accept that such liquidity insurance could encourage banks to take more risk, giving rise to moral hazard problems. This

---

[44] See also Turner (2009).

might provide a rationale for bank regulation, e.g. minimum standards of capital adequacy (Diamond & Dybvig, 1983; Tucker, 2004).

Diamond and Dybvig's early work characterised bank lending as a form of relationship-based funding for firms, particularly small and medium-sized entities. Under this approach, banks are more like private equity firms (Diamond & Dybvig, 1983). Loan originators have private knowledge about their borrowers' businesses, so they are best placed to recover their loans. This makes it difficult to sell loans in the secondary market (Diamond, 1984; Diamond and Rajan, 2001). This theoretical approach to bank lending did not reflect what was happening in Anglophone banking markets at the time, however. In London, the clearers' traditional company lending – via bills and advances – was rapidly being eclipsed by home finance and consumer credit. Larger companies were rejecting the practice of one banking relationship, and using multiple banks – a horses-for-courses approach. Centralised lending using automated underwriting techniques, such as credit scoring, was replacing branch-based personalised lending. Most significantly, increased use of securitisation meant that loan originators did not necessarily have to have direct access to funding provided by a large balance sheet. Newly originated mortgage loans could be sold to better funded institutions and non-bank investors. Lowell Bryan went so far as to suggest that this would allow the break-up of vertically integrated banks into their constituent parts: brokers for originating loans, factory-like operations for underwriting and administering loans, credit enhancement provided by insurers and financing by fund managers (Bryan, 1988).

Bryan's model with its functional specialists was presented as a radical departure, but there were parallels with London's traditional clearing bank model, with its clear demarcations between accepting houses providing bill underwriting and credit enhancement, discount houses providing liquidity and clearers using customer deposits to provide short-term working capital. The Bryan and clearing bank models shared a common approach in which specialist firms were intermediated through the money and credit markets. The glue that had kept the clearing bank model together was an orderly money market that maintained flows between its constituent parts, even in a crisis. The same could not be said of the post-1980s securitised credit market, which collapsed during the 2008 crisis. One response would have been to recreate an orderly money market, using a modern equivalent of prime bank bills, perhaps prime asset-backed securities. Another possibility, drawn from nineteenth-century experience, might have been to restrict banks to relatively short-term assets or to restrict liability management. None of these options gained any traction.

Instead, the Diamond and Dybvig approach enjoyed a revival, offering a reassuring rationalisation of the deregulated banking model. Significant maturity mismatching was accepted as part of modern banking life, and its management was seen to depend on reassuring depositors with deposit insurance and adequate capital (Diamond & Rajan, 2001; Diamond, 2007; Schularick & Taylor, 2012). It was argued that Bagehot's lender-of-last-resort policy had been the main factor contributing to London's century of stability and that deposit insurance – in its widest sense – was the modern equivalent of Bagehot's successful policy (Tucker, 2004; Vickers, 2011b).

## 5.5 CONCLUSIONS

J. W. Gilbart, author of *A Practical Treatise on Banking*, wrote in 1827 that 'it is contrary to all sound principles of banking for a banker to advance money in the form of permanent loan'. It was axiomatic for Victorian bankers that short-term deposits be matched by short-term assets. Banking practitioners addressed the risk of maturity mismatching by the simple expedient of excluding long-maturity assets (except undated British government securities in the form of highly liquid Consols) from prudently run banks' balance sheets. In addition, they restricted banks' ability to liability manage and encouraged them to hold money market instruments that retained their liquidity at times of stress. This approach contributed to a century of stability from the 1870s to 1971. The current orthodoxy on risk management rejects this approach. We are not convinced it will stand the test of time.

REFERENCES

Ackrill, M. and Hannah, L. (2001). *Barclays: The Business of Banking*. Cambridge: Cambridge University Press.

Allen, W. A. (2012). Government debt management and monetary policy in Britain since 1919. BIS Working Paper no. 65.

Balogh, T. (1950). *Studies in Financial Organization*. Cambridge: Cambridge University Press.

Battilossi, S. (2000). Financial innovation and the golden ages of international banking: 1890–1931 and 1958–81. *Financial History Review*, 7(2), 141–75.

Battilossi, S. (2002). Banking with multinationals: British clearing banks and the Euromarkets' challenge, 1958–1976. In Battilossi, S. and Cassis, Y. (eds), *European Banks and the American Challenge: Competition and Cooperation in International Banking under Bretton Woods*. Oxford: Oxford University Press, pp. 103–34.

Boleat, M. (1985) *National Housing Finance Systems: A Comparative Study*. London: Croom Helm.

Broadberry S. N. and Howlett P. (2005). The United Kingdom during World War I: business as usual? In S. N. Broadberry and M. Harrison, eds., *The Economics of World War I*. Cambridge: Cambridge University Press, pp. 206–34.

Bryan, L. (1988). *Breaking Up the Bank: Rethinking an Industry under Siege*. Homewood, IL: Dow Jones-Irwin.

Calomiris C. W. and Haber S. H. (2014). *Fragile by Design: The Political Origins of Banking Crises and Scarce Credit*. Princeton, NJ: Princeton University Press.

Capie, F. H. (2010) *The Bank of England: 1950s to 1979*. New York: Cambridge University Press.

Collins, M. (1990). *Money and Banking in the UK: A History*. London: Croom Helm.

Daunton, M. J. (1987). *A Property-Owning Democracy? Housing in Britain*. London: Faber and Faber.

Diamond, D. W. (1984). Financial intermediation and delegated monitoring. *Review of Economic Studies*, 51, 393–41.

Diamond, D. W. (2007). Banks and liquidity creation: a simple exposition of the Diamond–Dybvig model, *Federal Reserve Bank of Richmond Economic Quarterly*, 93(2), 189–200.

Diamond D. W. and Dybvig P. H. (1983). Bank runs, deposit insurance, and liquidity. *Journal of Political Economy*, 91(3), 401–19.

Diamond D. W. and Rajan, R. (2001). Liquidity risk, liquidity creation and financial fragility: a theory of banking. *Journal of Political Economy*, **109**(2), 287–327.

Dow, J. C. R. (1970) *The Management of the British Economy, 1945–60*. Cambridge: Cambridge University Press.

Einzig, P. (1971). *The New Markets in London*. Vol. 1 of *Parallel Money Markets*. London: Macmillan.

Fforde, J. S. (1983) Competition, innovation and regulation in British banking', *BEQB*, **23**(3), 363–76.

Fletcher, G. A. (1976). *The Discount Houses in London: Principles, Operations, and Change*. London: Macmillan.

Gilbart, J. W. (1827). *A Practical Treatise on Banking*, 1st ed. London: E. Wilson.

Goodhart, C. A. E. (1984) *Monetary Theory and Practice: The UK Experience*. London: Macmillan.

Goodhart, C. A. E. (2015). Competition and Credit Control: some personal reflections. *Financial History Review*, **22**(2), 235–46.

Goodhart C. A. E. and Crockett, A. D. (1970). The importance of money. *BEQB*, **10**(2), 159–98.

Goodhart, C. A. E. and Needham, D. J. (2017). Historical reasons for the focus on broad monetary aggregates in post-WW2 Britain and the 'Seven Years War' with the IMF. *Financial History Review*, **24**(3), 331–56.

Gordon, C. (1993). *The Cedar Story: The Night the City Was Saved*. London: Sinclair–Stevenson.

Hotson, A. C. (2017) *Respectable Banking: The Search for Stability in London's Money and Credit Markets since 1695*. Cambridge: Cambridge University Press.

House of Commons Treasury Committee (2008). *The Run on the Rock: Fifth Report of Session 2007–08*, vol. 1. London: The Stationary Office Limited. https://bit.ly/33oSBQ8

Keynes, J. M. (1936). *The General Theory of Employment, Interest and Money*, 1st ed. London: Macmillan.

Kim, S. W. (2017). *The Euromarket and the making of the transnational network of finance, 1959–1979*. Unpublished PhD thesis, University of Cambridge.

King, W. T. C. (1936). *History of the London Discount Market*. London: Routledge.

London Clearing Banks (1977). *Evidence by the Committee of London Clearing Bankers to the Committee to Review the Functioning of Financial Institutions*. London: Committee of London Clearing Bankers.

Macmillan Committee (1931). *Committee on Finance and Industry: Report* ('Macmillan Report'). London: HMSO.

Merris, R. C. (1979). Business loans at large commercial banks: policies and practices, *Federal Reserve Bank of Chicago Economic Perspectives*, **3**(21), 15–23.

Monopolies Commission (1968). *Barclays Bank Ltd, Lloyds Bank Ltd, and Martins Bank Ltd: A Report on the Proposed Merger.* London: HMSO.

Montgomery, C. J. (1977). *The Clearing Banks, 1952–77: An Age of Progress: The Presidential Address of C. J. Montgomery.* London: Institute of Bankers.

National Board for Prices and Incomes (1967). *Report No. 34: Bank Charges, Cmnd 3292.* London: HMSO.

Needham, D. J. (2014). *UK Monetary Policy from Devaluation to Thatcher, 1967–82.* Basingstoke: Palgrave Macmillan.

Needham, D. J. (2018). Mortgages and mismatching – the transformation of British clearing banks. *The Property Chronicle*, 19 October 2018. www.propertychronicle .com/mortgages-and-mismatching/

Nevin, E. T. and Davis, E. W. (1970). *The London Clearing Banks.* London: Elek.

Offer, A. (1981). *Property and Politics, 1870–1914: Landownership, Law, Ideology and Urban Development in England.* Cambridge: Cambridge University Press.

Offer, A. (2014). Narrow banking, real estate, and financial stability in the UK c.1870–2010. In N. H. Dimsdale and A. C. Hotson, eds., *British Financial Crises since 1825.* Oxford: Oxford University Press.

Radcliffe Committee (1959). *Committee on the Working of the Monetary System: Report* ('Radcliffe Report'). London: HMSO.

Rae, G. (1885). *The Country Banker: His Clients, Cares and Work from an Experience of Forty Years*, 2nd ed., London: Murray.

Reid, M. I. (1982). *The Secondary Banking Crisis, 1973–75: Its Causes and Course.* London: Macmillan.

Revell, J.R.S. (1972). A secondary banking system. In H. G. Johnson and Associates, eds., *Readings in British Monetary Economics.* Oxford: Clarendon Press.

Rogers, D. (1999). *The Big Four British Banks: Organisation, Strategy and Future.* Basingstoke: Macmillan.

Sayers, R. S. *Modern Banking*, 7th ed. Oxford: Clarendon Press.

Schularick, M. and Taylor, A. M. (2012). Credit booms gone bust: monetary policy, leverage cycles, and financial crises, 1870–2008. *American Economic Review*, **102**(2), 1029–61.

Sykes, E. (1947), *Banking and Currency*, 9th ed. London: Butterworth

Tucker, P. M. W. (2004). Managing the central bank's balance sheet: where monetary policy meets financial stability, *BEQB*, **44**(3), 359–82.

Turner, A. (2009). *The Turner Review: A Regulatory Response to the Global Banking Crisis.* London: Financial Services Authority. https://bit.ly/2NcXNRJ

Vickers, J. (2011a). *Interim Report: Consultation on Reform Options.* London: Independent Commission on Banking.

Vickers, J. (2011b). *Final Report of the Independent Commission on Banking*. London: Independent Commission on Banking.

Wolf, M. H. (2014). *The Shifts and the Shocks: What We've Learned – and Have Still to Learn – from the Financial Crisis*. London: Allen Lane.

## Other Sources

*Bank of England Quarterly Bulletin (BEQB)*
*Bank of England Statistical Abstract (BOESA)*
*The Economist*
*Financial Statistics*
*The Times*

# 6 Regulating Agency Relationships and Risk Culture in Financial Institutions

Kern Alexander

## 6.1 INTRODUCTION

This chapter analyses the concept of human agency in organisations and how it can be used to understand the development and regulation of risk culture in financial institutions. It does so by considering how human agency is relevant for understanding how weaknesses in risk culture caused serious risk management and operational failures in some of the largest and most sophisticated banking and financial institutions. The chapter then considers to what extent financial regulation can play a role in facilitating the development of organisational norms to enhance risk culture in banking institutions. Specifically, it assesses the regulatory responses and industry-led initiatives taken since the financial crisis of 2007–8 ('crisis') to address weaknesses in bank risk culture. The chapter suggests that shortcomings in risk culture – particularly as understood through the lens of human agency theory – in financial institutions are the result of collective agency problems. It discusses some of the regulatory measures adopted to address weaknesses in bank risk culture and how self-regulatory initiatives in the banking sector are beginning to play a role in influencing risk culture. The chapter suggests, however, that self-regulatory initiatives are inadequate to control and limit the agency problems that arise from the collective activities of many individuals who work in most financial institutions. The chapter considers how the UK Senior Managers Regime is designed to address collective agency problems within banking institutions by imposing civil liability on senior managers for failing to carry out due diligence in overseeing subordinate employees who have acted negligently or otherwise in violation of regulatory rules. Although self-regulatory bodies are in most cases best placed to develop norms and standards of behaviour to prevent collective agency problems within banks and other financial institutions, a vertical liability regime such as that created by the Senior Managers Regime may be necessary to ensure that banking institutions develop adequate oversight practices of employees and other actors who affect the risk culture of financial institutions.

## 6.2   HUMAN AGENCY AND ORGANISATIONS

Broadly speaking, the concept of agency can be understood in many areas of social interaction. Indeed, every time individuals or entities enter into relationships, even casually, potential agency problems exist. Within this broad sense, agency relationships may often lead to exploitative and socially costly behaviour. Traditional agency theory in the corporate governance and finance literature has analysed how asymmetric information provides firm owners with inferior information to monitor managers who have the opportunity to engage in unobserved and costly behaviour (Shleifer & Vishny, 1997). The idea that managers have an information advantage and that this gives them the opportunity to take self-interested actions at the expense of the firm's owners represents the typical principal–agent problem (Jensen, 1998: 47).[1] Contract theorists attempt to overcome the asymmetric information problem by designing a 'complete contract' that aligns the interests or incentives of the firm's agents with those of the firm's owners (Hart, 1995: 32–3, 73–83). For example, such incentive arrangements may take the form of tying a portion of a manager's compensation to the company's performance in the stock market through the use of stock options. A contract that does not align the interests of the firm's agents with those of the firm's owners can lead

---

[1]   See Jensen and Meckling (1994) and Jensen and H. (1976), focusing their analysis on the divergent interests of stockholders and managers in public corporations. Jensen postulates that because 'people are, in the end, self-interested they will have conflicts of interest over at least some issues any time they attempt to engage in cooperative endeavors' (Jensen, 1998: 47–8).

to suboptimal firm performance and diminished firm value, as agents will have an incentive to shirk their responsibilities and appropriate the firm's assets.

The classic agency problem arises from the moral hazard that arises when 'individuals engage in risk sharing under conditions such that their privately-taken actions affect the probability distribution of the outcome' (Ross, 1974; Hölmstrom, 1979; 74). Although it was first introduced into the insurance literature, moral hazard encompasses situations in which the incentives of the principal (the firm owner or creditor) diverge from the incentives of the agents (employee or person using property that belongs to others). Based on the assumption that a rational agent can be expected to maximise its own utility, and where its economic self-interest conflicts with that of the principal, the principal will incur costs. Agent moral hazard can also lead to a 'tragedy of the commons' where there is a collectivisation of losses for actions that cannot be monitored or controlled by the principals or other actors (Ross, 1974: 74). This collectivisation of losses reflects the problems associated with negative externalities and social costs.[2]

The collectivisation of losses that can arise from the tragedy of the commons can also occur within the organisational structure of large organisations or financial institutions in which the behaviour of many individual agents across the organisation can lead to a collective form of moral hazard, an incentive problem at the collective action level (Dow, 2000: 15). This would involve individual managers having inadequate incentives to monitor and solve problems because organisational norms and institutional structures are such that they constrain or limit behaviour that may 'rock the boat'. Also, organisational incentives might be structured in a unilinear or univocal way, running directly from firm owners to managers, which does

---

[2] The 'tragedy of the commons' results from the moral hazard that 'arises when it is difficult and costly to exclude potential users from common-pool resources that yield finite flows of benefits, as a result of which those resources will be exhausted by rational, utility-maximizing individuals rather than conserved for the benefit of all'. See Ostrom (2008: 3573).

not take account of the firm's organisational norms and institutional structure that can influence decision-making and strategy and which may lead to a collective form of moral hazard across the organisation. Similarly, the very personality traits that fulfil traditional corporate governance objectives, such as shareholder wealth maximisation, can result in disadvantaging the interests of other principals such as bondholders or other creditors or stakeholders such as customers and employees.[3]

In contrast, the sociological perspective of agency provides another lens through which to view agency problems. Indeed, the traditional sociological theory of agency considers 'the thoughts and actions taken by people that express their individual power' (Emirbayer & Mische, 1998). Emirbayer and Mische (1998) underline how the concept of agency is somewhat vague due to its application in a variety of contexts.[4] In an attempt to analytically disaggregate agency into its several component elements and to show the multiple ways through which the dimensions of agency interact with diverse forms of structure, they expand the concept of agency into 'human agency', which is defined as 'the temporally constructed engagement by actors of different structural environments – the temporal–relational contexts of action – which, through the interplay of habit, imagination, and judgment, both reproduces and transforms those structures in interactive response to the problems posed by changing historical situations'.

Most of the current studies on human agency find their source in the seminal work of Albert Bandura. He first elaborated the concept

---

[3] See generally Malmendier and Geoffrey (2009), Khurana (2002), and Tversky and Daniel (1974).

[4] They argue that 'the concept of agency has become a source of increasing strain and confusion in social thought. Variants of action theory, normative theory, and political–institutional analysis have defended, attacked, buried, and resuscitated the concept in often contradictory and overlapping ways. At the centre of the debate, the term agency itself has maintained an elusive, albeit resonant, vagueness; it has all too seldom inspired systematic analysis, despite the long list of terms with which it has been associated: self-hood, motivation, will, purposiveness, intentionality, choice, initiative, freedom, and creativity' (Emirbayer & Mische, 1998).

of human agency within the topic of self-efficacy (Bandura, 1986). According to his theory, human agency as self-efficacy is 'the human capability to exert influence over one's functioning and the course of events by one's actions' (Bandura, 2009). From this definition, he identified four main features of human agency: (1) intentionality, (2) forethought, 3) self-reactiveness and (4) self-reflection (Bandura, 2006). While 'intentionality' refers to intentions and, amongst others, addresses plans and strategies to put them into practice, 'forethought' is conceived as 'the temporal extension of agency'; in other words, it involves establishing targets and anticipating future outcomes. 'Self-reactiveness' stretches the effects of 'forethought' in the sense that agents are not just 'planners and fore thinkers' but also responders to contingent or changing circumstances. They need to have adequate self-management and motivation for translating their plans into practice and for responding to unexpected outcomes. Finally, 'self-reflection' involves an evaluation of the nature of human agency.

Bandura further articulated his theory by identifying three different forms through which human agency is exercised: (a) personal, (b) proxy and (c) collective (Bandura, 1997). Personal agency, also known as 'direct personal agency', is exercised on an individual basis. Significantly, personal agency assumes that individuals have direct control and influence over people and things. However, such control and influence cannot be direct in all contexts. Hence, the lack of direct control and influence is the basis to consider the concept of proxy agency. Where people do not have full control over the facts that relate to and affect their lives, they exercise proxy agency. Exercising proxy agency means 'relying on the efforts of intermediaries' (Bandura, 1999) who have resources and tools to guarantee the results others aim at achieving. Moreover, Bandura stresses that 'people do not live their lives in individual autonomy. Indeed, many of the outcomes they seek are achievable only through interdependent efforts' (Bandura, 2000). This is known as 'collective agency', which refers to effects produced by collective initiatives of people who share the same objectives or beliefs and therefore act as a group: 'A group's attainments are the product not only of shared knowledge and skills of its different members, but also of the interactive, coordinative, and synergistic dynamics of their transactions.' The 'interactive, coordinative, and synergistic' dimension of the group's behaviour are not necessarily driven by the economic incentives that compensation arrangements – or the opportunity to appropriate the principal's property affords – may induce but rather are influenced by the collective initiatives of the group within the organisation whose objectives are conditioned by social norms and cultural practices, and their actions to achieve their objectives are channelled by the institutional mechanisms through which the group can interact and coordinate its actions to achieve its objectives.

## 6.3   HUMAN AGENCY AND RISK CULTURE IN BANKING ORGANISATIONS

Banking organisations are complex institutions whose economic objectives of achieving shareholder wealth maximisation are only realisable through the collective efforts of many individuals who share the same objectives and beliefs and who can coordinate effectively their activities to promote the firm's economic success. However, the size and complex structure of large systemically important banks suggests a wide range of potential agency problems that involve several major stakeholder groups, including but not limited to shareholders, creditors, depositors and other customers, employees and management, and supervisory bodies. Agency problems arise because responsibility for decision-making is directly or indirectly delegated from one stakeholder group to another in situations where stakeholder groups have different objectives and where complete information that would allow the first group to exert control over the decision maker is not readily available. Traditional agency theory has underpinned the major features of the design of regulatory structures that attempt to align the incentives of principal and agent and to limit the incentive to take excessive risks at society's expense (externalities). However, problems of incentive conflict between different groups of employees, management and other stakeholders based on different understandings of ethics and norms of behaviour that undermine the firm's pursuit of its strategic objectives have become the focus of a growing literature on risk culture.

Human agency theory supplements traditional corporate governance agency theory by postulating that, as with other complex organisations, individuals who work within banking organisations do not pursue their objectives in a vacuum based on the design of a contract but rather are subject to societal norms and institutional values that influence how they coordinate their activities to achieve both the individual and collective objectives of the institution. Institutional outcomes that are achieved by the collective initiatives of individuals who share the same beliefs and values within an organisation are the product of a particular business or risk culture. This type of collective agency is driven by the collective pursuits of individuals throughout an organisation and is influenced substantially by the norms and standards that are fostered by the institution itself in the pursuit of its own business strategy and purpose, which are also conditioned by societal norms and cultural practices.

It is generally accepted that the culture within banking institutions during the period prior to the crisis of 2007–9 emphasised excessive risk-taking for short-term profits at the expense of longer-term firm performance and sustainable shareholder value. Moreover, the risk culture within institutions was driven by compensation arrangements that relied heavily on variable pay that was determined by short-term performance metrics that often rewarded behaviour that generated short-term revenue and profits while placing the firm's long-term viability at risk and disadvantaging customers. One of the lessons of the crisis, therefore, was that regulators should play a greater role in judging how culture drives firm behaviour and risk-taking and how this impacts society as a whole. Indeed, the ultimate goal should be that firms should understand their own culture and how its norms and practices can affect the firm attaining its objectives (Sants, 2010).

In the aftermath of the crisis, regulators and policymakers have urged banks and other financial institutions, in particular those regarded as systemically important financial institutions, to have a sound 'risk culture'. Likewise, supervisors and regulators have been encouraged to have, among other things, a systematic focus on financial institution culture. As a result, risk culture has become a central topic in debates on financial regulation, while regulators, policymakers and practitioners have been devoting more efforts to provide effective strategies to ensure a sound risk culture in regulated financial institutions.

The academic literature regarding the regulation of risk culture in the financial services industry is very limited (Ashby, Palermo & Power, 2014). Nevertheless, three areas have emerged in which the concept has been addressed. First, risk culture has been considered by referring to individual behaviour, ethics and company governance mechanisms (Banks, 2012: 23). It has also been considered a subset of the broader company's organisational culture and thus defined as 'the norms and traditions of behaviour of individuals and of groups within an organization that determine the way in which they identify, understand, discuss, and act on the risks the organization confronts and the risks it takes' (IIF, 2009). Significantly, firms converge on defining risk culture as everyone's responsibility, from management to employees – in other words, as a system of values and behavioural norms that help foster risk management processes and ensure an adequate level of risk control. In this context, risk culture is seen as an effective tool for reducing a firm's excessive risk-taking (Ernst & Young, 2014).

Second, risk culture can be analysed by evaluating the incentives that regulators and policymakers have provided. For example, the Basel Committee on Banking Supervision (BCBS) in 2009 encouraged regulators to strengthen risk management within banks and highlighted the importance of risk culture (as a 'critical focus') in banks' business strategies (BCBS, 2009). This was then transposed into some of the main post-crisis legislative reforms on financial regulation. For instance, Directive 2013/36/EU (CRD IV) requires

EU member states to 'promote a sound risk culture at all levels of credit institutions and investment firms'.[5] Clearly, regulators stress that risk culture is an aspect that cannot be ignored within a financial institution's broader cultural norms. In this respect, the Group of Thirty (G30) declared in 2013 that 'boards should identify and deal seriously with risky culture, ensure their compensation system supports the desired culture, discuss culture at the board level and with supervisors, and periodically use a variety of formal and informal techniques to monitor risk culture' (G30, 2013). In practice, regulators claim that an effective risk culture is ensured through an appropriate interaction between a firm's board and supervisors. The BCBS emphasised this in a 2014 consultative document on bank corporate governance that defined risk culture as 'a bank's norms, attitudes and behaviours related to risk awareness, risk taking and risk management and controls that shape decisions on risks'.

Risk culture influences the decisions of management and employees during day-to-day activities and has an impact on the risks they assume. Accordingly, to promote an effective risk culture it is the board's task to set the 'tone at the top'. On the other hand, supervisors should liaise with the board, its risk and audit committees, to verify whether or not the institution has adequate risk governance mechanisms and effective risk culture. (BCBS, 2014). Furthermore, the Financial Stability Board (FSB) set out clear guidance to help regulators and supervisors assess risk culture in financial institutions. In its 2014 *Guidance on Supervisory Interaction with Financial Institutions on Risk Culture*, the FSB stated that 'a sound risk culture bolsters effective risk management, promotes sound risk-taking, and ensures that emerging risks or risk-taking activities beyond the institution's risk appetite are recognized, assessed, escalated and addressed in a timely manner'. The FSB also recommended

---

[5] Directive 2013/36/EU of the European Parliament and of the Council of 26 June 2013 on access to the activity of credit institutions and the prudential supervision of credit institutions and investment firms, amending Directive 2002/87/EC and repealing Directives 2006/48/EC and 2006/49/EC, OJ 2013 No. L176/338, Recital 54.

supervisors to play an active role for assessing good risk culture among financial institutions.[6]

Third, risk culture can also be analysed by evaluating the role of ethics and culture in a bank's risk management practice and how it affects its strategic objectives as well. In a 2015 report on bank conduct and culture, the G30 drew a line between the roles of the board and management, and the role of regulatory authorities in relation to culture and risk culture. While the former have responsibility for the firm's cultural focus, regulatory authorities should not determine culture. Instead, they should perform monitoring functions as to the effectiveness of a firm's own culture to deter, among other things, inappropriate behaviour in violation of regulatory norms and standards (G30, 2015). This view suggests that the issue of risk culture from the regulatory perspective is more nuanced and complex when considering whether it hinders a firm in achieving regulatory objectives. This means that firms should manage risk culture from an internal perspective, while regulators should address risk culture in relation to whether regulatory objectives are being fulfilled and its systemic implications on the markets and financial system.

Recent financial scandals strengthened the link between firm culture and prudential regulation. Scandals such as the rigging of London interbank offered rate (LIBOR) and mis-selling of payment protection insurance in the United Kingdom prompted regulators to discuss risk culture in the context of misconduct risk. For instance, the European Systemic Risk Board (ESRB) has recognised that systematic misconduct throughout an institution (i.e. LIBOR rigging and mis-selling) can create systemic risk and other system-wide financial stability problems. The ESRB has recommended that banks monitor their collective behavioural practices and governance mechanisms to reduce misconduct risk (ESRB, 2015). Significantly, appropriate risk

---

[6] See FSB (2014): supervisors are recommended to conduct periodic reviews of an institution's culture, issue findings and review the extent to which culture is the underlying cause of the identified problems.

culture ensures adequate risk management and is also regarded by regulators as a tool for preventing financial institution misconduct having systemic implications (Nouy, 2015). This means that understanding culture – what one does 'when nobody is watching' – and ethics – the line between acceptable and unacceptable decisions – can help us to recognise, and even predict, some behaviour.

## 6.4   REGULATORY INITIATIVES FOR BANK RISK CULTURE

The United Kingdom has taken the lead amongst developed countries in adopting regulatory approaches to monitor and enhance risk culture in banking and financial institutions. Indeed, the connection between culture and prudential regulation is evident in the work of the UK regulatory authorities: the Bank of England's Prudential Regulation Authority (PRA) and the Financial Conduct Authority (FCA). The PRA declared that even though it does not have any 'right culture' in mind, it will act 'to tackle serious failings in culture through its normal activity, through use of its supervisory powers, and through enforcement action' (PRA, 2014). Similarly, the FCA has stressed the importance of focusing on financial institution culture and in particular risk culture to prevent behaviour in violation of regulatory rules and standards (McDermott, 2015).[7]

The impetus for this regulatory focus on risk culture has been driven by the recommendations of the Parliamentary Commission on Banking Standards (PCBS, 2013a, 2013b) report *Changing Banking for the Good*, issued in June 2013, whose aim was to enhance professional standards and promote sound culture in UK banks. The PCBS 2013 recommendations were adopted in the aftermath of the scandals surrounding the manipulations of the LIBOR and the foreign exchange

---

[7] The FCA's former director of enforcement has stated that 'we believe that a firm's culture is a key driver of staff behaviour and, in many cases, where things have gone wrong in a firm, a cultural issue was a key part of the problem' (McDermott, 2015).

rate indices[8] and the systematic mis-selling of financial products to bank customers. The PCBS was highly critical of most British banks, especially the largest and most sophisticated institutions, and in particular criticised bank senior figures who had 'shelter[ed] behind an accountability firewall'.[9] The PCBS concluded that flaws in the regulatory regime governing the conduct of senior management and individuals resulted in an inadequate level of accountability at senior management level for systematic malpractice within institutions.[10]

To implement the PCBS recommendations, Parliament enacted the Financial Services (Banking Reform) Act 2013 to address weaknesses in bank governance and to enhance bank risk culture. The Banking Reform Act authorised the UK Treasury to adopt in 2014 the Senior Managers and Certification Regime (SM&CR), which is designed to reinforce a sound culture and clarify the responsibilities of senior managers and board members in banks.

The SM&CR came into force on 7 March 2016. In light of the serious weaknesses in accountability and business culture identified by the PCBS, the new SM&CR framework was initially directed to banking institutions. However, a report commissioned by the UK Treasury entitled *The Fair and Effective Market Review* proposed that most elements of the SM&CR be extended to other regulated firms active in the wholesale fixed income, currency and commodities markets (FICC).[11] Subsequently, the UK government accepted this proposal with the view to shaping a 'more rigorous, comprehensive and consistent approach across the financial services industry' (HM Treasury, 2015: 9). To this end, the Treasury adopted a reformed approved persons regime that would be called the Senior Managers and Conduct Regime.[12]

---

[8] See Foreign Exchange Professionals Association (2015: 1–2), discussing manipulation of the foreign exchange fix. For discussion of LIBOR manipulation, see HM Treasury (2012).
[9] See PCBS (2013).    [10] See PCBS (2013).
[11] See HM Treasury, Bank of England and FCA (2015).    [12] See HM Treasury (2015).

The SM&CR aims to address the collective agency problem within regulated financial institutions by imposing civil liability on senior managers for the violations of regulatory rules committed by individuals – either acting or failing to act individually or acting or failing to act together or as a group within the institution – even if the senior manager had no knowledge or reason to suspect that the subordinates were committing violations of the relevant civil law or administrative rules. Senior managers can avoid liability by demonstrating that they have taken in advance preventative measures to protect against omissions or violations of the regulations and have undertaken an organisational plan to diminish the likelihood that subordinates working under their supervision violate the relevant legislative and regulatory provisions. The SM&CR is designed to enhance the accountability of senior managers, board members (including non-executive board members) and those responsible for managing and overseeing the taking of risks within regulated financial firms for the violations of those individuals or groups of individuals who work under their supervision. The SM&CR addressed the need for regulators to work with regulated institutions in developing adequate risk culture standards to support senior management and other employees and professionals working in the financial sector in meeting their ethical responsibilities to customers and complying with regulatory requirements.

Essentially, the SM&CR consists of three pillars: (1) the Senior Managers Regime, (2) the Certification Regime and (3) the Conduct Rules. The key areas that address collective agency problems can be summarised as follows. The SM&CR addresses individuals having high decision-making powers within an institution. Non-executive directors and individuals operating outside the United Kingdom may also fall into this category. Significantly, for institutions under the oversight of the FCA, the new Conduct Rules will cover senior managers, certified persons, directors and other employees. Individuals holding senior management responsibilities will be subject to supervision and pre-approval procedure by the FCA or PRA. To this end, firms will have to understand and pay considerable attention to concepts such as senior management functions, prescribed responsibilities and overall responsibilities (FCA, 2015). In so doing, they are required to set out a 'governance' or 'responsibilities map' indicating names of senior managers, roles and responsibilities, as well as lines of accountability within the firm. In addition, they must ensure that they have adequate procedures to assess the 'fitness' and 'propriety' of senior managers and other staff who might cause harm to the firm or its customers (HM Treasury, 2015: 4) Finally, Conduct Rules are another noteworthy feature of the SM&CR. These are high-level rules applying directly to all staff (with the exclusion of ancillary staff). Firms are expected to incorporate the Conduct Rules in their employment documentation and provide training. Senior managers and other individuals subject to the SM&CR will be accountable to the regulator if they breach Conduct Rules prescribed by the FCA or PRA in relation to their own area of responsibility. Among other things, senior managers hold a statutory duty of responsibility to take 'reasonable steps' to prevent the firm from breaching regulatory requirements within a senior manager's area of responsibility.

As mentioned above, the SM&CR must be explained in the context of a wider debate on bank culture triggered in the aftermath of scandals that ultimately undermined public confidence in the banking sector and in the financial services industry as a whole. Implementing the SM&CR will be unquestionably a major challenge for all the concerned firms. Senior managers will have to show how they take into consideration an effective culture and how this is operationalised within their firm. The SM&CR is considered a significant contribution to improving banking culture and thus increasing individual accountability by attributing liability to senior managers and the board for individual or group failure within the organisation to comply with regulatory rules, with potential personal liability for such violations. Indeed, it is designed to incentivise senior managers to instil a responsibility to do all they can to develop and implement a positive risk culture throughout financial organisations (Bailey, 2016).

## 6.5 THE ROLE OF PROFESSIONAL BODIES

The PCBS's 2013 report also highlighted the importance of creating not only stricter regulatory rules to enhance bank risk culture but also that 'a credible set of professional bodies' can help enhance professional standards and culture in the financial sector (PCBS, 2013b: 136). Within the current regulatory regime, the term 'professional bodies' has a wide meaning. For instance, Baxter and Megone (2016) stress that the term can be generically referred to bodies providing technical and ethical training in the banking sector or, more specifically, to organisations that elaborate behavioural standards with the view to influencing the conduct of professionals working in the banking and financial sectors. The post-crisis reforms paved the way for the set-up of such bodies as the Chartered Banker Professional Standards Board (CB:PSB), the FICC Market Standards Board (FMSB) and the Banking Standards Board (BSB). These contribute to raising standards, professionalism and accountability of individuals in the financial industry.

### 6.5.1  Banking Standards Board (BSB)

The BSB was launched in 2015 as a result of the PCBS's deliberations and reforms and the follow-up recommendations of Sir Richard Lambert's (2014) *Banking Standard Review* in 2014. The BSB aims at promoting adequate standards of behaviour and competence across UK banks and building societies so as to rebuild trust and reputation in the sector (BSB, 2016). In its 2015–16 annual review, the BSB set out its key areas of work for the next years: (1) conducting assessment exercise among member firms on key themes;[13] (2) promoting professionalism across all parts of the banking sector and at all levels; (3) exploring the relationship between law, regulation and ethics and what this means in the specific context of banking and banking

---

[13] These include (a) the alignment of a firm's purpose, values and culture; (b) the difference between a focus on culture and on compliance; (c) leadership and key person risk; (d) incentives and reward structures and practices; and (e) fostering challenge and speaking up for the provision, take-up and effectiveness of staff training and support. See BSB (2016).

culture; and (4) developing voluntary standards that will support a better service for customers and other relevant parties across the sector (BSB, 2016).

### 6.5.2    FICC Markets Standards Board (FMSB)

The FMSB was established in 2015 following the recommendations set out in the FEMR. The FMSB aims at promoting good practice standards for wholesale fixed income, currencies and commodities markets through coordination between domestic and global firms, as well as end users at the most senior level (FMSB, 2017). In November 2016 the FSMB published a draft standard for improving bank transparency so as to guarantee that an investor order is a true representation of their demand.[14] According to the standard, (1) banks' allocation policies should be made available to market participants, 2) issuer preferences in the allocation process should take priority, (3) when a mandate is granted, the lead banks and issuer should agree a document setting out the issuer's aims for the transaction and how the banks will achieve that, including allocation preferences and marketing strategy, (4) banks should disclose to the market their policy on how they select investors for market soundings and investor roadshows, (5) lead banks should agree a strategy on book disclosure frequency with the issuer (book updates should be disclosed publicly and should not be misleading), (6) investors need time to collate their demand for a transaction and (7) investors should put in orders that are a true reflection of their demand and should not be misleading (FMSB, 2017).

More recently the FMSB's Conduct and Ethics Sub-committee has also encouraged the strengthening of surveillance and training in wholesale markets to better address the risk of insider dealing and market manipulation. In December 2016, the FMSB issued guidelines

---

[14] 'This standard is the result of a unique joint effort by corporate users of the market, institutional investors and underwriting banks to bring greater clarity to the process for issuing debt and ensure it works fairly and effectively for all concerned. We believe it is a significant step in raising standards.' Mark Yallop, chair of the FMSB; see FMSB (2016a).

accordingly. With regard to surveillance, the guidelines recommend this function be independent from the front office and the systems be periodically reviewed to adapt to specific types of risks (FMSB, 2016c). As to training, this requires more involvement from senior managers ('who understand the business best') to junior levels. In fact, central to the guidelines is a bigger role for managers who must, among other things, engage in face-to-face discussion of conduct issues with staff.

### 6.5.3 Chartered Bankers: Professional Standards Body (CB:PSB)

The CB:PSB was jointly launched in 2011 by the Chartered Banker Institute and eight UK banks. Its aim is to create a strong culture of ethical and professionalism in the UK banking industry through the development and implementation of sustainable standards. To this end, the most salient initiative is the Chartered Banker Code of Professional Conduct (the Code). This lays down values, attitudes and appropriate behaviours for all professional bankers. Significantly, all CB:PSB member firms are expected to integrate the Code with their own codes of business. The Code conforms to the spirit and letter of the FCA and PRA Individual Conduct Rules. According to the Code, professionalism in banking is evidenced through the following conducts: (1) treating all customers, colleagues and counter-parties with respect and acting with integrity; (2) developing and maintaining their professional knowledge and acting with due skill, care and diligence while considering the risks and implications of their actions and advice and holding themselves accountable for them and their impact; (3) being open and cooperative with the regulators and complying with all current regulatory and legal requirements; (4) paying due regard to the interests of customers and treating them fairly; (5) observing and demonstrating proper standards of market conduct at all times; (6) acting in an honest and trustworthy manner and being alert to and managing potential conflicts of interest; and (7) treating information with appropriate confidentiality and sensitivity (CB:PBS, 2018).

In addition, the CB:PSB has recently published a revised version of its 2012 Foundation Standard, which 'sets out the CB:PSB's expectations of all individuals in relation to the Professional Conduct and Professional Expertise required by such individuals to apply the Code on a day-to-day basis'.[15] Following the PCBS inputs towards a better culture and professionalism in banking, the pathway proposed by the CB:PSB has brought some significant results.[16]

The overall progress of industry bodies in addressing weaknesses in bank risk culture suggests that policymakers should in the first instance rely more on industry initiatives, rather than binding regulatory rules, to enhance risk culture. Nevertheless, the following section suggests that regulatory rules and policy can play a useful role in creating incentives for banking institutions to improve their risk governance and culture. In particular, regulatory standards and guidance may be necessary in certain areas, such as remuneration and trusted financial products, to enhance risk culture in banking institutions, but that ultimately institutions themselves are best placed to channel the collective actions of individuals to improve the governance and operations of banks.

## 6.6   REGULATING BANK CULTURE – WHERE SHOULD THE FOCUS BE?

In considering the role of regulation in bank corporate governance, one should take account of the perception of regulatory safeguards by individuals within organisations and how this might lead to what

---

[15]  See CB:PBS (2016b).

[16]  'Over 500,000 bankers in the UK and globally are now covered by a common code of conduct, the Chartered Banker Code of Professional Conduct (Code). Around 70% of the UK banking workforce is covered by this common Code. In total, 246,000 individuals, 93% of the 'in scope' population, in CB:PSB firms across the UK and globally met the Foundation Standard in 2015.' Ibid.
   '10 Foundation Standard eLearning modules, have been developed and include provision of knowledge on Senior Managers and Certification Regime.
   Benchmarking of the Leadership Standard continues across CB:PSB firms, with the first bankers due to achieve the Leadership Standard in 2016.' See CB:PBS (2016a).

is known as the Peltzman effect, which results in behaviour that counterbalances the intended effect of the regulation. The Peltzman effect holds that assuming a perceived level of risk influences individual behaviour (i.e. risk compensation); the benefit from certain regulation that aims to increase safety may be offset by adjusting behaviour to the perceived decrease in risk by taking greater risks (Peltzman, 1975). This means that regulations that are aimed at reducing certain risks can result in moral hazard that can lead to behaviour that increases those risks.

With this in mind, the regulation of bank culture should emphasise a balancing of the responsibilities between consumers and firms that takes account of the effect that the perception of regulation might have on moral hazard within the firm and with consumers. A specific area that policymakers and regulators have addressed where such a balance can be struck is the regulation of remuneration structures in banks and financial firms. A number of studies have shown that remuneration structures in financial institutions can create morally hazardous behaviour, especially for managers and traders who can be induced by financial and other incentives to engage in risky behaviour that can threaten both the firm's viability as well as create significant social costs. This is because compensation and professional recognition or promotions within the firm are similar to an option contract. The individual in question shares profits (above a certain threshold) with the bank but not the losses brought about by the individual's conduct. In essence, the employment contract is akin to an asymmetrical bet as the downside is limited (getting fired and suffering damage to reputation). In addition, the promotion or earning of a bonus is presumably tied to extraordinary performance, making it worthwhile to take large risks. 'Going for broke' becomes a viable strategy (Dow, 2000: 17–18) On a macro level, banks are incentivised to gamble since the behaviour of competitors leads to a 'breakdown of the social order'. To remain profitable and competitive, banks are 'forced' to engage in risky behaviour, even if the individuals within the firm are opposed to such strategies.

After the financial crisis erupted, the then UK regulator – the Financial Services Authority – introduced a Remuneration Code in 2010 for senior staff at financial institutions. The PRA and FCA are responsible for enforcement of the code in which they 'will be responsible for ensuring that the remuneration policies ... are aligned with effective risk management and that they do not provide incentives for excessive risk-taking' (Bank of England & Financial Services Authority, 2011). Among the Remuneration Code's measures, at least half of variable remuneration should consist of shares rather than cash. The shares awarded in pay packets have to be retained for specified periods. As a result, the balance between cash and securities for bonuses has significantly changed in favour of securities with the deferral periods now extended to around seven years, and there is a greater emphasis on measures of good and bad behaviour being reflected directly in the bonus decision. (House of Commons, 2011).

### 6.6.1   Trusted Consumer Products

Another area where regulators may be able to strike a balance between regulating the responsibilities of regulators and consumers and the public at large is in the development of financial products to be sold to retail consumers. Indeed, it is accepted that complex products combined with a lack of financial literacy is a significant problem in financial markets. Under the Financial Services Act 2012, the FCA is required to have regard to the needs that consumers may have for advice and information from banks that is appropriately presented and provided in a timely, accurate, intelligible way. If the FCA is diligent about this duty, then it should make progress in helping consumers understand the products they are buying.

There is, however, more that could be done. Regulators can mandate that banks create trusted consumer products that would be granted a trusted seal of approval by a trusted products board. A trusted products board that could create a system of identifying and certifying simple, low-cost financial products is an attractive idea. This is not a role that the regulator should take on, but it is something the voluntary sector itself may be well placed to do. The FCA should be prepared to help the voluntary sector in these endeavours by providing information on products and their costs.

More generally, when considering where the regulatory focus should be, one should bear in mind that most banking crises have arisen from management decisions that reflect agency problems that result in weak risk management and a failure to incorporate a clear and sustainable set of standards and norms adhered to within the organisation. Inadequate risk culture can exacerbate existing agency problems in which managers have risk preferences different from other stakeholders, including owners, customers, creditors and the government representing the public at large. Even if managers' incentives are reasonably aligned with other stakeholders, they may have limited competence in assessing the risks involved in its decisions and yet have significant freedom of action because of the absence of internal control systems that are able to resolve agency problems.

## 6.7 CONCLUSION

This chapter considers how the concept of human agency can be used to understand the phenomenon of risk culture in banking and financial institutions. The chapter argues that the traditional understanding of agency problems in the corporate governance literature cannot fully explain the risk management and operational failures of banks during the crisis of 2007–8. The chapter suggests that human agency theory as it applies to the collective efforts of individuals within an organisation can provide a fuller understanding of the agency problems and moral hazard that continue to afflict banking and financial institutions. The chapter reviews international regulatory developments in the area of risk culture and the main legal and regulatory instruments adopted by the British government, including its SM&CR, and how it attempts to address the collective agency problem by imposing individual liability on senior managers and executive board members for violations of regulatory rules by individuals who work under their supervision within regulated institutions. It then considers the various industry-led self-regulatory efforts to improve risk culture within regulated financial institutions. The chapter suggests that there will be tensions and challenges in attempting to regulate risk culture in banking and financial institutions, and the scope of the regulatory mandate will likely remain uncertain. Nevertheless, UK banking and financial sector regulatory initiatives are beginning to change significantly how banks and other financial institutions address their own agency problems that arise from inadequate internal risk culture. It is submitted that the complexities of regulating the collective activities of many individuals regarding cultural standards and norms within large organisations can be more effectively achieved through a balance between official sector regulation and self-regulatory initiatives that build on existing institutional knowledge in the financial sector.

REFERENCES

Ashby, S., Palermo, T. and Power, M., (2014). Risk culture: definitions, change practices and challenge for chief risk officers. In J. Patricia, ed., *Risk Culture and Effective Risk Governance*. London: Riskbooks.

Bailey, A. (2016). Culture in financial services – a regulator's perspective. Speech at the City Week 2016 Conference, 9 May 2016. https://bit.ly/2rb72sZ

Bandura, A. (1986). *Social Foundations of Thought and Action*. Englewood Cliffs, NJ: Prentice–Hall.

Bandura, A. (1997). *Self-Efficacy: The Exercise of Control*. New York: W. H. Freeman.

Bandura, A. (1999). Social cognitive theory of personality. In L. A. Pervin and O. P. John, eds., *Handbook of Personality*. New York: The Guildford Press.

Bandura, A. (2000). Exercise of human agency through collective efficacy. *Current Directions in Psychological Science*, 9(3), 75–8.

Bandura, A. (2006). Toward a psychology of human agency. *Perspectives on Psychological Science*, 1(2), 164–80.

Bandura, A. (2009). Agency. In D. S. Carr, ed., *Encyclopedia of the Life Course and Human Development*. Detroit: Macmillan Reference USA.

Bank of England and Financial Services Authority (2011). *The Bank of England, Prudential Regulation Authority – Our Approach to Banking Supervision*.

Banks, E. (2012). *Risk Culture: A Practical Guide to Building and Strengthening the Fabric of Risk Management*. Basingstoke: Palgrave MacMillan.

Baxter, J. and Megone, C. (2016). *Exploring the Role of Professional Bodies and Professional Qualifications in the UK Banking Sector*. London: Banking Standards Board. https://bit.ly/2puA46B

BCBS (Basel Committee on Banking Supervision) (2009). *Enhancements to the Basel II Framework*. www.bis.org/publ/bcbs157.pdf

BCBS (Basel Committee on Banking Supervision) (2014). *Consultative Document: Corporate Governance Principles for Banks*. www.bis.org/publ/bcbs294.pdf

BSB (Banking Standards Board) (2016). *Annual Review 2015/2016*. https://bit.ly/2NIVhBN

CB:PBS (Chartered Banker Professional Standards Board) (2016a). *CB:PSB Progress Report*. https://bit.ly/32c6sId

CB:PBS (Chartered Banker Professional Standards Board) (2016b). *Foundation Standard Requirements for Professional Bankers*. https://bit.ly/2qjp9fY

CB:PBS (Chartered Banker Professional Standards Board) (2018). *The Chartered Banker Code of Professional Conduct*. https://bit.ly/2Ndp4mW

Dow, J. (2000). What is systemic risk? Moral hazard, initial shocks, and propagation. *Monetary and Economic Studies*, **18**(2), 1–24.

Dunkley, E. (2015). UK draws line under 'banker bashing' after scrapping assessment. *Financial Times*, 2015 December 30. https://on.ft.com/2NGehAL

Emirbayer, M. and Mische, A. (1998). What is agency? *The American Journal of Sociology*, **103**(4), 962–1023.

Ernst & Young (2014). *Shifting Focus: Risk Culture at the Forefront of Banking*. https://go.ey.com/32gtQof

ESRB (European Systemic Risk Board) (2015). *Report on Misconduct Risk in the Banking Sector*. https://bit.ly/2NIXFsf

FCA (Financial Conduct Authority) (2015). *CP15/22 Strengthening Accountability in Banking: Final Rules (including Feedback on CP14/31 and CP15/5) and Consultation on Extending the Certification Regime to Wholesale Market Activities*. www.fca.org.uk/publication/consultation/cp15-22.pdf

FMSB (FICC Markets Standards Board) (2016a). FICC Markets Standards Board proposes greater transparency in new issue process for debt. *FMSB*, 2016 November 18. https://bit.ly/2NhBN8n

FMSB (FICC Markets Standards Board) (2016b). *Statement of Good Practice for FICC Market Participants: Conduct Training*. www.femr-mpp.co.uk/wp-content/uploads/2016/12/16-12-08-SoGP-Conduct-Training_FINAL.pdf

FMSB (FICC Markets Standards Board) (2016c). *Surveillance Core Principles for FICC Market Participants: Statement of Good Practice for Surveillance in Foreign Exchange Markets*. www.femr-mpp.co.uk/wp-content/uploads/2016/12/16-12-08-SoGP_Surveillance-in-FX-Markets_FINAL.pdf

FMSB (FICC Markets Standards Board) (2017). *New Issue Process Standard for the Fixed Income Markets.* https://fmsb.com/wp-content/uploads/2017/04/FMSB_NewIssuesProcess_FIMarkets_2-May-FINAL.pdf

Foreign Exchange Professionals Association (2015). *Focus On: Foreign Exchange Benchmarks.* https://fxpa.org/wp-content/uploads/2015/06/fxpa-benchmarks-5-22final.pdf

FSB (Financial Stability Board) (2014). *Guidance on Supervisory Interaction with Financial Institutions on Risk Culture: A Framework for Assessing Risk Culture.* www.fsb.org/wp-content/uploads/140407.pdf

G30 (Group of Thirty) (2013). *A New Paradigm: Financial Institution Boards and Supervisors.* https://bit.ly/2JOXw5m

G30 (Group of Thirty) (2015). *Banking Conduct and Culture: A Call for Sustained and Comprehensive Reform.* https://bit.ly/2qpKBQh

Hart, O. (1995). *Firms, Contracts, and Financial Structure.* Oxford: Oxford University Press.

House of Commons (2011). Uncorrected transcript of oral evidence, to be published as HC 1447-xii. Oral evidence taken before the Joint Committee on the Draft Financial Services Bill, 8 November 2011. https://bit.ly/2CbrQmn

HM Treasury (2012). *The Wheatley Review of LIBOR: Final Report.* https://bit.ly/2r8S3Qd

HM Treasury (2015). *Senior Managers and Certification Regime: Extension to All FSMA Authorised Persons.* https://bit.ly/2C9kgZw

HM Treasury, Bank of England and FCA (Financial Conduct Authority) (2015). *Fair and Effective Markets Review: Final Report.* https://bit.ly/36yYg8t

Hölmstrom, B. (1979). Moral hazard and observability. *The Bell Journal of Economics,* **10**(1), 74–91.

IIF (Institute of International Finance) (2009). *Reform in the Financial Services Industry: Strengthening Practices for a More Stable System.* Washington, DC: IIF.

Jensen, M. C. (1998). *Foundations of Organizational Strategy.* Cambridge, MA: Harvard University Press.

Jensen, M. C. and Meckling, W. H. (1976). Theory of the firm: managerial behavior, agency costs, and ownership structure. *Journal of Financial Economics,* **3**(4), 305–60.

Jensen, M. C. and Meckling, W. H. (1994). The nature of man. *Journal of Applied Corporate Finance,* **7**(2), 4–19.

Khurana, R. (2002). The curse of the superstar CEO. *Harvard Business Review,* **80**(9), 60–6.

Lambert, R. (2014). *Banking Standards Review.* https://bit.ly/32i7gLG

Malmendier, U. and Geoffrey, T. (2009). Superstar CEOs. *Quarterly Journal of Economics*, **124**(4), 1593–638.

McDermott, T. (2015). Culture in banking. Speech to the British Bankers Association. https://bit.ly/36Af3YE

Nouy, D. (2015). Towards a new age of responsibility in banking and finance: getting the culture and the ethics right. Speech at Goethe Universität, Frankfurt, 23 November 2015. https://bit.ly/2PIcP3A

Ostrom, E. (2008). Tragedy of the commons. In *The New Palgrave Dictionary of Economics*. Basingstoke: Palgrave Macmillan.

PCBS (Parliamentary Commission on Banking Standards) (2013a). *Changing Banking for Good*, vol. 1. https://bit.ly/33hDwjy

PCBS (Parliamentary Commission on Banking Standards) (2013b). *Changing Banking for Good*, vol. 2. https://bit.ly/36xKjaT

Peltzman, S. (1975). The effects of automobile safety regulation. *Journal of Political Economy*, **83**(4), 677–726.

PRA (Prudential Regulation Authority) (2014). *The Use of PRA Powers to Address Serious Failings in the Culture of Firms*. https://bit.ly/36xjEef

Ralph, D. and Tuveson, M. (2015). Is regulation of risk culture the missing piece? Civil actions reconsidered. *Banking and Financial Services Policy Report*, **25**(1), 12–18.

Ross, S. A. (1974). On the economic theory of agency: the principle of similarity. In M. Balch, D. McFadden and S. Wu, eds., *Essays on Economic Behavior under Uncertainty*. Amsterdam: North-Holland.

Sants, W. H. (2010). Do regulators have a role to play in judging culture and ethics? Speech at the Chartered Institute of Securities and Investments Conference, 17 June 2010. www.fsa.gov.uk/pages/Library/Communication/Speeches/2010/0617_hs.shtml

Shleifer, A. and Vishny, R. (1997). A survey of corporate governance. *Journal of Finance*, **52**(2), 737–83.

Tversky, A. and Daniel, K. (1974). Judgment under uncertainty: heuristics and biases. *Science, New Series*, **185**(4157), 1124–31.

Walker, P. (2016). FCA drops banking culture review. *FTAdviser*, 2016 January 4. https://bit.ly/2JOMFZe

# 7 What Does Risk Culture Mean to a Corporation?

## Evidence for Business Value

Andrew Freeman

## 7.1 INTRODUCTION

Given the impressive accumulation of risk-related literature and associated flourishing of professional associations and qualifications, it is easy to lose sight of just how recent has been the rise of formalised risk management as a business discipline. Its penetration beyond financial services remained extremely limited until well into the twenty-first century and arguably remains so today. Terms such as 'risk culture', although normalised of late by constant repetition, are neologisms. The even more recent arrival of 'conduct risk' demonstrates the fluidity of supposedly well-understood ideas. There has been immense creativity at a fast pace as thinkers and practitioners alike have sought to wrestle risk into useful and usable categories and processes. To anyone but a risk evangelical, it should not be controversial to state that the combination of speed and contingency has not always produced clarity. As we will see below, there is plenty of muddle when it comes not just to articulating what is meant by 'risk culture' but more generally in making statements about the practical dimensions of culture-related risk management in any business or organisational environment.

It is vital to recall this context in any discussion of risk culture and its possible influence on corporate value creation. As this chapter will explore, interest in risk culture(s) in business can be characterised as essentially a post-2008 financial crisis effort by practitioners and regulators alike to identify glaring fault lines in the risk management discipline and seek to circumvent or repair some of the most evident gaps. This occurred in the financial services industry rather than across business in general, and, as I will show, we can see only small ripples of influence beyond that technocratic, formalised sector. Other business that had earlier interest in cultural factors (typically where the emphasis was on managing operational risks in order not to kill people through hazardous exposures) were relatively unaffected by the surge of activity around risk culture in finance. Interestingly, there has been precious little public questioning of the utility of the underlying risk management effort, and this is one benchmark suggestive of at least some disciplinary maturity based on operational and intellectual practices. Anyone who attends one of the large commercial risk-themed conferences will have personal experience of just how potent the unification around some central ideas about risk management has become. Iconoclasts are not necessarily welcome.

While it is certainly useful to explain some specifics in the rise of interest in risk culture, my main argument is that it is in the wider context where we should always be looking if we are to assess the impact of 'risk culture' on corporate value creation. 'Risk culture' is essentially an innovation intended to isolate some explanatory variables in financial services. It is already proving to be transient. In the United Kingdom, for example, it has been somewhat superseded by the regulatory notion of 'conduct risk'. At best this is a refinement; more worryingly it might be seen as a further unnecessary step in the evolution of risk management. It is tempting to chase risk concepts ever further down the latest available rabbit hole, but epistemologically and practically we lose sight of the bigger picture at our peril.

Therefore, this chapter offers a two-part discussion. First, I explore the establishment of risk culture as a powerful thematic post-2008. This necessarily begins with a reminder of the main academic lines via which we can trace cultural influences or context(s) for analysis of businesses in general. This is crucial for understanding how and why risk management developed as a technocratic rather than a sociological discipline – some might more optimistically say as a new branch of management science. Although this might appear to be well-trodden ground, I offer some new insights into certain aspects specifically relating to the emergence of risk culture as a topic of interest.[1] In particular, I examine in detail the years 2008–12 covering the main events of the global financial crisis and seek to illuminate the evolution of risk management through the lens of risk culture during this period of recent history.

Second, how therefore should we assess the evidence for risk culture and business value? Will a firm where there is an articulated and 'risk culturally defined' drive for value experience tangible differences from a rival firm where risk culture might be seen as more intrinsic and less value-oriented? Does such a firm even exist? As we will see below, I remain sceptical to claims that go beyond even some quite basic limits.

## 7.2  'ORGANISATIONAL' AND 'RISK' CULTURES

We can date quite precisely the period when interest in risk culture broke out from academic study and became a mainstream topic in business, albeit essentially limited to financial services. Significant academic interest in risk as a cultural phenomenon itself dates only from the 1980s and 1990s, building on earlier work in anthropology and sociology, notably by Mary Douglas during the 1960s.[2]

These early studies and their associated insights had very limited penetration into the world of business. This may have been less because the academics themselves were unaware of the potential

---

[1] For transparency, I was employed by McKinsey & Company from 2006 to 2009 and was either partially responsible for or experienced at first hand some of what I describe below. From 2007, I was active in the global risk practice, including as managing editor of the McKinsey Working Papers on Risk series. I would like to thank former McKinsey colleagues for their insightful comments and encouragement, notably Martin Pergler and Mark Lawrence. Thanks to Cameron Melville. Special thanks to Catherine Tilley for her particularly helpful suggestions following discussion and a careful reading of an early draft and, last but not least, Professor Michael Power of the LSE for his extremely generous suggestions and feedback.

[2] See, for example, the work of Douglas (1966), Douglas and Wildavsky (1982), Beck (1992) and various; for a good summary, see Lupton (1999).

importance for business of their work than, rather, because professional managers carried a set of 'hard' beliefs dominated by accounting and other performance metrics that made them unlikely at that time to seek out and explore 'soft' alternatives related to human behaviours and motivations. Power, Ashby and Palermo (2013) noted that during their 2013 study on risk culture in financial organisations, they found 'very little engagement with academics as risk culture advisors', contrasting this with the relative openness to academic expertise of the airline industry. Douglas and Wildavsky (1982) were certainly well aware of the wider implications of their work but saw these mainly in the sociopolitical rather than the business sphere.

We can go further. Academic and business writers have typically existed in their own silos, with practitioners occupying their own separate spaces. Work in one area that arguably should have made an impact in another often failed to break out from a perceived field. For example, Goffee and Jones's (1996) important and influential work on organisational cultures was classified in terms of 'change' and not 'risk' management. Not only did the authors seem to be largely unaware of or uninterested in risk as a closely related concept, but also early students of risk management did not pick up on the transferability of many of the core ideas stemming from their work – itself evidence that the origins of risk management were essentially quantitative and pseudoscientific. As I will show below, the emphasis within risk as a discipline was to change, but these origins are inescapable.

The idea that an organisation could have a 'corporate culture' susceptible to empirical examination was long influential everywhere except, it seems, in proximity to risk. Some date this alternative cultural history to the 1980s (Power, Ashby & Palermo, 2013: 15–18), when concepts derived from anthropology and sociology began to be applied to corporations (Lo, 2016). Many academics in that period referred back to a seminal 1952 work by Alfred Kroeber and Clyde Kluckhohn (1952) in which they classified definitions of 'culture' made after 1871, noting more than 300 variants, of which 164 were considered sufficiently formal as to be codified. Their own definition is useful for the purposes of this chapter, notably because it includes the idea of 'future action' under conditionality, a textbook risk management concept but one for which the implications are not spelled out because of the linguistic and intellectual context:

> Culture consists of patterns, explicit and implicit, of and for behavior acquired and transmitted by symbols, constituting the distinctive achievements of human groups, including their embodiment in artifacts; the essential core of culture consists of traditional (i.e. historically derived and selected) ideas and especially their attached values; culture systems may, on the one hand, be considered as products of action, on the other, as conditional elements of future action.
>
> *(Kroeber & Kluckhohn, 1952: 181)*

Among the most influential organisational culture researchers was Edgar Schein (1985), who, even in early iterations of his work, explicitly linked culture and leadership in what was taken up as a de facto call to action by chief executives.[3] Schein also stressed the importance of group validation as necessary for the coherence of an organisational culture. Willingness to teach new joiners, he suggested, is one indicator of the strength of group support for a current set of attitudes and behaviours. In order to study an organisation's culture, Schein (2004: 26) suggested, one would need to examine its artefacts, values and assumptions including unspoken assumptions. As an aside, we can usefully characterise a well-formulated risk appetite statement as a 'risk cultural' road map for all three of these elements, suggesting that this is one artefact offering a unique reference point for understanding the relevant organisation. Risk appetite statements have become common, indeed almost compulsory, in financial services but remain relatively rare in other sectors.

---

[3] Thereby potentially contributing to the start of the sharp rise in the ratio of CEO remuneration to that of the average worker.

Influenced by Schein, various leadership cults emerged in management theory, while regular excitement over individual high-flying managers was punctuated by occasional falls from grace or sudden infatuations with rival concepts such as innovation or customer-centricity. It is a reasonable generalisation that from the 1980s onwards, corporations began to be characterised as cultural and operational systems within which groups of individuals performed tasks determined by some sort of shared values or understanding, whether these came mainly from a charismatic leader or a consensus-driven workforce or, more likely, some combination of both. 'Culture' provided numerous ways to elaborate and promote explanations for those systems. Large corporations such as IBM and General Electric typified this approach by publicly embracing distinctive management styles and cultures, including making important contributions to the cult of the CEO.

Academic and practitioner interest in corporate culture grew to the point that the associated literature was susceptible to its own classification by scholars. It is clear in 'pure' organisational culture work that scholars were searching for evidence that culture could offer explanations not just for organisational structures and habits but also outcomes. This proved problematic. Demonstrating that it could be more lucrative to write about business than to practise it, in 1982 Tom Peters and Robert Waterman (1982) published *In Search of Excellence*, thereby entering the ranks of global management gurus alongside Peter Drucker. The eight principles or 'traits' outlined in the book were a mixture of practical and cultural factors. Unfortunately, several supposedly excellent companies profiled by Peter and Waterman imploded within two years of the book's publication, prompting mocking coverage in business journals, if not a decline in sales. But the ideas embedded in this work have proved remarkably resilient and have been much more influential in business than any academic articles or other body of work (with the possible exception of lean manufacturing). In the world of 'business excellence', culture was important but not pre-eminent. This approach to organisations was generally positive, seeking to light the path so that companies (and aspiring individuals) could navigate their way towards world-class performance. The inspiration for risk culture was, as we have seen, much less optimistic in nature.

A decade after Peters and Waterman, George Gordon and Nancy DiTomaso (1992) briefly surveyed the organisational culture/ performance terrain before offering their own findings of (limited and temporary) outperformance by a small sample of US insurance companies. In a thought-provoking article, Andrew Lo (2016) states that 'it is known that some cultural values are positively correlated to better economic outcomes' and cites Gordon and DiTomaso's work, albeit with an important and accurate caveat. In common with other scholars, however, Lo goes on to ignore the caveat and takes for granted that the performance/culture link is a positive one. Gordon and DiTomaso themselves note the relative paucity of hard evidence linking culture and performance before presenting their findings. It is surely relevant that the word 'risk' does not feature in their article. On close inspection, their conclusions are so bounded by strong caveats that in the end they can be accorded only weak status. This is true in general of academic study of this topic. Any methodological weakness stemming from the difficulty of agreeing on a definition of 'risk culture' as described in this chapter has been mirrored and even enlarged at the level of 'culture' overall.

## 7.3   CULTURAL STUDIES

A more recent survey confirmed this, even as it acknowledged that interest in the culture/performance connection had greatly expanded as scholars embarked on studies around the world. Sonja Sackmann (2011) identified 55 relevant academic articles published between 2000 and 2009 before classifying and analysing them. She noted that 'the measurement of organisational culture and performance is still diverse and problematic', adding that, to her surprise, 'most researchers developed their own idiosyncratic way for measuring organisational culture in the specific context of their research projects', meaning that there is little basis for comparison and consolidation of findings (194). A major methodological problem is a plenitude of performance metrics that calls into question the objectivity of the underlying research. Sackmann lists no fewer than 10 individual outcome, 11 financial and an impressive 29 non-financial performance measures across her sample of 55 studies, or almost 1 unique measure per study. A particular piece of research is in effect examining a single facet of a much bigger whole, allowing the rhetorical question as to whether it is 'really culture that was researched or rather parts of something that may be called culture?' (195).

This detail is important because Sackmann (2011) also found that most of the studies she reviewed did indicate at least some direct empirical link between culture and performance – this finding has been amplified in later citations to support the belief that culture is indeed a key determinant of corporate success. Supposedly, academic credibility now vindicates the gut feelings of many actual managers of corporations and other practitioners. This is to the detriment of Sackmann's cautious conclusions and observation that this entire field can be considered to be taking its 'first steps' and to be still at a 'rather superficial level of detail' (219–20). She argues convincingly that no single study will adequately capture all of the facets of organisational complexity – hardly surprising given the rich dynamic that makes up day-to-day organisational reality.

Following Sackmann, I do not wish to conclude that further engagement with linkages between culture, including risk culture, and performance (however defined) is fruitless. Indeed, helpfully, we can quite easily tease out some highly promising areas for future research. Lo (2016: 23) argues convincingly that mainstream economics has largely failed to explore such connections because it has been quite satisfied with its twin stylised sledgehammers – rational expectations and game theory. For economic purists, ideas about culture are 'much too touchy-feely'.[4] However, economic examinations of

---

[4] I include in this the sniffy reception and ongoing scepticism shown towards 'behavioural economics' by the academy.

business cultures have tended to leave out awkward realities. Herma-lin's (2001) synthetic classification of economic models of corporate cultures includes game theoretic as well as agent-based and adaptive evolutionary approaches. None allows adequately for non-stationarity, time variance, uncertainty and so on. Yet each of these factors is determinant for future outcomes as additionally shaped by human decisions and behaviours.

Mark Casson (1991) explicitly linked business culture and eco-nomic performance at macro and micro levels, arguing that the higher the trust between agents and institutions, the greater the positive performance via lowered transaction costs. Crémer (1993) also ana-lyses corporate culture from the perspective of informational transac-tion costs – free flows of information equate to efficiencies and competitive advantage. This is highly relevant for risk management, where access to and the analysis of information can determine whether a risk culture is meaningful (see Chapter 2). Indeed, the idea of information as the ultimate risk commodity, or alternatively as the most potent cultural vector for risk, is extremely compelling.

An important curiosity in thinking on business culture from an economic perspective has been the stark gap between the mainstream and the body of work known as 'administrative science' epitomised by Herbert Simon. In 1945, he published *Administrative Behavior*, introducing the idea of 'bounded rationality' to explain aspects of decision-making in organisations. In 1957, in an introduction to a new edition, he mocks, on the one hand, economists for their 'Thom-istic refinement' of competitive game analysis and decision theory and, on the other hand, alternative sociological explanations based on Freud that 'reduce cognition to affect' and do an injustice to the 'buzzing, blooming confusion that constitutes the real world' (Simon, 1957: xxiii–xxv). In chapter 10, Simon explores ideas of loyalty and organisational identification that are highly relevant for organisa-tional theory and business culture, but, remarkably, his ideas have been largely ignored in the latter field (even though he was honoured later in his career) (198–219).[5] As noted elsewhere, the linguistic gap – Simon did not use the term 'culture', and his terminology has dated dramatically – may have played an important part in limiting interdisciplinary connections, to the detriment of other fields of study, including that of risk management.[6]

Meanwhile, it is important to recall the gradual evolution of risk management as not just an emergent discipline but as an organisational impulse with powerful and essentially uncontrollable ramifications. It is generally accepted that the first chief risk officer (CRO) was appointed only in 1993 (Power, 2005: 132–48). Unsurprisingly, that position was created in a finance business, albeit a subsidiary of General Electric, but one where the main risks were clearly financial in nature. Thereafter, the CRO role quite quickly became more common, first in large banks and investment banks and later in other financial firms, before beginning a much slower period of acceptance in other industries (some of which had surprisingly mature risk cultures but were using a rival risk taxonomy to describe their operations). The organisational consequences of senior managerial posts with explicit risk management responsibilities were to prove as significant as they were accidental or unintentional. Often the role of a newly appointed CRO was to codify and formalise things that had long been done by others as much as it was to create and consolidate new activities. Early CROs were often making things up as they went along, asserting requirements and needs (such as flows of information) that had few precedents. The drive to create risk systems and metrics, with their associated artefacts, would have powerful consequences for how risk management itself would continue to claim legitimacy and

[5] I am extremely grateful to Catherine Tilley for this point.
[6] Michael Power has pointed out to me that a similar case can be made for the work of Philip Selznick (1957), whose major work *Leadership in Administration* was coincidentally published in the same year as Simon's second edition and is full of cultural-type analysis. Fuller tying of these research threads would require its own chapter.

jostle for attention among senior managers and stakeholders. 'Culture' arguably became another disputed area for CRO influence – why was it a risk, as opposed to, for example, a human resources, issue? The enterprise view of the CRO as essentially a technocrat who would legitimately claim organisational space overrode any sense that everyone was responsible for risk – a narrow functional perspective dominated a broader cultural opportunity.

I believe these backgrounds can help us understand why risk culture emerged so strongly as a topic of interest in financial services in or around 2008, before there had been meaningful debate in the same organisational space about the overarching idea of 'culture' itself. The professionalisation of risk managers, epitomised by the CRO figure, created its own epistemological space, a coherent and therefore imposing set of technical frameworks and standards and a willing set of contributors who had powerful motivation to fill out the content. There was similarly strong reason for regulators to follow an appealingly simple logic thread. The financial crisis offered systemic proof that prior incidents of organisational risk management failures had been miscast. In a general sense, in 2008 risk management had indisputably failed, and only then was it clear that post-mortems on past failures had wrongly focused on malign individuals. What was needed, instead, was an explanation that broadened the scope of analysis and showed how entire organisations could have developed the cultural conditions for widespread collapse. Answers would lie in 'risk cultures' rather than in 'cultures' per se. But risk cultures were grounded in the technical/technocratic model that risk management had defined – this would prove a limiting factor both within financial services and beyond.

Today we can see that 'risk culture' has some obvious a priori limitations. Important academic debate and regulatory guidance/ research is reaching back to what might in different circumstances have been the original step, that of mining for insights from organisational 'cultures' before gathering specific nuggets related to risk. And 'risk culture' itself is in interesting ways being sidelined by a new focus on 'conduct risk', made emblematic by the change of name in 2013 of the UK financial regulator from Financial Services Authority to Financial Conduct Authority (FCA).

## 7.4 REMEMBERING THE 'RISK REVOLUTION'

It is crucial to consider the strong influence of the financial services industry in embedding risk as an organising concept with potential to have beneficial effects on organised business activities more generally (Freeman, 1993). We can trace the beginnings of analysis of the impact of formal risk functions to the late 1990s and 2000s. Risk management was seen as naturally a highly technical discipline, dominated by quantification of credit and market risks for banks, while extensions of these activities soon included the management of operational risks that were to be modelled in the same way despite a palpable lack of data (Power, 2007: 103–127). The RAROC system developed at Bankers Trust represented one point on a spectrum that included the daily one-page risk report required by Dennis Weatherstone at JPMorgan, out of which value at risk (VaR) evolved and quickly became a standard way of measuring short-term exposures to some categories of risk despite well-advertised methodological limitations. In the rise of VaR, cultural needs were subsumed because of the need to justify, at an industry level, securities-trading businesses on economic and prudential grounds – in this case, senior bankers, with good grasp of lending risks, wanted a relatively simple summary of potential losses from trading activities they had taken on as Glass–Steagall was first neutered, then repealed. In offering up its ideas as a de facto industry standard, JPMorgan was not motivated by altruism but by necessary guild fervour. Put another way, VaR itself can be viewed as a created cultural artefact that served a collective industrial purpose (that of legitimising the consolidation of banking and brokerage). It is also an excellent example of how practitioners themselves can overlook crucial caveats once cultural tools and techniques become normalised, just as academics tend to pay lip service to significant, even crucial, caveats while extracting apparently solid conclusions from research projects.

Non-financial businesses were slow to adopt risk management approaches derived from finance, presumably because they were sceptical as to the benefits of doing so or thought the relevant disciplines had limited application beyond narrow financial concerns of interest mainly to chief financial officers. Simply put, while 'risk' was clearly a core concept for the business models of most financial firms, this was not the case elsewhere. A few outliers suggested that the application of financial risk management could produce strategic advantages in other business contexts, but these tended to come from data-rich industrial sectors heavily influenced by commodity price factors.[7] More generally, insofar as they considered risk at all, non-financial organisations looked towards organisational practices, influenced by case studies on high-reliability environments such as air traffic control or space engineering. By the late 1990s, academics could point to a powerful conceptual division between risk as a managerial/organisational discipline (often but not exclusively with a focus on safety and zero tolerance operating environments) and an accounting/audit discipline. An organisation's choices or positioning between these two would have profound implications for its operations and perhaps even its success, depending on the relevant metric. However, penetration of risk-informed thinking was limited and rarely included 'soft' concepts such as culture.

Specific interest in cultural aspects of risk management began to form slowly from 2005 onwards. There was a growing perception

---

[7] A good example is a case study of TXU, a US energy firm, featured in Freeman, Buehler and Hulme (2008c). The analysis highlighted risk-informed and finance-theoretical insights into strategic positioning based on superior understanding of industry dynamics. But it failed to pay equal attention to the vital role played by highly self-confident senior managers who embarked on steps that would have been deemed irresponsibly risky in many other organisations. Furthermore, TXU suffered from Peters and Waterman syndrome, in that no sooner had it been extolled than it was sold at a high price to private buyers and then essentially collapsed as its business model unravelled.

that the established financial industry risk management systems (i.e. mainly for credit and market risks and dominated by the accounting/audit end of the spectrum), by then summarised as the principal elements of 'enterprise risk management' (ERM), had potential limitations. They had not yet been implicated in a major economic or financial crisis as such, but there was a feeling that the organisational contexts in which risk functions actually worked were potentially just as important for any observable outcomes. Ironically, 'risk culture' became a topic not purely as a direct consequence of the 2008–12 financial crisis but, as we will see, in parallel with atmospheric hints before then that something was wrong with the formalised risk management approaches that were heavily entrenched, indeed were considered essential by banking and other financial regulators. Storms were brewing.

While I am happy to accept that there is little direct evidence for this claim, plenty of indirect signals point to its essential truth. Large, indeed by then global, banks were struggling with vast staff numbers, dispersed operations and complex IT systems that made it impossible to derive anything as simple as the original JPMorgan daily report. In some cases, bloated organisations had so escaped management control that risk managers themselves were aghast and began to reach for new ways to assert a grip on business lines' autonomy. As bankers realised that incentives were one way (perhaps the only way, given their industry) they could understand how their colleagues might actually conduct their risk-taking, they became aware that within their organisations were fiefdoms, or distinct groups of actors, tied together by behaviours agreed amongst themselves that might in fact be at odds with larger organisational objectives, including strategic ones.[8] This initial interest framed the issue as one of 'risk culture'. It started in

---

[8] The use of incentives in efforts to create or implement risk cultures in banking is highly suggestive that the industrial context trumped any perceived need to look more broadly for organisational solutions. In other words, bankers could have chosen alternative cultural tools but were predisposed to focus on the one economic motive that dominated their thinking as well as collective and individual behaviours.

financial services before taking on wider significance. Even within the same organisation, multiple risk departments could have utterly different cultures depending on where they sat, such that some CROs were unable to create coherent overarching functions from their central or group positions. One global bank had no fewer than 20 distinct risk teams when a new CRO arrived after the 2008 crisis; other banks certainly had more around the same time.

In fact, the reality of enterprise-level thinking on risk management in financial services in the period 1990–2005 was never monolithic. On the one hand, in front-line trading and lending activities, themselves heavily reliant on financial engineering using more or less complex derivatives to manage portfolio exposures, risk was seen mainly as 'opportunity' but was crucially restrained by capital charges and an emergent culture of compliance/risk policing (Cowell & Levins, 2016). The risk-taking impulses of leverage-loving banks were to be reined in by thick volumes of rules that sought to cap overall levels of risk for institutions and limit individual agency. Awareness of systemic risk remained nascent. Regulatory arbitrage ran amok.

On the other hand, risks associated with operations, i.e. with the actual day-to-day running of a business, including preparations for disruption, were seen as much more naturally aligned with compliance and control functions – here risk was viewed less as opportunity than as a related series of direct costs to business, albeit costs that were intriguingly difficult to measure. It is true that during the same period after 1995, accelerating from 2000 onwards, something called 'operational risk' was painstakingly elaborated and somewhat painfully bolted on to banking capital allocation-based approaches amidst widespread willingness to maintain methodological purity while looking past fundamental differences between risk categories.[9] But this was a fudge by all concerned from the beginning. It tended to obscure the

---

[9] In this period, leading banks were experimenting with capital modelling approaches, including scenario and operational loss attributions. It is perhaps natural that their preferred approaches shared core features with those already well established for credit and market risks.

operating reality within large financial firms, where the compliance and control model of risk management was always viewed as a necessary evil – necessary because essentially imposed by regulators and other nervous stakeholders, evil because the revenue-producing parts of a business saw the associated costs as value-eroding dead weight. This has had important ramifications for how risk culture, and more recently conduct risk, came to be promoted and debated.

Early interest in 'risk culture' began around 2000, fitfully to coincide with post-mortem analysis of occasional corporate collapses/catastrophes (Enron, Parmalat, LTCM, UBS, Barings, etc). Each case enjoyed a brief period of widespread coverage by the media. Typically, the focus was on the specifics of the firm's culture, the propensities for risk taking and the extent to which the environment allowed for the 'normalization of deviance' (Vaughan, 1996). A key episode was a trading scandal at National Australia Bank, when announced losses of A$360 million led to an inquiry by the Australian prudential authority and an internal bank inquiry (PwC, 2004). The regulator's report, made public in March 2004, found that 'cultural issues are at the heart' of the bank's failings, noting among warning signs that aggressive traders had effectively 'warned off' the internal audit function and that risk management controls had been viewed internally as 'tripwires' to be negotiated (Australian Prudential Regulatory Authority, 2004: 6 *passim*).

Interest in 'rogue traders' at banks led to other firms asking whether they could suffer a fraud or were vulnerable to a terrible episode with financial and reputational consequences. The frequency of rogue traders set one frame for thinking about how it might be possible to identify those amoral or psychopathic individuals with the propensity to do wrong – the 'bad apples' syndrome.[10] But there was also some, albeit limited, awareness of the need to understand

---

[10] See interesting and provocative work by Timothy Lupfer (2009), who was early to realise that neuroscience could be implicated in efforts to understand and potentially treat deviant behaviours.

broader cultural systems that might make an organisation vulnerable in a general way. Could a business be successful if it had a toxic culture? Or was there a causal relationship between good cultures and business success? These questions became more systematic with the increasing visibility of strains in the financial system that were in fact harbingers of a disaster that would fully explode in the second half of 2008 and then continue to unfold over the coming years. However, there was no widespread adoption of the term 'risk culture'. It is only with hindsight that we can see these early signs of interest for what they were.[11]

## 7.5    RISK IN CRISIS MODE, 2008–12

In this section, I explore in some detail the flowering of risk culture in the context of the global financial crisis that began in 2007 before running wild in 2008 and beyond. I do not wish to suggest that this somehow forms a discrete or bounded period, for inevitably its origins lay in the rumblings I referred to above, and the topic certainly carried on so that it remains somewhat alive today. However, interest in risk culture dramatically intensified during 2008, stimulated by the fast-emerging financial crisis (Power, Ashby & Palermo, 2013), and then demonstrably dropped off a few years later. We can see both the utility of the related ideas and debates, as well as their limitations, by examining specific events and documents. Harder, but important, is to recall that the financial crisis was an immensely dangerous, destabilising and unsettling process, somewhat like being in a car driving at night on an unlit road and finding that the headlights suddenly switch off. Actors could not see where they were going and felt they could no longer anticipate the next bend because they had been plunged into

---

[11] Mark Lawrence has pointed out to me that a few informal networks of senior bank executives, including a CRO invitees-only group sponsored by the IFCI Foundation's International Financial Risk Institute (ICFI Risk Institute, 2004), were important channels for discussions among professionals at this time and that the NAB case was one trigger for shared acknowledgement of a need for greater awareness of cultural factors. More study is needed in this area.

total darkness. That sense of an imminent, potentially fatal, crash pervaded the social and cultural space in which 'risk culture' appeared as an interrogative domain. Any reference below to a dry industry report, for example, is unlikely even fractionally to convey this atmosphere, but this context is essential if we are to grasp the subject.

In this crisis phase, risk culture was promoted in a governance/ organisational context in which risk management could be done well or badly. Actors reached for this new dimension of risk in search of explanations for the disasters unfolding before them. It did not seem plausible to assign blame to credit risk management in isolation, while some banks and asset managers were clearly in much worse shape than others despite having very similar business models. Introducing the idea of 'risk culture' moved analysis of the crisis to a comfort level by effectively screening the financial system as a whole – what caught attention was the projection of plausible explanatory factors that worked for a troubled single institution even though it was clearly part of bigger sectoral groups. Now it was possible to imagine two essentially identical sets of financial obligations, where one organisational owner would be bankrupt and the other, with a stronger 'risk culture', resilient. What were the attributes of a strong risk culture? Was it sufficient to remove an autocratic bullying chief executive who had run his bank as a personal fiefdom, or would that bank's culture have been so deeply infected as to demand more fundamental changes?

The mundane consequences that could flow from a particular risk culture – that an organisation might therefore do better or worse – were rarely spelled out with any precision and were even less often justified with empirical evidence. Indeed, perhaps no such evidence was called for. The sharp rise of interest in risk culture occurred against a catastrophic pandemic-like background in which institutions were bankrupted by their own risk management errors, implicating public finances when bailouts or rescues were deemed essential to the functioning of the financial system as a whole. Hence, perhaps, the initial view was that sick risk cultures could be 'diagnosed' and potentially cured by the right combination of searching questions and expert prescription, including the intervention of organisational experts who could shove or nudge behaviours, often using compensation as the heavy medicine of choice. At the bottom of organisations, this approach was concerned with individuals and their incentives/behaviours. At the top, it developed the notion of managing risk at the enterprise level (the 'ERM debate'). But the central embedded claim was clear – fix or improve risk cultures within a few bad institutions, and there would be marked/measurable improvements in important areas such as financial stability, earnings volatility, perhaps even crimes such as fraud and mis-selling of financial products, notably mortgages. Risk culture mattered, and it was not the time to split hairs as to why or how much. Even well-run institutions could benefit from an explicit engagement with the same ideas.

Responding to pressures felt by clients, leading consulting firms began to examine ideas of risk culture more systematically. In parallel, financial services trade associations, including the Institute of International Finance (IIF), initiated working groups to analyse the causes of the financial crisis and present pre-emptive countermeasures that could be offered up by leading financial firms. It is easy to be cynical about such efforts but arguably more helpful to examine with hindsight what resulted from the application of significant resources and practitioner expertise. There was a welcome refusal to suggest that simply firing a malign corporate leader could adequately address institutional malaise. Despite the well-publicised and rather popular defenestrations of several such bank bosses, this was necessary but not sufficient. Boards and chief executives could set a 'tone at the top', but they could not dictate everything that happened further down their organisations. Sensible inquiry therefore should extend into the nether regions of suspect organisations. Nevertheless, it is worth pointing out that risk culture acquired momentum at precisely the time when the simplest alternative stabiliser of global banking and finance – much higher levels of core capital in the banking system – was stubbornly resisted by the industry (and given only tepid support by some regulators, who also keenly embraced risk culture). Culture provided a persuasive way of generalising the causes of the crisis and helping key parties to construct new ways of intervening whilst avoiding other potential remedies that were viewed as far less palatable.[12]

## 7.6 OUTSIDERS LOOKING IN

An important nexus was that between McKinsey & Company and the IIF. McKinsey had founded a global risk practice in 2006–7 following extensive internal study of the market opportunity for consulting work. A central idea of its advocates was that risk management using corporate financial and other 'engineering' tools had the potential to change businesses of all kinds, so that, to the extent finance was in the vanguard, some of its ideas and experiences could usefully be harnessed in other sectors. Coincident with the financial crisis, McKinsey began to publish a series of working papers that laid out an intellectual framework for risk as an organising concept in business and finance. Risk management had to be helped to show its potential in industries other than finance, so it was no surprise that two of the senior McKinsey directors who pushed the risk practice ahead had strong backgrounds as consultants to the energy sector. Close collaboration across industry lines was almost a precondition for success of the risk practice, something that would test McKinsey's own culture.

In mid-2006 McKinsey hired Mark Lawrence, a former CRO of ANZ Group, as a partner in the risk practice. Always something of an outsider (he left the firm in October 2008), he nevertheless played a key role in furthering the emergence of 'risk culture' as a topic of interest within McKinsey and as a broader public concern and rallying concept for the financial industry. Lawrence had previously been active on IIF working groups, and he found himself uniquely

---

[12] As well as much higher capital requirements, possible options included a return of the Glass–Steagall division between commercial and investment banking via which large banking groups would have been broken up.

positioned as the crisis unfolded. Several McKinsey colleagues took up influential roles on IIF projects in 2008–9 thanks to his involvement.[13]

With regards to risk culture, they could do so with some credibility because in early 2008 the risk practice had begun to conduct research on risk culture (in which I had an instrumental role). This gained momentum as anecdotal evidence accreted from clients trying to articulate that something had gone badly wrong and that it seemed to have something to do with how they were organised and how their staff behaved because of, or despite, management instructions. Was there a way to analyse systematically these different cultural anecdotes? What, indeed, was culture anyway, and what was its relationship to 'risk'? At some point, risk and culture were mentioned in the same breath and a new field effectively brought into existence. Where a head of HR might ask rhetorically, 'What is our culture?', a CRO instead asked, 'Is our culture a source of risk?' and 'What is our risk culture?', and answers flowed quite liberally.

From the beginning of dedicated risk work at McKinsey, there was an awareness that cultural factors could act as grit in the otherwise smooth gears of carefully calibrated 'risk-return management' strategies. Take, for example, this commentary (emphasis added):

> In an ideal world, all business managers or decision makers would analyze the impact of a proposed project or investment on the overall level of the company's risk and make precise trade-offs that would help the company maintain optimal risk exposure. In the real world, this is true only in *companies that have a strong risk culture that informs how managers at all levels make decisions.* This includes incentive systems that encourage individuals to value the whole enterprise rather than personal fiefdoms and to

---

[13] This is not to imply that McKinsey had some sort of special access to the IIF. In fact, Oliver Wyman and EY both carried out significant work for the reports referred to in this chapter but in other work streams, and this was openly acknowledged.

make decisions with an eye to long-term economic outcomes
rather than short-term performance.

*(Freeman, Buehler & Hulme, 2008b: 32)*[14]

The same paper went on to note some common failings in risk culture, contrasting, for example, the short-term risk-based approach
taken in a trading operation versus the need for board members to
take a risk-informed view of strategy whilst often isolated from the
necessary dialogue with much better informed senior managers. If risk
management is often essentially a cost to business, then a sensible
organisation will seek a sound cost–benefit trade-off once it under-
stands where risk is delivering, or might deliver, a benefit that can be
measured or made tangible in some way. Note that finance jargon
has entered the field, bringing in concepts of risk-adjusted returns
from investment management, 'value added' from the shareholder/
stakeholder debate and so on. Culture sits in the background as a
potential inhibitor.

These comments had not appeared by accident. Overarching
ideas that supported the risk consultants were regularly seeded with
new insights fed back directly from clients. Because leading global
banks figured prominently among these, questions and concerns
about culture became obviously relevant and more pressing as
months went by and the financial crisis deepened.

During the first half of 2008, Lawrence was looking for input
to support the IIF's Committee on Market Best Practices, set up in
October 2007 in response to the first phase of the financial crisis (Bear
Stearns had been bought by JPMorgan in March 2008). An interim
report was produced by the IIF in April 2008 (IIF, 2008b), followed by a
full report in July (IIF, 2008a). It is important to note that during this
period there was widespread confusion as to what was going on and

---

[14] This paper was simultaneously published as a pair of articles in *Harvard Business
Review*, appearing in slightly amended form. The core ideas had been circulated and
refined within the risk practice since 2005–6 and had been embryonic well before
then (Freeman, Buehler & Hulme, 2008a, 2008c).

how it should be interpreted. Lawrence suggests that the realisation that culture was a major factor was 'rather stumbled upon' and was significantly challenging for CROs, who came predominantly from quantitative backgrounds.[15] Analysis for the IIF reports was conducted and written under extreme pressure of time and circumstances. Regulators such as the New York Federal Reserve Bank seized upon some of the materials, e.g. asking major banks to conduct a gap analysis of their risk management capabilities in light of IIF recommendations in the July 2008 report.[16] Lehman Brothers failed in September 2008, followed by the collapse of the Icelandic and bailout of the UK banking systems in October.

A measure of Lawrence's growing influence is that where he was originally included in the list of main committee members in the April report, by July his name appeared in four of five dedicated working groups – no other individual was so widely involved. Moreover, he was included in a new group set up in December 2008, a so-called steering committee on implementation, which was charged with continuing the IIF's crisis work.[17] It was in this context that the risk culture connection with McKinsey was to solidify.

When the steering committee's report was eventually published in December 2009, it acknowledged that despite mention of risk culture in earlier reports, the concept had not been further explained or explored (IIF, 2009). Indeed, the July 2008 report had included only the following two statements, a 'principle of conduct' and a 'recommendation':

---

[15] Interview with author, September 2018.

[16] Id. It was in part because the banks reported back to the Fed that they needed more guidance that there was pressure for the second IIF report in December to contain much more material, including a clear definition of risk culture.

[17] The history of this aspect of the crisis has yet to be written. An important actor was Charles Dallara, IIF managing director, who was early to spot in 2007 that something appeared to be badly wrong with risk management and commissioned the various IIF working groups and consequently sat at the centre of the broader industry response to the crisis.

**Principle 1:** A robust and pervasive risk culture throughout the firm is essential. This risk culture should be embedded in the way the firm operates and cover all areas and activities, with particular care not to limit risk management to specific business areas or to restrict its mandate only to internal control.

**Recommendation I.3:** Risk management should be a priority for the whole firm and not be focused only on particular business areas or made a purely quantitative oversight process or an audit/control function. Mutually reinforcing roles within each organisation are essential to creating a strong, pervasive risk culture. (IIF, 2008b)

Now, however, the IIF said that risk culture would be 'essential to the efficacy of any future risk management recommendations' (IIF, 2009: 31). During the first half of 2009, McKinsey was pursuing its work to the point that it could give a credible definition of risk culture and a coherent explanation of how this had been derived and how the concept could be made actionable in real organisations by a combination of survey data and diagnostic analysis.[18] Much of the internal working material eventually found its way directly or in modified form into the IIF report. Ironically, it thereby became public in this way before McKinsey itself had published any of its work – a working paper eventually appeared in February 2010 (Lamarre, Levy & Twining, 2010). The box below gives a short extract from the main text of the IIF report, but much more detail can be found in appendix III, which devotes 12 pages to the topic. The overlap in terms of ideas and material with the working paper eventually made available by McKinsey is clear (Lamarre, Levy & Twining, 2010).[19]

---

[18] The definition was 'the norms of behaviour for individuals and groups within an organisation that determine the collective ability to identify and understand, openly discuss and act on the organisation's current and future risks'.

[19] As is the depth of the interrelationships I am mentioning. Much of the risk management work in the IIF report, including four detailed appendices (respectively 'Risk Appetite', 'Risk Culture', 'Risk Models and Statistical Measures of Risk' and 'Risk Management across Economic Cycles'), was delegated to a Working Group on Risk Management (of which I was a member, by then in a post-McKinsey role at Deloitte). Mark Lawrence was co-chair of that working group, which also included

---

**Extract from the IIF Report on Reform in the Financial Services Industry**

**New Recommendation A:** Risk culture can be defined as the norms and traditions of behaviour of individuals and of groups within an organisation that determine the way in which they identify, understand, discuss, and act on the risks the organisation confronts and the risks it takes.

**New Recommendation B:** Management should take an active interest in the quality of the firm's risk culture. Risk culture should be actively tested and objectively challenged in a spirit of fostering greater resilience and encouraging continuous improvement, reflecting the strategic aims of the organisation.

**New Recommendation C:** Firms should ensure that relevant personnel have their formal responsibilities for risk clearly elaborated in their job descriptions and be evaluated for their fulfilment of these responsibilities as part of firms' periodic performance reviews.

**New Recommendation D:** Any material merger or acquisition should be the occasion of a serious analysis of the risk culture in the new organisation; the opportunity to take action to correct problems and foster a positive risk culture should not be overlooked. (IIF, 2009: 32)

---

A further piece of evidence for how a few dominant ideas about risk culture were codified and then embedded in important financial industry post-crisis responses is a consultative document issued in November 2013 by the Financial Stability Board (FSB, 2013), established by the G20 in 2009 and affiliated to the Bank for International Settlements. The paper offered *Guidance on Supervisory Interaction*

two members of McKinsey's risk practice and a then PwC director who was soon to join McKinsey's risk practice (see appendix VIII). These materials were widely disseminated in the banking industry and related policy circles. Lawrence makes the important point that the IIF working group materials went through multiple iterations and received input from many different sources before being finalised.

*with Financial Institutions on Risk Culture*, in the context of earlier work on systemically important institutions, citing numerous round tables and bilateral discussions. Acknowledgements include gratitude to the IIF and McKinsey & Company, while the authors make a slip when they cite in a footnote a definition of risk culture, referencing the 2009 IIF report but then inadvertently giving the definition first spelled out in the McKinsey 2010 risk working paper mentioned above. The reference had been corrected by the time the consultative document was finalised in April 2014 as a *Framework for Assessing Risk Culture* (FSB, 2014). This might seem like a trivial point, but I argue it is highly revealing as to the closeness of the links between these and other implicated institutions at a crucial time for regulatory responses to the crisis. These responses would have a direct impact on the prospects and performance of leading global financial institutions.

In terms of content, the McKinsey risk culture work produced a summary diagnostic framework (see Figure 7.1). It helpfully allowed

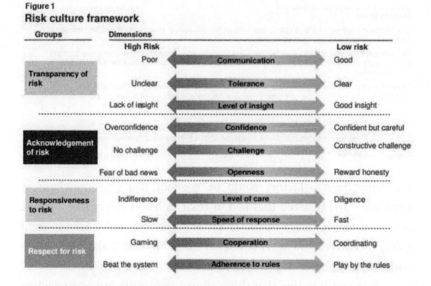

FIGURE 7.1 McKinsey risk culture framework.
Figure from Lamarre, Levy and Twining (2010). Copyright © 2018 McKinsey & Company. All rights reserved. Reprinted by permission

**Established processes and controls**

Business processes are effectively controlled and controls keep pace with change and complexity in the business.

**Identify and assess risk**

There are clear processes to identify and assess risk. There is a clear framework with which risks are evaluated and controls are managed.

**Integrity and ethical values**

Behaviours in practice reflect espoused values and ethics, and these are actively reinforced by management.

**Communicate mission and objectives**

Strategy is clearly defined and communicated. Staff understand how their objectives link to the business unit and the organisation's strategy.

**Commitment to competence**

Staff are appropriately qualified, skilled and experienced to effectively perform their role. There is a focus on continuous improvement.

**Information and communication**

Communication and symbols reinforce the organisation's values, ethics and behavioural expectations. "Zero tolerance" behaviours are understood. Communication between functions is effective.

**Assignment of authority and responsibility**

Roles and accountabilities are clearly defined and communicated to all staff. Staff are clear about what decisions they can make and what they need to escalate.

**Human resource policies and practices, and performance measurement**

Leaders and staff have clear performance expectations and targets. Leaders effectively supervise and coach staff and appropriate behaviour is reinforced.

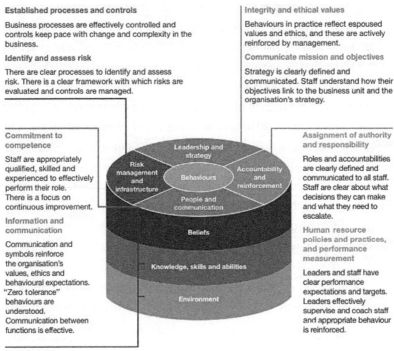

**Maturity levels**

**Environment** Organisations have appropriate support infrastructure in place such as policies, processes and systems that guide how to respond to risks.

**Knowledge, skills and abilities** People have a comprehensive understanding of what risk management policies and procedures mean to them. They can accurately identify risks and have the skill and ability to respond to risks.

**Beliefs** People value and truly believe in risk management and have internalised knowledge, processes and practices so that doing the right thing in terms of risk management is part of how they naturally operate.

FIGURE 7.2  PwC risk culture framework.
Figure from PwC (2015). Copyright © 2015 PricewaterhouseCoopers.

for oppositions – factors could be good or bad or somewhere in between – and insisted that bad or toxic cultures rarely had a single issue but would likely be the result of several related weaknesses in rules, incentives and accepted behaviours. Figure 7.2 shows an alternative approach developed around the same time by PwC.

It is worth noting that these efforts were quite innovative when they appeared and did an effective job of capturing most of the relevant beliefs and behaviours. Later risk culture frameworks have added little while becoming ubiquitous. We can see that practitioners (as opposed to academics) were trying to integrate the technocratic and social/organisational views of risk. Although there was perhaps not an explicit connection made at the time, the balanced scorecard and similar systematic management tools were in vogue at many organisations, including non-financial ones, around this period. The McKinsey framework emphasised behaviours, while PwC used a general culture framework into which it added risk where there were the most obvious spaces. Both frameworks work just as well in the later context of 'conduct risk', and both were sincere efforts to see risk as more than a purely technocratic discipline, albeit using quite different approaches.

Lawrence remained active after leaving McKinsey, particularly in Asia and Latin America, where he consulted widely and was engaged by central bank supervisors to help build their awareness of risk, with a focus on risk appetite, to which risk culture was somewhat secondary (APEC, 2013). In a wide-ranging interview from 2015, he noted that risk culture was 'like the crucial, largely hidden, software that makes risk management processes really work efficiently'. Tellingly, he suggested that if senior managers and directors who want to ensure that their risk management processes and systems are contributing to effective risk management are asked whether they know that their culture is supporting that central objective, often 'they don't know the answer and they don't know how to know' (Cowell & Levins, 2016: 152).

## 7.7  PERFORMANCE ARTS: RISK, CULTURES AND ORGANISATIONS

Power, Ashby, and Palermo's (2013, p. 4) study of risk culture in financial organisations notes that the authors' academic preconceptions included that 'risk culture is a way of framing issues of risk and culture in organisations and not a separate object'. Nor is it a static thing but a 'continuous process, or processes', some formal and easy to observe, others informal and visible only in 'small behaviors and habits'. These insights remind us that the growing volume of material on 'risk culture' has always itself been a subset of content not just on organisational culture but also on the schism in risk work between 'risk as compliance' and risk 'as business partner' concepts (Power, 2016).

In the rest of this chapter, I address more fully the linkages between risk culture and corporate performance, beginning with my observation above that, while financial services jumped directly to 'risk culture' before the more logical starting point of 'culture', this was not the case elsewhere. A consequence is that financial services as an industry might have a distinct approach to the cultural dimensions of organisational makeup. In simple terms, we can consider culture at societal level, beneath which are identifiable corporate cultures, within which there are typically subcultures of which 'risk culture' may be one element, crucially with a transversal characteristic that makes it potentially different in important ways from, say, a functional team subculture. In a large corporation, an individual could in practice belong to several subcultures or minority cultures and thereby be exposed to distinct but overlapping influences.

By extension, there may even be distinct sub–risk cultures, particularly in an organisation where risk is a measured commodity in some way. One only has to think, for example, of the large investment banks in which sometimes small specialised units for tax arbitrage, corporate recovery or complex trading strategies had (often rampantly toxic) cultures that were starkly at variance with those prevailing in other units or the remainder of the organisation. There are self-evidently rich connections both between these institutional strata and across the myriad populations that make up observable sets of organisations. By thinking about 'layers' and their interconnections inside and outside a particular organisation, we might gain insight into events where small subcultural groups exhibit behaviours across an industry – the toxic case of LIBOR fixing where electronic message boards allowed specialised traders to collude among themselves outside their corporate office walls, for example.

This leads to an important observation. If risk management is viewed as an essentially technocratic function done by specialists, with more or less defined scope in an organisation, then it is by definition itself something of a minority culture. This could explain why in many firms CROs have had difficulty in gaining acceptance for their frameworks or systems either in their pure technocratic forms or in softer forms where there is perhaps awareness on the part of the risk specialists of cultural resistance. Risk functions play a particular role thanks to the nature of their assumed purposes. I mentioned above the appointment of the first CRO. The presence of such an officer is always something of a forcing device for a corporate culture but with so many potential dimensions that it is small wonder we seek to reduce them to manageable proportions. The impact of a CRO appointed internally from a position of influence versus that of an outsider coming in to a new post, for example, is certain to be utterly different. Equally, an outsider might arrive to take on a well-established risk management system or be tasked with introducing something *de novo*, either explicitly rejecting a previous approach or simply starting from a blank sheet of paper. Governance arrangements are critical, but even when these are considered *ex ante*, there are numerous pitfalls awaiting an apparently sensible set of choices.

In the post-crisis period, a global financial firm, for example, brought in to its ranks a new CRO who reported directly to the chief operating officer and thence to a small group of senior executives who had founded and run the firm for decades.[20] To all appearances, the governance and reporting arrangements were impeccable. The firm believed that it already had a strong risk culture but wanted to improve its formal risk management systems. The mission for the CRO was to create a centralised risk function that would oversee all aspects of the firm's risk-taking. She was given resources (including the right to make additional external hires) and encouragement that

---

[20] For obvious reasons I have anonymised this material in order to maintain confidentiality of the real persons involved.

was clearly signalled across the firm. But after less than three years, the role was ended by mutual consent.

Several errors had become obvious. Although the CRO had a strong external track record and reputation, this had been built in a different area of financial services – skills did not map well to the 'industrial' problem to be solved. Further, she failed to grasp how the internal politics of the firm worked and therefore did not manage effectively the task of centralising the risk function. Certain departments were uncooperative, some passively, others more actively resisting and exploiting the CRO's lack of previous experience in the specific activities of the firm. Good IT delivery was a *sine qua non* for success, but some IT professionals, used to strong decision rights in their support of front-line operational teams, effectively undermined the central risk function's establishment. An additional and important factor was that shifting regulatory requirements created uncertainty around the disposition of risk and compliance functions, opening up contested space that distracted from the core mission. The firm has since abandoned a centralised function and has not appointed a replacement CRO.

Although it does not seem at all shameful, this episode has never been publicly acknowledged, presumably because it is deemed a failure that would be unacceptable to stakeholders who are impatient of anything other than success. It could, in fact, just as well be argued that senior management gained valuable insights into the cultural realities within the firm, which has functioned quite well by reverting to its original risk and operating structures. Nevertheless, many millions of pounds were committed before these lessons were learned. The complexity of any related cost–value claims speaks for itself.

The cultural specificity of this firm is obvious and telling. But the same is true, for example, of institutions that were created by several governments as responses to the financial crisis, either in the form of bailout institutions or as stimulus vehicles. In the case of one such UK organisation, risk 'best practices' were adopted in an explicit attempt to foster a risk culture, including an empowered CRO supported by strong and generically crafted risk policies. After only a few years, the institution was sold by the UK government, and its governance arrangements were dismantled by the new owner, so this experiment in the creation of a risk culture was thereby terminated. We have no way of knowing what may or may not have helped to create 'value'.

Here we can connect the study of organisational culture directly back to 'risk culture' as it has played out in financial services. In parallel with the McKinsey/IIF work described above, there was an important – because radical – effort begun by the Dutch National Bank (DNB) as its own response to the financial crisis. In its original position paper published in November 2009 (i.e. roughly at the same time as the IIF and McKinsey reports), the bank argued that it was important to include 'ethical behavior and culture in supervision (of banks)' (De Nederlandsche Bank, 2009). Given the high level of awareness among central bankers of the IIF/FSB work, it is interesting that the DNB made no reference to 'risk culture' as such. Instead, in 2011 it created a department of governance, culture and organisational behaviour and embarked on a series of research projects to explore how it might improve the stability of banking not just by raising capital levels but also by understanding bank cultures and how these might be shaped and improved. Importantly it cited a legal motive related to the duty of a bank supervisory authority to protect the public interest via its supervision of banks. It also emphasised psychology over accounting.

The DNB's approach is now admired and to some extent copied elsewhere. In the United Kingdom, the FCA has not only placed the concept of 'conduct' at the heart of its own supervisory regime but is also sponsoring ongoing work on what this means for the cultures of financial institutions. A recent discussion paper included a wide range of contributions on *Transforming Culture in Financial Services* (Financial Conduct Authority, 2018). Many of the 28 contributors noted and analysed the importance of regulating firms with retail customers – I have deliberately not addressed this in detail here, but it is important to note that this is a topic with its own rich literature.[21]

The DNB contributed an update on its culture research (Financial Conduct Authority, 2018: 53–6), stating conventionally that organisational culture is not a monolithic but rather a multifaceted construct, is not static and does not exist in isolation but is the result of responses to time-determined environmental influences. If we accept that culture is evolutionary, then this has 'implications for the manner in which bank supervisors can, or perhaps even should, supervise culture'. We can note that is consistent with the *ex ante* and *ex post* approaches set out by Power, Ashby and Palermo (2013) in their study of risk culture.

Two aspects of the DNB's work are noteworthy. First, it assumes that there is good academic justification for asserting a link between culture and performance. Indeed, it strongly states this case (De Nederlandsche Bank, 2009: 53 (citing Sackmann without the caveats)) in terms of organisational culture and human behaviour being 'crucial for a company's *sustained success*' (53 (my emphasis)). Second, it sets out the main components of its supervisory/cultural approach:

- In the context of board effectiveness, it focuses on behaviours with respect to leadership, decision-making and communication.
- In the context of change effectiveness and culture change, it focuses on whether certain group behaviours contribute to or impede organisational transformations, eg relating to the firm's business model, performance or culture.

---

[21] In an important article, Ring, Bryce, McKinney and Webb (2016) set out in detail the different ways the UK regulator has engaged with risk and organisational culture since the mid-2000s, their key point being that by focusing on retail customers, the FCA was culturally aware much earlier than other national regulators. I find this debatable, not least because at critical moments the authors rely on eliding culture and risk culture in order to make their argument.

- In the context of risk culture, it focuses on how particular groups handle the trade-offs in decision making with respect to risk and reward.
- In the context of risk culture, it focuses on whether group behavioural patterns and their cultural drivers increase the risks for unethical conduct.

*(Financial Conduct Authority, 2018: 54–5)*

This is useful from several perspectives. Notably, it puts risk culture into precisely the context I suggested above, as subordinate to broader categories. In addition, it uses informal language such as 'trade-offs' to describe complex topics that are susceptible for more formal economic analysis. It leaves rather vague the element of time, given that typical organisational change programs take years to effect and more years to assess for effectiveness.

## 7.8 THEORETICAL NICETIES, AWKWARD REALITIES

In the end, I predict that much further study in the area of risk culture and performance is likely to remain categorically confused. One reason is the complexity of operations inside real as opposed to notional corporations/ organisations. A second reason is the inherent difficulty of creating meaningful comparisons given the disparity of risk practices within diverse organisational forms and functions. Even the term 'corporation' is susceptible to a wide range of interpretations. Companies can be public or private, large or small, and utterly different in their modus operandi.

When academics or consultants conduct surveys or interviews or adopt other field techniques, they rely on the subjects to tell honestly their experiences and feelings. Even a thorough examination and an assumption of a degree of evasion is set to fail to capture the richness, good and bad, of corporate activity and the daily or hour-by-hour realities of a living corporate culture or risk culture. Complexity exists everywhere, but it can be focused on specific areas at different times as an organisation moves around its objectives. Capturing this fully is exceptionally challenging, arguably nigh impossible.

Shifting organisational contexts and cultures represent one awkward reality. I mentioned above numerous concepts of value, but these are also shifting so that capturing insights is extremely difficult. Students of 'risk' will be familiar with the idea of manufactured risks (Beck, 1992; Beck, Adam & van Loon, 2000) – these are risks that emerge thanks to our own activities, whether generating nuclear power or requiring banks to hold Tier 1 capital. A lot of today's formal risk management is conducted in response to such risks. Activities that merely fulfil regulatory requirements, for example, make up a significant part of risk work in a typical financial organisation. Power has alluded to the way in which these have been rationalised in a 'pervasive 'logic of opportunity', namely widespread claims that risk management 'adds value' and 'makes business sense" (Power, 2005: 157–8). This is insightful and helpful, but there is an equally pervasive and valid reaction inside organisations that reads 'is pointless for the business' and 'adds a layer of cost' just like the parallel compliance and internal audit functions. These thoughts tend to be voiced less because they convey negativity, however justified. Stakeholders will respond less positively to truth telling than to a narrative of good practice and normative behaviour that can be recorded and monitored. The dominance of the accounting/audit/control aspects of risk management also weighs heavily in this respect. Risk as a function or a culture is unlikely to influence corporate strategy, for example, if the preponderant operating model is that it instead should be checking whether a trading book is correctly tallied or whether the health and safety checks have been carried out according to rules.

Hence my second awkward truth, perhaps unremarkable to risk experts but easily overlooked or discounted effectively to zero in many contexts. We cannot escape the reality that the contribution to value of a risk management function/culture might be mainly thanks to what its existence causes *not* to happen. Take, for example, the threat that an organisation faces a regulatory intervention and potentially reputation-busting sanction. As Power (2005: 158) writes:

In general, if institutional mechanisms exist to value risk management arrangements which conform to legitimate blueprints, then it is entirely rational to invest in such systems regardless of any internal benefits. Positive net economic consequences exist provided that the benefits exceed the cost of creating the appearance of conformity.

Appearing to conform is not quite the same as merely paying lip service. The actuality of conformity is critical in most organisations because this is seen as relatively tangible. It is not acceptable to be non-conforming; therefore, a measure of success is that a regulatory exam is passed without sanction. Insofar as risk management is a part of such an exam, then it is inevitably further embedded as an extension of compliance and internal control and will thus be measured by the same yardstick. But most organisations at a given point in time are not under regulatory exam – the process and whether it will even lead to a sanction is utterly uncertain as to timing and outcome. It is the mere threat of an exam and a negative finding that holds sway.

This fundamentally clouds the value proposition of risk. From a narrow perspective, 'the performativity of CROs is shrouded in the problem of counterfactuality, so they must work hard to establish a legitimate form of performativity in the organisation' (Power, 2005: 142). Wider, when it comes to risk more generally, this unknowledge of future outcomes and the need to make *ex ante* justifications for a nevertheless costly activity set is profoundly in tension with the private attitudes noted above. If risk culture is essentially pointless but necessary for compliance with sometimes fuzzy regulatory guidelines, then it must be tolerated but not further encouraged because costs must be contained. (This puts it on a par with, say, the provision of other group services in an otherwise decentralised corporate organisation – it's fine for payroll to be imposed by the centre, but it is only tolerable if that service is provided at a reasonable cost and with some degree of efficiency.) Debate then centres on how much risk management of this type is necessary for the right degree of appearance. Note that we are a long way away from any niceties about risk culture and value creation. The calculation is almost equivalent to thinking through a degree of insurance coverage relative to a set of premia but crucially without the common understanding that accompanies internal dialogue on coverage levels and the related scenario assumptions.

As well as stressing that this counterfactual element should never be airbrushed, I think, awkwardly, there is also an inevitability about the unobservability of (or at best the extreme difficulty of observing) much risk work that is essential for our understanding of how cultures, call them 'risk cultures' if you will, work in organisations. This point has been made theoretically, but is under-explored in academic research.[22] We need to know more about who does what, the behind-the-scenes routines and areas where there are contested risk ownership spaces, the informal norms that support sense-making and legitimate behaviours even while formalised frameworks and mappings appear to be the dominant mode of risk management. Survey-based research is unlikely to get far in this respect. We need almost to embed observers in organisations over lengthy periods of time whilst ensuring that they do not suffer from capture. Ethnographers should replace change managers.

These challenges to the risk culture/value relationship link inextricably to the emergence/invention of operational risk management two decades ago and to the new contemporary category of 'conduct risk', which has now largely overtaken risk culture as a focus of concern. As noted, these aspects of risk management face the inescapable problem of counterfactuality. Banks have already spent a fortune modelling operational risks, jamming together error management with one-off accident responses and near misses and seeking to justify manageable levels of reserves. Now they are busy, at least in

---

[22] See Power (2016: 8) for a short summary of this point and some suggestive avenues. The theoretical notion of 'back office' work is clearly aligned with the rise of a compliance-dominated risk management model.

the United Kingdom, institutionalising a function to manage conduct risk, mainly because they believe with some justification that this is desired by the regulator so that they would suffer harm were they to disregard or pay only superficial attention to this evolution of their risk cultures.

Although from the outside it appears to be a failure of imagination and management vision, perhaps we should not be too taken aback that banks in the main have replicated the structured frameworks and compliance-heavy procedures they pioneered for earlier risk types. Just as with operational risk, for example, organisations seem to take comfort using familiar technical tools and approaches even if they know there is little intellectual coherence behind their activities. Conduct is conceptually as open-ended as culture and as likely to prove spurious as it is enlightening. But because it has been invented and then embraced by regulators, it must be taken seriously. That predisposes actors to assume, if not to assert, that it has some value. It is therefore, perhaps, not so surprising after all that measuring that value has proved to be so elusive.[23]

## 7.9 CONCLUSION

I have tried to show why I am sceptical as to our current ability to make any strong empirical claims about the relationships between risk culture and corporate performance. My scepticism is based on the analysis of my opening section, where I examined the rise of risk culture in financial services to underline some of the theoretical and

---

[23] An interesting parallel can be drawn with reputational risk. One school of thought has it that harm to a person's or an organisation's reputation is a consequence of a risk failure so at best is a secondary or tertiary effect in a risk cascade. In this case it is the initial risk that is susceptible to management, mitigation, etc., whereas reputation per se is an intangible that will suffer negatively in the event of a real or perceived risk failure. A rival approach insists that reputation is in fact something tangible that can be treated as a special class in a risk taxonomy. A practical compromise for risk managers can be to determine a small number of key risks that link to obvious reputational harm were they to materialise (fraud or a major confidential data breach, for example) and to factor this into how these risks are assessed.

methodological challenges that face central elements of risk management as an emergent professional and managerial discipline. The
sectoral specificities of risk culture are vital if we are to appreciate
its special (and limiting) place in that emergence. Risk has been
bureaucratically, rather than socially, internalised in banks and other
financial institutions to the extent that we could argue there has been
no successful adoption of risk culture at all.

I also outlined the parallel development of corporate cultural
studies with its curious absence of risk-informed thinking.

I then suggested that if either 'culture' or 'risk culture' is to be
useful for analysing corporate value creation (or preservation), then it
must be demonstrably conceptually robust, testable and defensible to
all stakeholders. I also explored some of the challenges that arise from
what really goes on in the administrative life of corporations. It is
insufficient to observe or claim that an organisation has a particular
risk culture. Simply, this requires subjectivity and is therefore of
limited use if we seek to generalise. Divining the consequences of a
particular risk culture for business value is quite another matter and
arguably a stretch too far. Risk culture is at best a subordinate concept
invented at a specific time to serve a purpose that was not openly
articulated perhaps because it was not even a conscious construct. We
might think of it almost as a placeholder, a concept that proved useful
in a situation of crisis and confusion to encompass a range of activities, behaviours and outcomes, but the usefulness of which has
proved rather transient.[24] If 'risk culture' has had any performance-
related impact, it might be in its contribution to the avoidance of
harsher capital standards or other punishments for a banking industry
whose multiple misbehaviours are still playing out today.

We cannot make an honest diversion around the deep uncertainties facing us when we consider 'culture' as a tool for organisational understanding. Risk, in whatever form we seek to pin it down,
remains a plastic concept. And despite the impression created by

[24] Thanks to Michael Power for this idea

torrents of risk and culture materials, we are at an early stage in terms of our ability to map and measure these things: we know they exist; we try to explain them; we learn from experience even as situations evolve in real time' we stumble over counterfactuals and other obstacles. So, although I am a sceptic, I am encouraged that scholarly and other efforts are helping to further our understanding. Frustration at diverse definitions and methodologies is neither novel nor confined to this field.

## REFERENCES

APEC (Asia–Pacific Economic Cooperation) (2013). *Enhancing Supervision of Financial Institutions' Risk Appetite Frameworks*, APEC#213-SO-01.1. https://bit.ly/36BNMoR

Australian Prudential Regulatory Authority (APRA) (2004). *Report into Irregular Currency Options Trading at the National Australia Bank.* Sydney: APRA.

Beck, U. (1992). *Risk Society: Towards a New Modernity.* London: Sage.

Beck, U. (2000). Risk society revisited: theory, politics and research programmes. In B. Adam, U. Beck and J. van Loon, eds., *The Risk Society and Beyond: Critical Issues for Social Theory.* London: Sage, pp. 211–29.

Casson, M. (1991). *The Economics of Business Culture: Game Theory, Transaction Costs, and Economic Performance.* New York: Oxford University Press.

Cowell, F. and Levins, M. (2016). *Crisis Wasted! Leading Risk Managers on Risk Culture.* Chichester: John Wiley & Sons.

Crémer, J. (1993). Corporate culture and shared knowledge. *Industrial and Corporate Change*, 2(3), 351–86.

De Nederlandsche Bank (2009). *The Seven Elements of an Ethical Culture: Strategy and Approach to Behaviour and Culture at Financial Institutions 2010–2014.* https://bit.ly/2NHHj39

Douglas, M. (1966). *Purity and Danger: An Analysis of Concepts of Pollution and Taboo.* London: Routledge.

Douglas, M. and Wildavsky, A. (1982). *Risk and Culture: An Essay on the Selection of Technical and Environmental Dangers.* Berkeley: University of California Press.

Financial Conduct Authority (2018). *Transforming Culture in Financial Services*, DP18(2). www.fca.org.uk/publication/discussion/dp18-02.pdf

Freeman, A. (1993). New tricks to learn: a survey of international banking. *The Economist*, 10 April 1993, 1–37.

Freeman, A., Buehler, K. and Hulme, R. (2008a). The new arsenal of risk management. *Harvard Business Review*, **86**(9), 93–100.

Freeman, A., Buehler, K. and Hulme, R. (2008b). *The Risk Revolution*. New York: McKinsey & Company.

Freeman, A., Buehler, K. and Hulme, R. (2008c). The strategy: owning the right risks. *Harvard Business Review*, **86**(9), 102–10.

FSB (Financial Stability Board) (2013). *Increasing the Intensity and Effectiveness of Supervision: Guidance on Supervisory Interaction with Financial Institutions on Risk Culture*. www.fsb.org/wp-content/uploads/c_131118.pdf

FSB (Financial Stability Board) (2014). *Guidance on Supervisory Interaction with Financial Institutions on Risk Culture: A Framework for Assessing Risk Culture*. www.fsb.org/wp-content/uploads/140407.pdf

Goffee, R. and Jones, G. (1996). What holds the modern company together? *Harvard Business Review*, **74**(6), 133–48.

Gordon, G. and DiTomaso, N. (1992). Predicting corporate performance from organizational culture. *Journal of Management Studies*, **29**(6), 783–98.

Hermalin, B. (2001). Economics and corporate culture. In C. Cooper, S. Cartwright and P. Earley, eds., *The International Handbook of Organizational Culture and Climate*. Chichester: John Wiley & Sons.

ICFI Risk Institute (2004). About the Institute. Website. http://ifci.ch/about.htm

IIF (Institute of International Finance) (2008a). *Final Report of the IIF Committee on Market Best Practices: Principles of Conduct and Best Practice Recommendations*. Washington, DC: IIF.

IIF (Institute of International Finance) (2008b). *Interim Report of the IIF Committee on Market Best Practices*. Washington, DC: IIF.

IIF (Institute of International Finance) (2009). *Reform in the Financial Services Industry: Strengthening Practices for a More Stable System*. Washington, DC: IIF.

Kroeber, A. and Kluckhohn, C. (1952). *Culture: A Critical Review of Concepts and Definitions*. Cambridge, MA: Harvard University Press.

Lamarre, E., Levy, C. and Twining, J. (2010). *Taking Control of Organizational Risk Culture*. McKinsey Working Papers on Risk, No. 16. https://mck.co/2JS3NNv

Lo, A. (2016). The Gordon Gekko effect: the role of culture in the financial industry. *FRBNY Economic Policy Review, August*, **22**(1), 17–42.

Lupfer, T. (2009). Managing the bad apples and protecting the barrel. *Deloitte Idea Labs*.

Lupton, D. (1999). *Risk: Key Ideas*. London: Routledge.

Peters, T. and Waterman, R. (1982). *In Search of Excellence: Lessons from America's Best-Run Companies*. New York: Warner.

Power, M. (2005). Organizational responses to risk: the rise of the chief risk officer. In B. Hutter and M. Power, eds., *Organizational Encounters with Risk*. Cambridge: Cambridge University Press, pp. 132–48.

Power, M. (2007). Putting categories to work: the invention of operational risk. In *Organized Uncertainty: Designing a World of Risk Management*. Oxford: Oxford University Press.

Power, M. (2016). *Riskwork: Essays on the Organizational Life of Risk Management*. Oxford: Oxford University Press.

Power, M., Ashby, S. and Palermo, T. (2013). *Risk Culture in Financial Organisations: A Research Report*. London: Centre for Analysis of Risk and Regulation, London School of Economics.

PwC (PricewaterhouseCoopers) (2004). *An Investigation into Foreign Exchange Losses at National Australia Bank*. https://bit.ly/2qllKxl

PwC (PricewaterhouseCoopers) (2015). *Risk Culture: Where to from Here?* www.pwc.com.au/pdf/2015-risk-culture-and-conduct-report.pdf

Ring, P., Bryce, C., McKinney, R. and Webb, R. (2016) Taking notice of risk culture – the regulator's approach. *Journal of Risk Research*, **19**(3), 364–87.

Sackmann, S. (2011). Culture and performance. In N. Ashkanasy, C. Wilderom and M. Peterson, eds., *The Handbook of Organizational Culture and Climate*, 2nd ed. Los Angeles: Sage, pp. 188–224.

Schein, E. H. (1985). Organizational culture & leadership. *The Academy of Management Review*, **3**(3).

Schein, E. H. (2004). *Organizational Culture and Leadership*, 3rd ed. San Francisco: Jossey–Bass.

Selznick, P. (1957). *Leadership in Administration: A Sociological Interpretation*. New York: Harper & Row.

Simon, H. (1957). *Administrative Behavior*, 2nd ed. New York: Free Press.

Vaughan, D. (1996). *The* Challenger *Launch Decision: Risky Technology, Culture and Deviance at NASA*. Chicago: University of Chicago Press.

# 8 Values at Risk

*Perspectives on the Ethical Turn in Risk Management*

Anette Mikes

## 8.1 INTRODUCTION

Risk managers are flirting with organisational ethics.

In the wake of the 2007–9 financial crisis, and in subsequent rate rigging, money laundering and other compliance scandals, there has been a growing recognition that what has gone wrong can neither be understood nor prevented without considering what has gone *ethically* wrong. Accordingly, there are normative calls for risk management to provide a systematic analysis of the ethicality of individuals or organisations implicated in these disasters. Mike Power, Simon Ashby and Tommaso Palermo (2013: 4), as part of their agenda of reconnecting risk-taking with control processes, highlighted the role of risk managers in creating a 'new moral narrative of organisational purpose'. Their claim that 'risk management is being repositioned as a carrier of organisational ethics' (8) recognises that risk culture reform must go beyond incentives – whereby risk metrics enter the performance measurement system – to 'renewed corporate narratives for focusing on clients along with respect for internal control processes'.

However, as the sociologist Philip Selznick (2000: 15) points out, it is not enough to simply 'elaborate a purpose': we have the problem of infusing values into the life of organisations. In the context of the ongoing risk culture reform in financial services, it has become important to talk about the integrity of the firm. Writing almost twenty years ago, Selznick foreshadowed the problem of risk culture by noting that banks had been in the process of forgetting the very ideals and ends that they were supposed to be serving:

Insofar as bankers think of loans as products, for which marketing
becomes a fully accepted part of what it means to do banking,
we're probably losing touch with certain central functions that a
banking institution ought to perform. ... We are moving toward
saying all transactions are fungible and it doesn't matter how you
make money so long as you make money, whereas the true problem
of integrity might ask us to focus instead on how we make money
and whether in making money we're also being true to the
commitments we ought to have.

*(Selznick, 2000: 16)*

In another stroke of visionary foresight, Selznick (2000) took
aim at the then emerging tech companies (citing 'amazon.com'),
which he believed were not only in the business of selling merchan-
dise through a revolutionary channel but also in the business of
creating customer databases, which in due course could be marketed
lucratively. Again, for tech companies, the question of integrity is to
know their commitments and stand by them, rather than keep asking,
'What do we have here that would help us to make more money?' (17).

The well-known corporate-governance advisory group the Committee of Sponsoring Organisations (COSO, 2016: 35) has recently
revised its 2004 guidelines on enterprise risk management (ERM),
explicitly urging risk managers to get involved in 'challenging [those]
decisions' that involve choice among the multiple commitments
and priorities of their organisation by asking whether a business
proposal 'infringe[s] on the entity's standards of conduct'. 'Is it legal?
Would we want our shareholders, customers, regulators, external
parties, or other stakeholders to know about it?'

Why do such questions matter to risk culture reform and risk
managers? In this chapter, I shall argue that an organisation's commitments, core values and priorities offer a window into its espoused
culture: be that 'risk culture' in a narrow sense, motivating attitudes
to risk-taking and risk control, or culture in a more general sense,
manifest in a wide-ranging set of organisational norms, values and

priorities. The problem of (risk) culture emerges when an organisation starts drifting from its original intentions and espoused commitments, when its values and priorities get regularly and habitually compromised in action. I shall call this drift the problem of *value displacement*.[1] For risk managers to take on the mandate of safeguarding organisational values, priorities and commitments (including the risk culture), they would first have to clarify the espoused value system and priorities; and second, they would need to be able to detect and visualise the gaps between the espoused and the actual values that drive decisions and actions in their organisation.

In this sense then, are we experiencing an ethical turn in risk management? Can risk managers bring espoused and in-action values into high-level risk discussions, and can they create a measure of organisational integrity (by indicating if their organisation is in fact living up to those values)? Do they already? What are the challenges of channelling concerns with value displacement into high-level discussions?

In order to answer these questions, we need to understand both how the elevation of values (espoused and lived) into the risk management process manifests empirically and what it might entail conceptually. In this chapter, I set out to establish, define and empirically investigate the phenomenon that one might call the ethical turn in risk management.

In brief, some risk management practices – particularly those that supposedly operationalise 'risk appetite' and influence 'risk culture' and 'the core values of an organisation' – can no longer sidestep organisational values and commitments. The question of *what* risks an organisation is taking is increasingly seen as intertwined with the question of *whose* risks an organisation is managing other than its

---

[1] The term 'value displacement' is inspired by organisational theorists' concept of goal displacement. Goal displacement occurs as a result of regressive organisational processes that make the end in view less attainable, leave original intentions unachieved and often make the situation worse.

own. According to some observers (Power, Ashby & Palermo, 2013), risk managers are expected to ask these questions despite the fact that risk management, as conceptualised in many finance textbooks and governance guidelines, appears to be a fundamentally 'amoral' management practice. Or, to be precise, it is a management practice that focuses primarily on one value: the financial value to be delivered to the company's owners.

Consider the risk-calculation tools known as value at risk (in banks) or earnings at risk (more broadly). Their very names betray that the financial outcome is the primary – or perhaps only – value at risk. Enron, Goldman Sachs, Wells Fargo and others have shown us what such cold calculations can produce. Managers at Goldman Sachs, for example, were able to monitor and contain the firm's own financial risks during the sub-prime mortgage crisis using superior risk-quantification processes. But these tools said nothing about the conflicts of interests that arose when the firm placed large bets to maximise its own bottom line at the expense of certain client groups (National Commission on the Causes of the Financial and Economic Crisis in the United States, 2011; Soltes, 2016). Both the firm and its many victims have paid heavily for that blindness (US Department of Justice, 2016a, 2016b, 2016c).

But risk managers who now intend to argue that values other than the bottom line matter will need both a mandate and the technology. Some have already implemented and are advocating tools that can add an actionable ethical dimension to their decision-making and strategy processes. These practices, as we will see below, were not imposed from outside or above; they came from risk practitioners who are expanding their traditional mandate to incorporate other-than-financial values at risk.

This chapter's three main sections pursue the contributions I hope to make. First, I show how certain concepts in risk management practice (e.g. risk appetite) already offer a natural bridge to organisational ethics by implicating the organisation's core values, key priorities and multiple stakeholders.

Second, based on my case studies at two Canadian high-reliability organisations, I show that some risk managers have created tools and processes that make a tangible (not just conceptual) connection between organisational values and management control. This enriches the risk management literature by highlighting a new phenomenon and by putting some empirical meat on the conceptual skeleton of risk appetising.

Third, drawing on behavioural ethics, I outline a richer conceptual framework that links risk management and organisational ethics through instrumentalising inquiries into value displacement. Values-at-risk considerations are relevant in decision-making and strategising, but without control tools, that may go unnoticed. We therefore need to better understand what it takes to develop tools that can amplify concerns with value displacement at the decision-making table. I highlight two areas in which an explicit consideration of values-at-risk tools and processes might be necessary to generate constructive debate and action: corporate failures due to conflicts of interest, and the incubation of man-made disasters.

## 8.2  FROM RISK APPETITE TO RISK APPETISING

At the heart of risk management practice is risk 'appetite', a concept by which organisations seek to (a) identify all material risks to their objectives and (b) design controls to keep those risk within the bounds of a 'target risk appetite'. For example, the international risk management standard ISO (2009: 73) defines risk appetite as 'the amount and type of risk that an organisation is willing to pursue or retain'. Subsequent international standards also mention risk appetite but offer no guidance on how it can be expressed (Hillson & Murray-Webster, 2012).

Following the great financial crisis, financial institutions have been under increased pressure to reform their 'risk cultures'. Risk appetite has been implicated in risk culture reform, which aims at rebalancing 'the pre-crisis emphasis on ... risk-taking with ... precaution and risk control' (Palermo, Power & Ashby, 2017: 154).

Indeed, risk appetite implies a control model operating like a thermostat, which adjusts to changes in the environment subject to a target temperature (Power, 2009). Risk managers have long prided themselves on this cybernetic, rational approach, itself the product of broader engineering conceptions of control theory (Hood, 1996; Robinson, 2007). The prominence of this conception of risk among corporate-governance advocates and policymakers also reflects the long-standing managerial preoccupation with quantification and boundary setting.

Between 2007 and 2013, most self-respecting consulting firms pontificated on risk appetite (Oliver Wyman, 2007; Buehler, Freeman & Hulme, 2008; IBM Financial Services, 2008; PwC, 2008; SAS Institute, 2011; KPMG, 2013). McKinsey's approach was typical: 'Determine your capacity and appetite for risk. Is the corporation maintaining the proper amount of risk capital, or is it overinsured or underinsured? How much risk would it like to own?' (Buehler, Freeman & Hulme, 2008: 23). Their answer:

> To understand whether it has the optimal level of risk capacity, a company must first quantify its *operating-cash-flow risk*. ... In addition ... many companies should manage their risk capacity against other dimensions of enterprise risk. A company in a cyclical industry might want to manage its overall *equity value at risk* ... Alternatively, a company might place a high premium on meeting earnings-per-share guidance and thus want to assess and manage *earnings at risk*.
>
> *(27–8, my emphases)*

These risk appetite measures were widely adopted in banks but less so elsewhere. A CFO survey jointly undertaken in 2005 by Deutsche Bank and the Global Association of Risk Professionals chastised non-financial services firms for being 'slow to embrace modern risk-management tools', finding that only 45 per cent had adopted value at risk, 43 per cent had adopted cash flow at risk and 36 per cent had adopted earnings at risk.

Overall, the following trends are discernible in these documents. First, there is significant confusion over terminology, with some using risk capacity, risk tolerance and risk appetite as synonyms, and others trying – with varying success – to differentiate them. This failure to offer a clear definition is 'disappointing at best and confusing at worst' (Hillson & Murray-Webster, 2012: 22).

Second, most consulting firms advocate risk appetite as something to be measured but do not show the methodological pluralism required by the plurality of circumstances. Respondents to a consultation document issued by the UK Financial Reporting Council 'pointed out that, within financial sectors, [risk appetite and risk tolerance] tended to be associated with specific metrics and modelling techniques' and were 'concerned that these might be imposed on companies in other sectors for which they are not suitable' (Hillson & Murray-Webster, 2012: 12).

Third, there seem to be two camps emerging also in terms of whose risk is to be managed: a shareholder-focused view (associated with quantitative expressions of risk appetite, as exemplified in McKinsey's 2008 report (Buehler, Freeman & Hulme, 2008)) and a wider stakeholder view, with no quantitative commitments and, in fact, displaying – as do other areas of risk management – a great deal of calculative scepticism (Mikes, 2009, 2011). COSO (2009: 5) defined risk appetite as the 'amount of risk, on a broad level, an organisation is willing to accept in pursuit of *stakeholder* value', but only two out of the six prominent consulting firms active in this field advocated explicitly that, because different stakeholders would have different risk appetites (PwC, 2008), 'the perspectives of all stakeholders need to be considered' (Oliver Wyman, 2007: 3).

But in fact, risk appetite is an inherently pluralistic control concept because it raises the question of whose appetite counts (Power, 2009: 851), though this is seldom acknowledged in the normative practitioner literature. Leaving aside issues of defining and measuring a 'target risk appetite' and 'the amount of risk taken', one cannot subject risks to cybernetic control without determining which stakeholders deserve protection from risk and which should be exposed. Why and to what extent?

Such discussions invite conflict among different stakeholders who have different appetites for risk and therefore require a pluralistic model of control (Hood, 1996). Yet the conception of appetite as a singular input into risk management simply assumes that plurality away, defining risk appetite as the *amount* of risk an *entity* is willing to bear (COSO, 2009); that is, a threshold that senior management can set like a thermostat.

In this spirit, prior to the financial crisis of 2007–9, many financial services firms used control models to elaborate on the differences between a company's target risk appetite and the type and amount of risk it actually took. Like other control tools, risk appetite frameworks were supposed to act not only as boundary-setting and monitoring devices but also as filters for issues meriting managerial attention (Marsh, 2009). The diversity of such risk appetite frameworks is notable, particularly in light of the manifest failure of many organisations to contain risks to their own value, not to mention the risks to so many innocent bystanders. Attention devoted to certain risks is a way of not seeing others, which are then left – undefined and unframed – to quietly incubate.

Following the financial crisis, academics and other observers were quick to ask, 'Where did risk management fail?' (Sabato, 2010). Some highlighted that risk appetite and risk tolerance involved 'confused concepts and poor reasoning', which needed to be rectified by 'further clear advice' (Purdy, 2010: 885) in order 'to articulate risk appetite' (Sabato, 2010: 316).

Finally, we see the elevation of setting and monitoring risk appetite (and by implication, monitoring 'risk culture') to the board level. Shortly after the publication of COSO (2009) in the United States, the National Association of Corporate Directors (NACD, 2009: 26) suggested that (a) risk appetite ought to be subject to an ongoing process, given that risks are themselves constantly changing, and (b) directors are responsible for this process. Other regulators and professional bodies agreed.[2]

Clearly, there is much room for practice variation but also a recognition that the stakes are potentially high, particularly as boards can be held accountable for failing to set and monitor risk appetite(s). Risk appetite is thus becoming a code word for the challenging acts of monitoring 'risk culture' and of drawing a line between whom an organisation does and does not need to protect from risk.

As Turner (1976: 379) warned, the central difficulty in avoiding disasters is discovering (a) which aspects of the problems facing an organisation are prudent to ignore and which should be attended to and (b) how an acceptable level of risk-taking could be established as a criterion for making this choice. Weick (1998: 74) went even further: 'Organisations are defined by what they ignore.'

Thus, there is an inescapable ethical dimension to the processes of setting risk appetite and monitoring 'risk culture'. As Power (2009: 849) argues, it is 'the consequence of a dynamic organisational process involving values as much as metrics'. He advocates conceptualising risk appetite not as a specific threshold but as a process, proposing (as did the NACD) to call this ongoing process 'risk appetising'. Such a process inevitably invites multiple voices and interactions, within and without an organisation, which collectively shape its view of which stakeholders should be exposed to (acceptable) risk and which must be protected from harm, no matter what. Such a view of risk appetite then defines both operational and ethical boundaries fortified by the espoused commitments, values and priorities of the firm.

---

[2] See the European Commission's (2011) green paper *The EU Corporate Governance Framework*.

## 8.3 VALUES-AT-RISK TOOLS IN ACTION: CASE STUDIES ON EMERGING PRACTICES

### 8.3.1 Case Sites and Methodological Notes

While the consulting firms were busy prescribing an ever-wider range of solutions to the corporate risk management problem, I was engaged in two field studies, observing the emergence of risk practices at two Canadian organisations, Hydro One and the Toronto Transport Commission (TTC) – a 'matched pair' (Ahrens & Dent, 1998) from which we can draw out similarities and contrasts. They both embarked on their risk management journey voluntarily; as non-listed companies, they were not required to embrace and disclose ERM practices. However, as crown corporations and industry champions, they felt the need to exemplify risk management 'best practice'.

Both operate in high-reliability industries: lack of operational reliability could lead not only to financial and asset damage but also to injury and death. Both have to manage a complex web of conflicting interests – the agendas of government ministers, regulators, consumers and passengers, environmental groups, aboriginal ('First Nation') landowners and the capital market debt holders that had subscribed to their bond issues.

I started fieldwork at Hydro One in spring 2008. Through twenty-three interviews, I aimed to reconstruct the history of ERM there from its consultant-led introduction in 2002 to its maturation into what was widely regarded by 2012 as the gold standard of risk management practice.

In 2012, one of Hydro One's pioneering risk managers, Rob Quail, published an article on risk appetite in *Corporate Governance Canada*. He was at the time director of risk management, having replaced John Fraser, who had retired earlier that year. Cutting the Gordian knot of confusion in the risk appetite debate, Quail's (2012) purpose was to address 'the practical realities of making trade-offs across business objectives'. He recognised that the risk appetite discourse was essentially about 'tough choices', such as 'How much financial risk should we take to meet environmental goals?' and 'How should we trade off our customers' level of satisfaction against our employees' well-being?'

I was keen to follow up and see how Quail's normative ideas had been put into practice. In August 2016, I had the opportunity to talk to Quail and to Carmine Marcello, who had been CEO of Hydro One when Quail introduced a process and a tool called the 'risk appetite radar' (RAR). By this time, both men were retired from the firm and were happy to share memories and supportive non-confidential documents pertaining to the risk appetite process at Hydro One. That autumn I carried out four recorded interviews with Quail and one with Marcello. The interviews were conducted on Skype and were subsequently transcribed. Though my main interest was in the elaboration and use of the risk appetite methodology at Hydro One, Quail mentioned a few times how other risk managers at other companies started to apply his approach, partly because of the apparent impact of the *Corporate Governance Canada* article and partly because an independent risk consultant also started to advocate the RAR. One of the early adopters was Mohamed Ismail, the head of risk management (formally titled as 'principal risk adviser') at the TTC, the Toronto public transport company. Having read Quail's article in 2012, Ismail was impressed and invited Quail to discuss the approach, speaking as one risk manager to another. He decided to implement the RAR at the TTC.[3] A period of project elaboration followed, in which Ismail discussed it with the executive management team and identified a conceptual confusion in the approach. However, instead of abandoning RAR, Ismail quickly corrected (clarified) the methodology and proceeded to work it into the budgeting process over the next four years.

[3] Ismail worked closely with Bem Case, senior adviser to strategic initiatives at the TTC. Their joint objective was (according to Case's job description) to 'facilitate ... cross-functional initiatives for modernization and continuous improvement of the TTC in such areas as corporate governance, enterprise risk management, and priority setting, among others'. Although the case description focuses on Ismail, it is important to note that he developed his ideas in collaboration with Case.

Quail put me in touch with Ismail during summer 2016, and I interviewed him several times on Skype (recording and transcribing all exchanges). Ismail agreed to help me arrange a one-week field visit in January 2017, allowing me to formally interview ten senior executives (including the CEO, CFO and COO), who all have come into contact with the RAR approach. Altogether, I conducted fifteen deep interviews (ranging from 1 hour to 2.5 hours) at the TTC, documenting the elaboration and stabilisation of their version of risk appetite.

### 8.3.1.1 Case 1. Hydro One

Quail (2012) hit upon the ethical dimension that surfaces as soon as an organisation recognises not only the plurality of its objectives but also the plurality of its stakeholders and values. He went on to argue, 'Providing 'naked' objectives isn't enough to allow [decision-makers] to understand ... what kinds of risks we like and what kinds of risks we don't like as an organisation' (26). Recognising (a) that risks could be seen as good and less good, bad and less bad and (b) that 'softer' risks to reputation or to customer relationships couldn't be quantified or monetised, Quail debunked two myths about risk appetite.

First, 'there is no such thing as a single 'catch-all' statement that will meaningfully communicate risk appetite; the term Risk Appetite Statement is itself misleading' (Quail, 2012: 26). Risk appetite can only be defined in the context of individual objectives by asking questions such as 'When faced with multiple options, how willing are we to select an option that might place this [particular] objective at risk?' and 'How willing are we to trade off the achievement of this objective against other objectives?' (27). Second, he pushed back on the quantification spirit of those wishing to metricise the discussion and pointed out that 'circumstances where risk appetite can be expressed as a fixed numerical limit or ratio are few' (26).

He proposed the following monitoring-and-control process for discussing risk appetite, starting at the executive-team level:

**Step 1.   Define the 'Target' Enterprise Risk Appetite** Quail proposed that the executive team should rate each strategic objective based on the 'mission, vision, and values of the organisation', in terms of their willingness to place that objective at risk – to trade it off against another – should the need arise.

This requires managers to be clear not only about their strategic objectives but also about their *core values*. Then, considering the two together, they prioritise the objectives on a 1–5 scale, with lower numbers indicating objectives (values) that a firm is less willing to trade off (see Figure 8.1).

The average ratings for all objectives are rendered in a radar chart that Quail called the RAR.

The example given in Figure 8.2 shows that Hydro One values safety as a core value; one of its stated objectives was 'number 1 in safety in our industry' (Mikes, 2012). Thus the value associated with this objective is considered 'sacred' – not to be traded off

| Rating | Philosophy | Tolerance for uncertainty | Choice | Trade-off |
|---|---|---|---|---|
| | Overall risk-taking philosophy | Willingness to accept uncertain outcomes or period-to-period variation | When faced with multiple options, willingness to select an option that puts objectives at risk | Willingness to trade off against achievement of other objectives |
| 5  Open | Will take justified risks | Fully anticipated | Will choose option with highest return; accept possibility of failure | Willing |
| 4  Flexible | Will take strongly justified risks | Expect some | Will choose to put at risk but will manage impact | Willing under right conditions |
| 3  Cautious | Preference for safe delivery | Limited | Will accept if limited, and heavily out weighed by benefits | Prefer to avoid |
| 2  Minimalist | Extremely conservative | Low | Will accept only if essential, and limited possibility/extent of failure | With extreme reluctance |
| 1  Averse | 'Sacred' Avoidance of risk is a core objective | Extremely low | Will select the lowest risk option, always | Never |

FIGURE 8.1 Quail's rating scale for articulating Hydro One's espoused strategic priorities.
Source: Quail, 2012

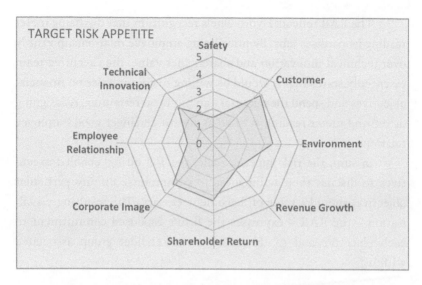

FIGURE 8.2 Hydro One's risk appetite statement (illustrative).
Source: Quail, 2012

against any other objective – and it implicates the specific stakeholder group whose safety is at stake: employees. Employee relationship has a similar rank; that is, it is a non-negotiable objective. This reflects the primacy of employees as a core value of the firm and the importance that management attached to keeping good relations with a highly unionised workforce. Keep in mind that these are *espoused* values.

Technical innovation is a close-to-sacred objective. This reflects a certain moment in Hydro One's history. Although the firm had never been known for technical innovation, it had committed itself in 2010 to become the first electricity company in Canada to introduce 'smart meters', which would automate and digitise its meter-reading activities (Mikes, 2012). For now, at least, the firm had very little willingness to compromise on technical innovation.

Financial objectives – revenue growth and shareholder return – have higher risk appetite scores than employee safety and employee relations; that is, they are espoused to take a back seat to those objectives.

The RAR reflects Hydro One's recognition that digitising meter reading jeopardises jobs. By prioritising employee relationship *visibly* over technical innovation and shareholder value, the executive team essentially states that it would be willing to compromise on financial objectives and spend the necessary amounts on retraining, reassigning or retiring meter-reading staff so as not to endanger good employee relations.

In sum, the risk appetite scale (the 1–5 rating) enabled executives to discuss their willingness to compromise on any particular objective, should a trade-off become necessary. The resulting visualisation – the RAR – expresses the firm's espoused commitment to each objective and to the value or stakeholder group associated with it.

**Step 2.   Assess the 'Exhibited' Risk Appetite** Actions speak louder than words. Having made Hydro One's *espoused* risk appetite visible, he wanted to do the same for its *exhibited* risk appetite. 'Where there have been tough choices, where multiple objectives came into play', he wanted to know, 'which ones prevailed?'

Quail (2012: 29) considered employee surveys but then realised that, as a risk workshop facilitator, he could ask people directly, 'gathering data on risk appetite perception' and using the same 1–5 scale'. Aggregating the data he had collected in person, he produced a crude gap analysis showing the difference between espoused and exhibited risk appetites (see Figure 8.3):

**Step 3.   Address the Gaps** The two outlines don't line up everywhere. For example, it doesn't look as if employee relations got the priority in actual decision-making that the executive team had espoused; at least, the employees Quail spoke with didn't think so. He referred to the difference between an objective's espoused ranking and its exhibited ranking as a 'delta'. The deltas are made visible in the RAR wherever the solid line connecting all the espoused rankings and the broken line connecting all the exhibited rankings don't line up. In this case, the data point to the possible reluctance of managers

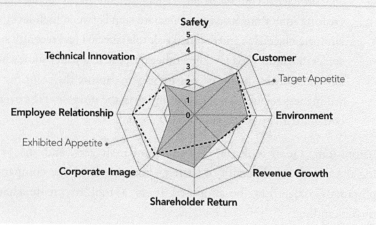

FIGURE 8.3 Quail's risk appetite statement: an example of espoused versus exhibited pluralistic values.
Source: Quail, 2012

to spend the necessary funds on retraining, reassigning and retiring employees respectfully.

Thus, with the RAR, managers can decide not only to adjust the firm's risk exposure among multiple constituents but also to improve its adherence to its own core values.

Two further insights arose from my discussions with Quail and Marcello. First, the RAR was the product of Hydro One risk managers' 'toolmaking' drive (Hall, Mikes & Millo, 2015). They saw it as a trailblazing 'opportunity'. The following recollection illustrates how opportunistic Quail and his former boss, chief risk officer John Fraser, were when initially conceiving and operationalising the RAR:

> John Fraser and I had read about the concept of risk appetite in external literature, but it always seemed to us to be a solution in search of a problem, and many authors seemed to have a vague idea of what they should look like and how they should fit into a mature ERM process. So one day, as a thought exercise in John Fraser's

office, I said aloud, 'If we were to develop something called 'risk appetite', what could it be for?' That's when I hit on the idea of creating something as an intermediate step between high-level strategic objectives and detailed risk tolerances. I had recently seen spider diagrams used for some other purpose in a paper somewhere and thought this might be a novel way to capture the company's willingness to put each objective at risk in the interest of the overall corporate mission and vision.

Before long, Quail took the tool to senior managers, and, discovering the surprising diversity of their prioritisations of the company's pluralistic objectives, he proposed it as a tool to create shared understanding:

> I thought that such a tool could be used to draw out a more meaningful discussion at the executive level. As a first step in developing the idea further, I established a scale for measuring 'appetite', similar to the one I later described in the paper [Quail, 2012], and began interviewing senior executives, as an add-on in the biannual risk profile review sessions, to capture their sense of what the 'spider diagram' should look like. ... I expected a fair degree of alignment among the executives on how they might rate the risk appetite for each objective. I was wrong. There was tremendous diversity. John and I recognised this as an *opportunity*. This led to the second purpose of the risk appetite approach: to provide a tool to facilitate alignment among senior executives on risk attitude and gain a deeper understanding of the strategy.

Toolmaking is more than just 'trailblazing' (Mikes, Hall & Milo, 2013); it also assumes that risk managers work with potential tool users and incorporate suggestions and feedback, which in turn leads to further changes in the tool and also strengthens commitment amongst would-be users to use it. Such user input triggered the final step in the evolution of Quail's methodology – the gap analysis:

At [one of the initial] workshop[s], one of the executive team asked a very useful question; another 'aha' moment for me. He asked me, 'When we vote on and discuss risk appetite, are we voting on how it is today – as shown by the decisions and actions we take – or how it should be to fulfil our mission and vision?' This one question led to the extra exercise of asking for both 'target' and 'exhibited' risk appetite and examining the gaps.

The second insight is that the ethical dimension was not planned; it emerged gradually, almost accidentally. That is, using the RAR tool made a hitherto invisible issue visible. Much as reading old letters can make you realise how your actions have diverged from your intentions, the superimposing of the two spider diagrams on one RAR made visible the difference between which stakeholders Hydro One *said* it prioritised and which ones it really *did* prioritise when it came down to it.

In fact, such discussions had started in meetings as soon as executives got a look at the 'target RAR' and started challenging each other on whether or not they believed in the priorities it showed. As Quail recalled:

Often there would be a discussion about – 'Okay, our risk appetite towards health and safety is this'. And someone else round the table would say, 'Ah, but here is an example of a decision you made recently that doesn't align with that'. So it is that challenge of the strategy and whether we really believe in it and how it translates into specific programs and what it means for stakeholders. That's a very fruitful discussion.

It was these discussions that reinforced Quail's belief that the gap analysis was needed to contrast the target risk appetite with the exhibited risk appetite, and it required him to collect information directly from employees in Hydro One's risk-identification workshops:

After I introduced it [the target risk appetite radar], quite by accident I came up with the idea of evaluating employee

perceptions of risk appetite – what they see at different levels. And
that yielded all kinds of benefits, too. Primarily about education.
So – and again, it's about the strategy, it's about the conversations
I had at workshops with employees across the company, talking
about how these values and how the objectives and how decision
making aligned down the line. [The question was whether]
management is living up to its values, rather than just whether
employees are submitting expense claims properly or whether the
financial statements are accurate.

As these accidental discussions became more intentional, Quail
was looking for evidence of 'misalignment': 'What does exist in the
company that signals or reinforces our risk appetite? What are
the controls, what are the documents, what are the elements of plans
that were in place that signal what the company is prioritising and
paying attention to? And part of the discussion at the workshop
became to look for misalignment.' As CEO, Carmine Marcello supported the risk appetite process, even though he understood it could
open a Pandora's box:

The [RAR] tool, as a visual representation of a ton of information,
was very effective in getting people to say: 'Why is there a gap here?
What is it that people are seeing differently?' And ... 'Let's put
those issues on the table'. [Rob Quail] never shied away from just
putting the bad news on the table, for the lack of a better word. And
highlighting the deltas, again, that's something I personally
appreciated. I am not necessarily sure everybody did.

The discussion around the deltas was now inevitable, as illustrated
by the episode in which employee relationship was found to be compromised in practice. The CEO recalled:

Quite frankly, when Rob put the employee relationship [delta] on
the table and he showed a gap, he showed us that people were
thinking differently. He was basically saying, 'Emperor, you have
no clothes.' And to be able to have that conversation – really delve

down into it and solve the problem and close the gap – it was pretty important and pretty powerful. And I think this tool allows you to see that very quickly. ... From a user perceptive, I think the power comes from the visualisation.

The next year (2013), the exercise was repeated at the board level, to discuss 'how the target risk appetite might have to change due to the changing situation of the company'.[4]

Hydro One's new digitisation strategy, for example, required some tough decisions. There would be teething problems with these smart meters, which might, in turn, aggravate customers. At the time, Hydro One had an objective of '90% customer satisfaction', which it had been able to achieve for several years. Now it seemed necessary to give that a lower priority than technological innovation (as seen in Figure 8.2). Management also discussed and understood that once the smart meter project was implemented, the company would have to prioritise customer satisfaction again; in the meantime, the company would ramp up its call centre capacity to deal with the expected complaints (Mikes & Hamel, 2012).

Explicating the deltas became part of Quail's risk management workshop activities. This enmeshing in the annual ERM process marks the successful formalisation of risk appetite at Hydro One. The series of discussions facilitated by the RAR tool amounted to a strategic control process: articulation of a target risk appetite, followed by the risk manager's data gathering to detect the exhibited risk appetite and visualise the gaps, which would then be discussed at the level at which strategic decisions could be made about how and when to close them. Because such decisions were made with reference to strategy, the RAR also served to connect strategic discussions and objectives to the values and priorities they implicated. Strategy had been made aware of its own ethical dimension.

---

[4] Quail, interviewed on 14 September 2016.

### 8.3.1.2    Case 2. The Toronto Transport Commission (TTC)

In 2012, following the publication of his *Corporate Governance Canada* article, Rob Quail (and his then boss, John Fraser) were invited by the CEO of the TTC to give a presentation to the management team on risk management. In the audience sat Mohamed Ismail, the TTC's newly appointed principal risk adviser. (Ismail chose the title himself to signal that risk management was really not his but line managers' responsibility.)

After the presentation, Ismail set out to develop a similar approach at the TTC. He sat down with each executive director to ask them about (1) the top risks they perceived, (2) which of the seven corporate objectives these risks jeopardised and (3) the rank order of those objectives. Figure 8.4 shows the seven objectives and the ranking scale Ismail developed initially, based on Quail (2012) but inverting the scale (1, open; 5, averse).

In March 2013, he arrived at an executive retreat armed with Quail's article and the results of his analysis. First, he showed the 'top risks' on a traffic light diagram, rank-ordered on a five-by-five risk map. Rather than focusing on the differences in the risks, Ismail pointed out the similarities; for example, how many risks were scored as 15 (assessed as 3 (probability) × 5 (impact). He then asked the executives to prioritise among those same-scored risks. The discussion was heated, and Ismail let it run until he was able to make the point he had meant to make: any comparison or differentiation was futile because they were 'comparing apples and oranges'. The reductionism of the risk assessments (probability × impact grades) produced several subsets of non-comparable risks mapped on to the limited grid of the risk map.

Having highlighted this problem in the TTC's risk assessments, it was time for Ismail to present his solution: each risk must be weighted by an 'objective weight' derived from the RAR of the TTC. Having collected the objective rankings in his one-on-one interviews, he now presented the results: all the spider charts (in one diagram) that the individual executives espoused.

# APPETITE RATING

| Rating | Philosophy | Tolerance for uncertainty | Choice | Trade-off |
|---|---|---|---|---|
| | Overall risk-taking philosophy | Willingness to accept uncertain outcomes or period-to-period variation | When faced with multiple options, willingness to select an option that puts objectives at risk | Willingness to trade off against achievement of other objectives |
| 5 | Averse | 'Sacred' – avoidance of risk is a core objective | Extremely low | Will select the lowest risk option, always | Never |
| 4 | Minimalist | Extremely conservative | Low | Will accept only if essential, and limited possibility/extent of failure | With extreme reluctance and where not reasonably practicable |
| 3 | Cautious | Preference for safe delivery | Limited | Will accept if limited, and heavily outweighted by benefits | Prefer to avoid |
| 2 | Flexible | Will take strongly justified risks | Expect some | Will choose to put at risk, but will manage impact | Willing under conditions |
| 1 | Open | Will take justified risks | Fully anticipated | Will choose option with highest return; accept possibility of failure | Willing |

Originally developed by Rob Quail, Hydro One. With modifications.

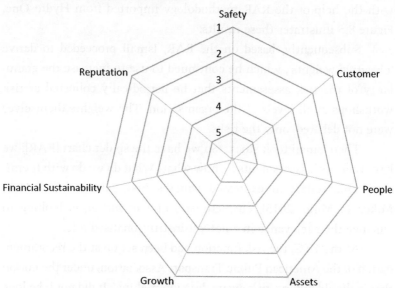

FIGURE 8.4 Scale used at the TTC to rank-order objectives/values.
Source: TTC internal documents

FIGURE 8.5 Individual assessments (illustrative, not actual) by TTC executives of the ranking of core values. The consensus (post-debate) view is indicated in dark grey.
Source: TTC internal documents

This initial (pluralistic) RAR indicated that executives were 'all over the place: they were pulling in all directions [in terms of their objective rankings] . . . But we had a very good debate. They came to see each other's priorities.' In the end, the meeting resulted in a 're-vote of the [ranking of the] objectives'. The executives were now unanimous on the rank order of five of the seven corporate objectives. For the other two, they agreed to average the scores. Thus the TTC's pluralistic values got their rank-ordering and a visible representation with the help of the RAR methodology imported from Hydro One. Figure 8.5 illustrates these results.

Subsequently, based on the RAR, Ismail proceeded to derive 'objective weights', which he continued to use to increase the granularity of the risk assessments that he periodically collected at risk workshops at all levels of the organisation. The weights themselves were not debated, only the risks.

Then Ismail took stock: 'So we have the spider chart [RAR], we have these risk assessments . . . now what? What do we do with them?'

This reflection expressed Ismail's 'toolmaking drive' (Hall, Mikes & Millo, 2015), characteristic of risk managers looking to enhance their relevance in a not-yet-institutionalised role.

At the TTC, the risk function had been set up at the recommendation of the American Public Transport Association, under the notion that it should 'inform risk-aware decision-making'. It did not take long before Ismail, a veteran TTC engineer himself, recognised an 'opportunity': to make risk-aware decisions in the capital allocation process, in which multiple engineering projects were constantly competing for funding: 'In early 2013, I noticed that [the TTC] was really struggling with decisions of resource allocation – you know, the 'kill or keep' type decisions – especially where a decision had obvious importance but an unclear connection to the set of corporate objectives that the [the TTC] had established. I realised this was an opportunity for risk management to help.' Ismail argued that the capital allocation methodology had the same problem as the previously non-comparable risk assessment scores:

> Apples and oranges. We have hundreds of initiatives about fleet maintenance, about stations ... Even after engineers do the risk assessments [assessing the amount of risk that the project would eliminate], we are presented with several projects, which in our traditional rating and ranking system all come up with the same numbers (2s or 3s, whatever). So then, between the 2s, ... which one takes priority?

He proposed that the TTC capital allocation methodology incorporate 'objective weights', derived from the RAR.

The weights were incorporated into the capital allocation methodology, but this subtle revision was rendered implicit: the software that produced the ranking of projects did not display the objective weights (those were part of the software architecture and non-negotiable during the resource allocation process). Figure 8.6 illustrates.

| Project | Cost (millions) | Impact of TTC's Strategic Objectives | | | | | | | Weighted Score | Prioritisation Benefit Ranking |
|---|---|---|---|---|---|---|---|---|---|---|
| | | Safety | Customer | People | Assets | Growth | Financial | Reputation | | |
| Surface Track | $54 | 5 | 3 | 0 | 5 | 0 | 0 | 5 | 190 | 1 |
| Second Exits | $112 | 5 | 3 | 1 | 3 | 0 | 0 | 3 | 108 | 2 |
| Bus Overhaul | $261 | 2 | 3 | 1 | 5 | 2 | 1 | 3 | 98.5 | 3 |
| Vision | $115 | 2 | 4 | 1 | 2 | 2 | 3 | 3 | 77.5 | 4 |
| Purchase of 99 Buses for Customer Service Initiatives | $95 | 1 | 3 | 1 | 0 | 1 | 0 | 2 | 29.5 | 5 |

*Note: information presented in the table above is for illustrative purposes only. Finite and ongoing projects have been included for demonstration of the prioritisation process.*

FIGURE 8.6 TTC project ranking after the introduction of objective weights. Note: the weights are not made explicit.
Source: TTC internal documents

Conscious of the importance of the RAR, Ismail orchestrated an 'update' of the corporate priorities by reopening the risk appetite discussion two years later (in line with the approved risk management policy).

These discussions produced a surprise: executives started to question the methodology. The TTC's initial risk appetite rating scale (shown in Figure 8.4) now caused a confusion: some executives realised that they rated an objective low (i.e. 'willing to trade off against other objectives') not exactly because they were ready to compromise it but because they felt the organisation had to be more open to take risk (and therefore must put the objective at risk) in order to foster innovation – thus wanting to show 'openness to take justified risks'.

In particular, the director of customer services argued that the customer objective was important ('a 4, to be traded off with extreme reluctance'), but the situation was 'untenable' without more risk-taking. His conclusion: 'on this objective, I am willing to take more risk: it is a 2'.

Ismail recognised that the methodology had a problem that required a correction: 'The first four columns [in Figure 8.4] talk about what's the philosophy around risk taking, while the last column asks: 'When these objectives compete together, which one is the higher priority?' So then and there we decided to separate these two questions from each other to avoid the mistake we made in the first round.' Instead of one spider chart, two were produced: one talking about the executive's willingness to put an objective (such as 'customer' or 'safety') at risk in order to innovate ('rating as tolerance' or openness to risk-taking), while the other concerned the willingness to make the trade-offs required by the capital allocation process ('rating as willingness to trade off' a value against others). Assessment of objectives by willingness for risk-taking became part of the executive- and board-level strategy discussions. The objective weights (based on the trade-off ratings) remained part of the capital allocation methodology. Thus the conceptual confusion was resolved, the methodology was corrected and as far as everyone was concerned, it improved.

## OBJECTIVE WEIGHTING

| | Rating as Tolerance | Rating as Trade-Off |
|---|---|---|
| | Willingness to accept uncertain outcomes or period-to-period variation | Willingness to trade off against achievement of other objectives |
| 1 | Open | Willing |
| 2 | Flexible | Willing under right conditions |
| 3 | Cautious | Prefer to avoid |
| 4 | Minimalist | With extreme reluctance and where not reasonably practicable |
| 5 | Averse | Never |

Courtesy of Hydro One. With modifications.

FIGURE 8.7 Two rankings of the TTC's objectives (values): tolerance view versus stakeholder view.
Source: TTC internal documents

In sum, the elaboration of risk appetite at the TTC raised two policy concerns and spawned not one but two tools – and two different risk appetite charts – to express them: one that displayed the willingness to take risk (a 'tolerance' view of risk appetite), and the other, which prioritised values that underlay the objectives (a stakeholder view of 'risk appetite'). The first view became an expression of executives' willingness to take risks in order to innovate – or not, as the case may be – to be discussed in discretionary strategic decision-making, while the second became enmeshed in a wider organisational process (capital budgeting). Figure 8.7 illustrates.

## 8.4  DISCUSSION

A good deal of both interest and confusion surround the concept of risk appetite, especially with regards to how a company can define the 'degree' of 'broad-level' risk that is acceptable 'in pursuit of its goals' and in the context of risk culture reform. As an organisation's culture is shaped by the interplay between its espoused and lived values, Mike Power argued that risk culture reform is essentially an ethical question and requires a process of 'risk appetising', i.e. a continuous reflection on values. The espoused values in question are not universal but rather specific to a given organisation in which they are upheld as ends in themselves. Drawing on Philip Selznick's concept of value infusion, I further argue that organisations are important vehicles through which various values are pursued, but some of these values, in some organisations, are more secure than others in other contexts. As organisational life involves tough choices and trade-offs between stakeholders and core values, espoused priorities, left alone and unchecked, may get compromised in action. Thus the risk-appetising process has to be unflinchingly honest about a most-lamented pattern of human affairs: value displacement. This challenge takes risk managers (as well as top management) well beyond their comfort zone. That is, organisations do not only need clarity around their espoused values and priorities, but they also need visibility into value displacement as and when their actual practices and decisions result in material drifts from their intended commitments and priorities. Yet, at the field level, there is still much ambiguity as to how to include value displacement relative to espoused priorities in risk management activities.

Both Hydro One's and the TTC's risk officers managed to grasp that at the heart of the risk appetite discourse there had to be a stakeholder discussion and an understanding of the need for making trade-offs between multiple values. The challenge for them was to create a tool (or set of tools) that could *stand for* risk appetite yet preserve what is essential in its substance: the inevitable pluralism of values at risk.

In addition, at the TTC, the pluralism of values at risk raised a problem for those executives who thought of risk appetite as a signifier of willingness to *take risk in order to innovate*, rather than *to put objectives at jeopardy*. The two views were irreconcilable. Ismail cut this Gordian knot by separating the risk appetite concept into two discussions – one expressing the willingness to innovate (toler-ance view), the other explicating values at risk (trade-off view). He inscribed the results of these discussions into two different tools and channelled the results of the latter into the capital-budgeting process while keeping the former to inform top-management-level strategy discussions about discretionary innovation projects.

RAR was put into consequential action in both companies. But this happened *in an emergent fashion*: gradually, almost tentatively, working the processes into the fabric of the organisation. Initially, RAR helped facilitate executive-level discussions about the priorities inherent in the espoused strategy of the firm, but given that these discussions raised substantive issues, the risk managers spotted opportunities to increase RARs influence on action.

At Hydro One, the risk managers added a new dimension to the target risk appetite: the 'exhibited' appetite and the 'deltas'. These further developments required that the risk appetite assessments travel between different locales: from the executive board room to dozens of risk management workshops and back. As nobody ques-tioned the methodology (the rating scale), they facilitated interven-tions (e.g. on improving employee relations) without the need to go back to the original data (the comments heard and surveys conducted at risk management workshops), because someone (Rob Quail) could be trusted to have surveyed and accumulated those employee voices pertaining to the 'deltas'. Finally, the progressive embedding of risk appetite (RAR) in strategy discussions (aligning executive perceptions of the strategic priorities) stabilised the new practice by enmeshing it in management infrastructure (Power, 2009).

At the TTC, the emergence of the risk management practice was punctuated by recurring self-reflection, critique, questioning and correction of the tools developed in order to enumerate risk assess-ments and risk appetite. Hydro One's approach to formalising risk assessments and risk appetite was taken as only preliminary at the TTC: the risk managers and the executive users found 'bugs' in the methodologies. They found problems with both the adequacy of risk

assessments (too much reductionism) and with the multiple mean-
ings inherent in the risk appetite scale (it did not sufficiently differentiate between important and relevant states of the world – some
ratings signified innovation, and some stood for jeopardy). However,
both approaches took a trajectory of cognitive improvement (Stinchcombe, 2001) when Ismail corrected them in response to critique,
thereby increasing the perception of their adequacy and relevance.

With the creation of the RAR tool, Hydro One's risk managers
created a link between risk management and values, meaning that
they made the particular commitments and priorities espoused
by their top management team visible (in spider charts) and channelled these prioritisations to influence consequential decisions lower
down in the organisation. On one hand, toolmaking can make visible
not only the core values and their rank order but also the gaps
between the espoused and the exhibited (in-action) priorities – as
evidenced by the bottom-up communication process at Hydro One
that surfaced employees' view about the in-action (actual) priorities,
as perceived in the trenches.

On the other hand, at the TTC, there was evidence of 'black-
boxing' the value priorities. In the course of capital budgeting, core-
value rankings were turned into 'objective weights' (which reflected
the relative importance of the organisation's values) and subsequently
got incorporated into the budgeting software. This made the values
imbedded in the infrastructure of an organisational control system
(planning), and invisibly, yet powerfully, present in a prominent corporate process. These practices suggest that giving visibility to gaps
between espoused and in-action values is just one way to instrumen-
talise values at risk – incorporating them into the architecture of
existing tools and processes is another.

## 8.5   APPLICATIONS OF RAR: FIGHTING AGAINST
## VALUE DISPLACEMENT

The formalisation of risk appetite at Hydro One and the TTC accords
well with the finding from the behavioural ethics literature that the

considered evaluation of ethical choices requires a social process. Social psychologist Jonathan Haidt and, more recently, neuroscientists argued that formal processes of social interaction were needed in order to bring about reasoned judgment in organisations, particularly when multiple values are involved (Haidt, 2001; Grant Halvorson & Rock, 2015).

It is important that risk managers can now impress on decision makers that overly unbalanced value systems (e.g. the only-profit-matters approach (Andersen, 2013)) become a pervasive way of seeing, but also a way of *not* seeing, which can, in turn, cause value displacement. An unduly increased focus on one value dimension, such as profit, is likely to gradually undermine other organisational commitments, and if allowed to dominate unchecked, such focus may subvert sensitivity to how profits are made and at what (and at whose) cost.

Value displacement has two sources. One is self-inflicted: a matter of how we frame and reframe issues that are too complex to be captured by simple tools. That is, as Rob Quail and Mohamed Ismail discovered, it is a *toolmaking problem*. The other source is psychological: a special case of bias, called *bounded awareness* (Chugh & Bazerman, 2007). Overall, research shows that when certain options or stakeholders fall outside our awareness in a given situation, we are *ethically bounded* and may make decisions and act in ways that prove to be inconsistent with our values (Bazerman & Sezer, 2016). For example, oil executives who view themselves as environmentally and fiscally responsible may nevertheless betray those values without realising it (Wade Benzoni, 1999). Bounded ethicality (and the psychological forces that underpin it) has a tendency to lead to rigid framing – reinforcing blind spots and supressing any questioning of the *bounded value system*. As Mark Twain observed: 'It ain't what you don't know that gets you into trouble. It's what you know for sure that just ain't so.'

I highlight two areas of concern in which an explicit consideration of *values at risk* (possibly with the use of tools such as the RAR) may be necessary, if not sufficient, for generating constructive debate and action: (a) corporate failures due to conflicts of interest and (b) the incubation of man-made disasters.

### 8.5.1 Corporate Failures and Conflicts of Interest

On 14 January 2016, Goldman Sachs announced it would pay over $5 billion to settle claims that it misled mortgage bond investors during the great financial crisis. The US Department of Justice and state officials had already extracted settlements from a number of large US banks. These legal actions rested on a fundamental concept: *conflict of interest*. Such conflict came in many forms: executive self-interest at the expense of the firm and its shareholders; proprietary self-interest (putting the firm's interest ahead of clients'); and allowing one client to benefit at the expense of another.

Consider the case of the hypothetical financial firm selling complex financial instruments during the financial crisis to enable client A to bet against the fall of the market. The firm itself also believes this fall to be inevitable and is making similar bets of its own. Yet it has to find client B to take the other side of the bet. The trader discloses information, but his own self-serving biases (perhaps even undetected by him) may lead him to disclose incomplete information to client B. After the financial crisis, Wall Street firms that really did make and benefit from such transactions were widely criticised (Goodley, 2012). Yet their examples illustrate the ethical choices traders face in the presence of structural conflicts of interest embedded in their business; these are complex dilemmas that create tension within the firm's commitment to serve its multiple and diverse commitments, including its own financial interests.

Board directors and risk managers who now intend to argue that values other than the bottom line matter may urge managers to forego proprietary profit opportunities that would involve certain clients to suffer significant losses. To make such arguments persuasive, they will need new tools that can add an actionable ethical dimension to the decision-making and strategy processes.

It is possible that a tool, such as RAR – with the inescapable visibility it gives to the plurality of the firms' values (and stakeholders) at risk – may reveal the latent ethical dimension in such decisions. Yet further research is required to determine what processes it takes to make such tools capable of inducing traders to 'put clients first' – be that client A or client B – ahead of their own proprietary or individual self-interests.

### 8.5.2 Man-Made Disasters

The lethal explosion on BP's *Deepwater Horizon*, the tragic fire at the Grenfell Tower and the Volkswagen emissions scandal are all examples of man-made disasters that were, in principle, preventable. Why, then, did they occur? Researchers agree on a common feature: a long incubation period in which risks and anomalies went unaddressed by managers and the senior leadership. The implication is that there are certain 'organizational preconditions and patterns' preceding disasters that are not only the outcome of human errors (Pidgeon, 1997: 1) but are produced, systematically, on the 'dark side of organizations' (Vaughan, 1999). Disasters happen when those preconditions begin to interact in a complex way that modifies the situation (Pidgeon, 1997), leaving the initial beliefs and values out of kilter with actual, enacted commitments (Turner, 1976). Put in another way, risk incubation is the result of value displacement: it happens when the organisation's in-action values and priorities drift from its espoused commitments.

By pressuring employees to 'buy into' particular ways of seeing and doing things (for example, by imposing cost pressures in a culture in which the 'bottom line' appears to be the only value that matters), managers might reap some rewards in terms of increased focus and efficiencies – but only in the short term. In the long run, the result is that even safety-critical organisations will surrender the espoused 'safety first' principle to cost pressures. In day-to-day action, employees will regularly take shortcuts on safety in order to comply with what they perceive to be a more important core value: the bottom line.

While people might overlook individual, small safety problems and may rest easy in the short term, in the long term, these problems will build up. As this happens, the gulf between rhetoric and reality becomes hard to deny – once employees, customers and others realise this, they stop trusting the organisation. But there is an even more dangerous consequence of the unquestioning, myopic pursuit of one-dimensional (typically, financial) goals: it creates the conditions for crises and the kind of disasters I mentioned above.

From a risk management viewpoint, a particularly important discussion concerns the possibility of 'busting' risk incubation, i.e. identifying incubating risks that are still within the recovery window between a threat and a major accident during which constructive action may be feasible (Edmondson et al., 2005). For example, in the much-studied cases of NASA's *Challenger* and *Columbia* disasters, crucial, although admittedly somewhat ambiguous, risk-relevant information reached decision makers who failed to act upon it (Vaughan, 1996; Edmondson et al., 2005).

Although it is always easier to do this *ex post* with the benefit of hindsight, I believe that organisations may proactively search for the common elements and drivers of risk incubation that typically surface in man-made disasters. The focus of this search would be the gaps between the espoused and the in-action value priorities. Bringing about such reflection is not easy. Tools are essential but require careful design. For example, a common problem plagues formal risk-reporting systems: risk managers can be inundated by a tsunami of un-prioritised issues. Also, when employees are asked to carry out 'risk assessments', reporting proclivity often plummets because most people find risk assessments too abstract and difficult.

In principle, organisations can design values-at-risk reporting systems that would prioritise issues (or reported risks) by linking them to the organisation's predefined values and priorities (e.g. safety (priority no. 1) or financial viability (priority no. 3)), as was the case at the TTC. The risk controllers in the back office would therefore see issues flagged and sorted by organisational priorities, which then could direct attention and follow-up action.

## 8.6  CONCLUSION

Despite the recognition that risk culture reform requires a sensitivity to the espoused commitments of organisations and to the very real threat of value displacement, most companies still find it difficult to include pluralistic values and multiple stakeholder considerations in their risk management activities. Based on the literature and case studies presented in this chapter, we can only conclude that creating visibility for values at risk is merely the first step in a long and winding road towards gaining control over 'risk appetites' and, ultimately, over the culture of an organisation.

The ethical turn in risk management involves bringing the ethical dimension to the fore by explicitly visualising – during strategic decision-making and formal control processes – the plurality of values at risk. Yet decision-making biases and the difficulties inherent in moral reasoning remain.

Neuroscientists argue that organisations can become aware of biases in ways that individuals cannot, by adopting bias-countering processes and practices (Haidt, 2001; Grant Halvorson & Rock, 2015). In other words, context and practices influence the extent to which people do or do not fall prey to their own biases in decision-making and in moral reasoning.

This variation in actors' ability to affect framings through defined processes and practices provides an important conceptual link between organisational ethics and risk management. Risk management is dependent on framing, which is predicated on *toolmaking*, i.e. the creation and reconfiguration of tools that frame risk issues for decision makers (Hall, Mikes & Millo, 2015). It is possible to conceptualise risk management as ongoing framing and toolmaking, in which what is at stake are the boundaries drawn around 'values at risk'.

The ethical turn in a company's risk management occurs when a major revision to the initial frame is orchestrated by extending the initial focal object of risk inquiry – 'What is the primary value at risk?' – to include multiple values at risk – 'Given the firm's strategy and conduct, what are the values and stakeholders at risk?' Reframing is particularly important in the wake of man-made disasters, which highlight the need for a 'full cultural adjustment' (Turner, 1976). There is, of course, no guarantee that any attempt at reframing will provide a full cultural adjustment or that it will grant visibility to the ethical dimension. Lip service to the full range of relevant stakeholders and values at risk notwithstanding, a company's limited conception of what is at risk often survives the disaster it creates, and we see the company settle back into the very habits that got it into so much trouble.

Yet, the fledging literature in neuroscience suggests that new organisational practices can shift ingrained thinking (Grant Halvorson & Rock, 2015). Rob Quail's RAR tool can thus be expected to inspire other risk managers to follow suit in their quest to complete what might be called 'the ethical turn in risk management'. Or, if we want to stick to the pragmatic motivation of Quail's creation, it adds a hitherto missing visibility to how closely strategic priorities (which executive managers have set) are followed in day-to-day action. Gaps indicate confusion on the ground – and that can be an indication of incubating risks.

Gaining this visibility is particularly important for safety-critical organisations. Many of them just fool themselves by stating 'safety first', while, in everyday practice, trade-offs of less safety for lower costs prevail. The consequences of such gaps between espoused and in-action value systems have been illustrated by a long stream of man-made disasters (Mikes, Oyon & Jeitziner, 2017).

By clarifying an organisation's values, RAR can prepare managers and employees to live by them. It may also (a) prepare decision makers for the inevitable backlash that follows 'defining moments' (Badaracco, 1997) when trade-offs prove to be really tough decisions with win–lose outcomes and (b) give decision makers the confidence to defend those actions. Creating such awareness and confidence requires intrusive, interactive and intensive debates about the organisation's multiple values and stakeholders, about the decision makers' attachment to each of them and about the potential long-term consequences of a difficult decision made at a defining moment. The risk appetite radar provides a summary of the conclusions from such debates and may therefore serve as a continuous guide for management in such high-stake decisions.

To nuance our argument, it is useful to separate the ethical dimension into two components: (a) individual ethical and legal decisions and (b) organisational ethical decisions (the potential impact of company strategy on the environment and disadvantaged communities). These are separate issues and require different types of risk management controls and mitigation. Internal control and whistle-blowing programs help to alleviate individual violation of ethical and legal norms but are inadequate for addressing organisational ethical considerations arising from strategy. This is the role for the values-at-risk agenda, now being embraced by a growing constituency of risk managers.

Based on these reflections, risk managers' flirtation with organisational ethics may turn into a long-term relationship, albeit a tumultuous one. By advocating the need to assess the ethicality of proposals and decisions, risk managers enter potentially explosive discussions on what values and stakeholders their organisation is prepared to stand for and which ones it is willing to (or must) compromise on. It won't be easy. But it will be a huge and healthy step forward. As the philosopher Paul Tillich argued, it takes *courage* to affirm one's essential being – to affirm one's inner aim – in spite of many self-serving temptations and ambiguities. As risk managers and board members are increasingly expected to affirm the values and priorities of their organisations, they too need this essential courage.

REFERENCES

Ahrens, T. and Dent, J. F. (1998). Accounting and organizations: Realizing the richness of field research. *Journal of Management Accounting Research*, **10**(1), 1–39.

Andersen, E. (2013). What happens when leaders only care about money? *Forbes*, 2013 December 18. https://bit.ly/2Nhgzr0

Badaracco, J. L., Jr. (1997). *Defining Moments: When Managers Must Choose between Right and Right.* Boston: Harvard Business School Press.

Bazerman, M. H. and Sezer, O. (2016). Bounded awareness: implications for ethical decision making. *Organizational Behavior and Human Decision Processes*, **136**, 95–105.

Buehler, K., Freeman, A. and Hulme, R. (2008). *The Risk Revolution.* McKinsey Working Papers on Risk, No. 1. https://mck.co/2Chfg57

Chugh, D. and Bazerman, M. (2007). Bounded awareness: what you fail to see can hurt you. *Mind and Society*, **6**(1), 1–18.

COSO (Committee of Sponsoring Organizations) (2009). *Strengthening Enterprise Risk Management for Strategic Advantage.* https://bit.ly/2JSW8i6

COSO (Committee of Sponsoring Organizations) (2016). *Enterprise Risk Management: Aligning Risk with Strategy and Performance (Public Exposure).* https://bit.ly/2PO3BCL

Edmondson, A. et al. (2005). The recovery window: organizational learning following ambiguous threats. In W. H. Starbuck and M. Farjoun, eds., *Organization at the Limit: Lessons from the* Columbia *Disaster*. Malden, MA: Blackwell, pp. 220–46.

European Commission (2011). *Green Paper: The EU Corporate Governance Framework.* https://bit.ly/2CiH2hO

Grant Halvarson, H. and Rock, D. (2015). Beyond Bias. *Strategy+Business*, 2015 July 13. www.strategy-business.com/article/00345?gko=ed7d4

Haidt, J. (2001). The emotional dog and its rational tail: a social intuitionist approach to moral judgment, *Psychological Review*, **108**(4), 814–34. DOI: 10.1037/0033-295X.108.4.814

Hall, M., Mikes, A. and Millo, Y. (2015). How do risk managers become influential? A field study of toolmaking in two financial institutions. *Management Accounting Research*, **26**, 3–22.

Hillson, D. and Murray-Webster, R. (2012). *A Short Guide to Risk Appetite*, 1st ed. Abingdon: Routledge.

Hood, C. (1996). Where extremes meet: 'SPRAT' versus 'SHARK' in public risk management. In C. Hood and D. K. C. Jones, eds., *Accident and Design*. London, UCL Press, pp. 208–27.

IBM Financial Services (2008). *Risk Appetite: A Multifaceted Approach to Risk Management.* https://bit.ly/2rjoVWR

ISO (International Organization for Standardization) (2009). *Risk Management – Principles and Guidelines*, ISO/FDIS 31000:2009. Geneva: ISO.

KPMG (2013). *Developing a Strong Risk Appetite Program.* https://bit.ly/2WQhNgi

Marsh (2009). *Research into Definition and Application of the Concept of Risk Appetite.* https://bit.ly/32hoRDt

Mikes, A. (2009). Risk management and calculative cultures. *Management Accounting Research,* **20**(1), 18–40.

Mikes, A. (2011). From counting risk to making risk count: boundary-work in risk management. *Accounting, Organizations and Society,* **36**( 4–5), 226–45.

Mikes, A. (2012). Enterprise risk management at Hydro One (A). Harvard Business School Case 109-001.

Mikes, A., Hall, M. and Millo, Y. (2013). How experts gain influence. *Harvard Business Review,* **91**(7–8), 70–4.

Mikes, A. and Hamel, D. (2012). Enterprise risk management at Hydro One (B): how risky are smart meters? Harvard Business School Supplement 112-073.

Mikes, A., Oyon, D. and Jeitziner, J. (2017). Risk management: towards a behavioral perspective. In T. Libby and L. Thorne, eds., *The Routledge Companion to Behavioral Accounting Research,* Abingdon: Routledge.

NACD (National Association of Corporate Directors) (2009). *Risk Governance: Balancing Risk and Reward.* Arlington: NACD.

National Commission on the Causes of the Financial and Economic Crisis in the United States (2011). *The Financial Crisis Inquiry Report.* Washington: US Government Printing Office.

Oliver Wyman (2007). *What's Your Risk Appetite?* https://owy.mn/32gTgBX

Palermo, T., Power, M. and Ashby, S. (2017). Navigating institutional complexity: the production of risk culture in the financial sector. *Journal of Management Studies,* **54**(2), 154–81.

Pidgeon, N. (1997). The limits to safety? Culture, politics, learning and man-made disasters. Journal of Contingencies and Crisis Management, 5(1), 1–14.

Power, M. (2009). The risk management of nothing. *Accounting, Organizations and Society,* **34**(6–7), 849–55. https://doi.org/10.1016/j.aos.2009.06.001

Power, M., Ashby, S. and Palermo, T. (2013). *Risk Culture in Financial Organizations: A Research Report.* London: London School of Economics.

Purdy, G. (2010). ISO 31000:2009 – setting a new standard for risk management. *Risk Analysis,* **30**(6), 881–86. https://doi.org/10.1111/j.1539-6924.2010.01442.x

PwC (PricewaterhouseCoopers) (2008). *Risk Appetite – How Hungry Are You?* https://pwc.to/33mAQB7

Quail, R. (2012). Defining your taste for risk. *Corporate Risk Canada,* Spring 2012, 24–30.

Robinson, D. (2007). Control theories in sociology. *Annual Review of Sociology,* **35**, 157–74.

Sabato, G. (2010). Financial crisis: where did risk management fail? *International Review of Applied Financial Issues and Economics*, **2**(2), 315–27.

SAS Institute Inc. (2011). *The Art of Balancing Risk and Reward: The Role of the Board in Setting, Implementing and Monitoring Risk Appetite*. Cary, NC: SAS Institute Inc.

Selznick, P. (2000). On sustaining research agendas: their moral and scientific basis: an address to the Western Academy of Management. *Journal of Management Inquiry*, **9**(3), 277–82.

Soltes, E. (2016). *Why They Do It: Inside the Mind of the Quail-Collar Criminal*, New York: PublicAffairs.

Stinchcombe, A. L. (2001). *When Formality Works: Authority and Abstraction in Law and Organizations*. Chicago: University of Chicago Press.

Turner, B. (1976). The organizational and interorganizational development of disasters. *Administrative Science Quarterly*, **21**(3), 378–97.

US Department of Justice (2016a). Goldman Sachs agrees to pay more than $5 billion in connection with its sale of residential mortgage backed securities. Press release, 2016 April 11. https://bit.ly/2CsykxD

US Department of Justice (2016b). *GS Settlement Agreement*. www.justice.gov/opa/file/839891/download

US Department of Justice (2016c). *Statement of Facts*. www.justice.gov/opa/file/839901/download

Vaughan, D. (1996). *The* Challenger *Launch Decision: Risky Technology, Culture, and Deviance at NASA*. Chicago: University of Chicago Press.

Vaughan, D. (1999). The dark side of organizations: mistake, misconduct, and disaster. *Annual Review of Sociology*, **25**, 271–305.

Wade Benzoni, K. (1999). Thinking about the future: an intergenerational perspective on the conflict and compatibility between economic and environmental interests. *American Behavioral Scientist*, **42**(8), 1393–405.

Weick, K. (1998) Foresights of failure: an appreciation of Barry Turner. *Journal of Contingencies and Crisis Management*, **6**(2), 72–5.

# Conclusion

## Michelle Tuveson, Daniel Ralph and Kern Alexander

Risk culture warrants a broad and multidisciplinary view. Our authors have provided insights and brought new thinking to this topic as an antidote to approaching the subject with linear thinking and prescriptive solutions. Their chapters provide multiple lenses for understanding and exploring risk culture as an organisational phenomenon.

Some readers may have hoped that this book would provide practical advice on management of risk culture, including its measurement, how that would feed into risk exposure versus risk appetite and perhaps even quantitative correlations to a company's performance. This highlights the broader question of quantitative measurement and data analysis of the culture of a firm and to what extent they can add value to qualitative approaches while accounting for the context of governance and structure and interactions with wider stakeholders. One can argue that academic studies have not yielded the proof that risk culture exists as an entity, let alone scientific evidence that attention to risk culture impacts on firm performance (see more on short- versus long-term performance below). Nevertheless, we would be negligent to ignore recent compliance and regulation-oriented trends on managing risk culture; hence, we have dedicated an entire chapter to this institutional view. Also, regardless of a firm's performance, efforts to secure a good risk culture may be considered a proxy for good governance.

The editors speculate that if a good risk culture is associated with lower organisational risk, then it may detract from the firm's short-term performance by manifesting in less aggressive business practices – shifting focus away from commercial gain today to ensure longer-term viability. For instance, a stronger risk culture, though beneficial in the longer term, may negatively impact the quarterly balance sheet and share price. Many such dichotomies exist around business decisions made regarding climate, environmental and wider sustainability considerations. Indeed, there is growing evidence of firms that are declining project financing in what are deemed to be low-sustainability businesses while seeking investments that are hedges for future climate actions and litigations. This thinking aligns with persistent scepticism towards the mantra that the share price of a publicly traded firm captures all future uncertainty around its performance.

Long-term considerations are consistent with a wider stake-holder view of the firm that is challenging the shareholder-only view of the purpose of the firm. Such considerations influence the expect-ations of employees and wider society regarding the behaviours and responsibilities of firms. Moreover, the social compact that underlies a firm's licence to operate is subject to rising expectations. This leads to the idea of retrospective assessment, in which past decisions are subject to a different view than that of the managers who took those decisions. This also suggests a way to test today's risk culture in an organisation: to what extent can retrospective sanctions or plaudits tomorrow be imagined by management today? In shaping tone from the top, can a CEO imagine being fired in two years' time for their decisions or behaviour this year? Anticipating future retrospectivity is an aspect of risk culture that addresses the long-term view of the firm and its place in society.

We continue the discussion of the long term by noting the declining trend in corporate longevity; no business is immune. It perhaps follows that one of the most valuable assets of a firm with regard to long-term viability is its ability to innovate. This point is somewhat at a tangent to the traditional focus of risk management on protection, e.g. reducing the likelihood or impact of harmful future events on existing assets or capabilities. The ability to innovate, however, is an intangible asset with profound impacts on whether a firm is able to adapt opportunistically to changing external factors.

We note an intuitive link between a good risk culture and a culture that promotes individual courage, e.g. an environment of sufficient psychological safety to allow individuals to both call out risky or unethical practices and to propose ideas that challenge current thinking. With just one chapter in the present volume on innovation, and the overwhelming focus of professional risk management on protection, we believe there is an appetite for risk management practices that speak directly to innovation, value creation and ultimately firm strategy.

We conclude by highlighting three specific themes that cut across social culture into firm culture and will doubtless be the subject of continuing and deep scrutiny. The first is broadly described as the 'rise of liability', which relates to retrospectivity, mentioned above. We are familiar with the insurance industry expressing its fears of the future by asking, 'What might be the next asbestos?', while businesses appear less forward-looking. An endemic feature of organisations is the pay and opportunity gap between women and men. Might a more litigious environment facilitate class action law suits to redress retrospective pay discrimination? What time scale might this happen over, and which organisation could survive it? If not gender pay, what other organisational dimensions might be challenged by the rise of liability?

The second is associated with what has been dubbed 'surveillance capitalism' (Zuboff, 2019), which is exemplified in the business model of Facebook. Given the ubiquity of rating systems in information platforms, from 'liking' social media posts to rating hosts and guests in Airbnb, we can expect that more and more of an individual's day-to-day activities will be rated by others and that this, via artificial intelligence (AI), will affect their future access to services. This is already happening in China under the guise of social credit (Parton, 2018), which relies on an extensive network of cameras and other identification and tracking technology. An individual who is deemed to exhibit poor behaviour, perhaps in debt repayment, can suffer reduced access to services such as public transportation and

financial credit or perhaps even have their university degree gradu-
ation blocked.

Analogously, organisations are already tracking various aspects
of their employees' activities through company-provided devices,
whether email accounts, phones, personal fitness monitors and so
on. While intensive monitoring of employees is standard in some
narrow arenas, such as stock trading in a bank, we can expect tracking
and social comparison to gradually extend to real-time monitoring and
associated rating by organisations of their employees' behaviours that
looks beyond their professional activities, at their social media presence and leisure time. Are we in danger of sleepwalking into a corporate culture of 'AI indictment', in which AI, with its biases and lack of
transparency, will guide the personal and professional development of
staff, including sanctions for poor behaviour?

Third, the complexity of interactions from micro to macro, and
from human scale to geophysical, put us in mind of the 'malicious
demon' that would interfere with our senses and our ability to obtain
objective knowledge, leaving us with radical uncertainty about the
outside world. In today's globalised economy, traversing many cultural, social, economic and political boundaries, and acknowledging
emerging technologies and their impact on social and political discourse, one does not need the existence of Descartes's demon to appreciate the profound doubt that confronts decision makers and the need
for reliable standards, norms and values to guide decision-making.

Societal institutions mediate between individuals and organisations via frameworks of law, regulation and policy and more fluid
political discourse. These institutions underwrite standards, norms
and values, providing the glue that holds organisations together when
confronting the challenge of making decisions in the face of uncertainty. The precautionary principle suggests there is a dialectical
relationship between uncertainty and institutions in that evolving
institutional frameworks 'too fast' may cause social or economic
dislocation, while going 'too slow' invites a shadow system with
unregulated power brokers to develop at the cost of incumbents,

including individuals. The latter is exemplified, according to many commentators, by the rise of global data platforms like Amazon, Facebook and Google, whose dominant reach is an effective, if not explicit, shaper of social discourse.

Despite the dearth of global frameworks with teeth, globalisation appears to lead convergence in governance practices, norms and mechanisms that influence risk culture. This seems to be driven by the gains of international trade via wide standards and agreements involving individual nations and also regional blocs, with its roots in international security and fiscal frameworks that emerged after World War II. At the level of firms and sectors in an economy, while firms address their own risk culture from an internal perspective, it is one of the responsibilities of regulators to take an external perspective of risk culture that takes account of the systemic implications that a firm's – or a group of firms' – conduct can have on the stability and sustainability of their sector or ecosystem. When that ecosystem turns out to be globally connected, beyond the economic value of trade, as exemplified by global warming due to carbon dioxide emissions or damage to national economies from international tax havens, then 'global risk culture' is seen to have meaning,

There are no easy answers to the problem of weak risk culture in organisations or systems or to growing strong risk cultures. This book – and, we anticipate, further work – presents opportunities to managers and policymakers to bring into alignment the profit- and efficiency-oriented objectives of firms with the social and cultural values that are necessary for a sustainable society.

REFERENCES

Parton, C. (2018). State credit is just one part of China's new state control. *The Spectator*, 2018 November 17. https://bit.ly/36AoWpi

Zuboff, S. (2019). *The Age of Surveillance Capitalism: The Fight for a Human Future at the New Frontier of Power*. New York: PublicAffairs.

# Index